Creolized Sexualities

Critical Caribbean Studies

Series Editors: Yolanda Martínez-San Miguel, Carter Mathes, and Kathleen López

Editorial Board: Carlos U. Decena, Rutgers University; Alex Dupuy, Wesleyan University; Aisha Khan, New York University; April J. Mayes, Pomona College; Patricia Mohammed, University of West Indies; Martin Munro, Florida State University; F. Nick Nesbitt, Princeton University; Michelle Stephens, Rutgers University; Deborah Thomas, University of Pennsylvania; and Lanny Thompson, University of Puerto Rico

Focused particularly in the twentieth and twenty-first centuries, although attentive to the context of earlier eras, this series encourages interdisciplinary approaches and methods and is open to scholarship in a variety of areas, including anthropology, cultural studies, diaspora and transnational studies, environmental studies, gender and sexuality studies, history, and sociology. The series pays particular attention to the four main research clusters of Critical Caribbean Studies at Rutgers University, where the coeditors serve as members of the executive board: Caribbean Critical Studies Theory and the Disciplines; Archipelagic Studies and Creolization; Caribbean Aesthetics, Poetics, and Politics; and Caribbean Colonialities.

For a list of all the titles in the series, please see the last page of the book.

Creolized Sexualities

• •

Undoing Heteronormativity in the Literary Imagination of the Anglo-Caribbean

ALISON DONNELL

Rutgers University Press

New Brunswick, Camden, and Newark, New Jersey, and London

Library of Congress Cataloging-in-Publication Data

Names: Donnell, Alison, 1966– author.
Title: Creolized sexualities : undoing heteronormativity in the literary
imagination of the Anglo-Caribbean / Alison Donnell.
Description: New Brunswick : Rutgers University Press, [2022] |
    Series: Critical Caribbean studies | Includes bibliographical references and index.
Identifiers: LCCN 2020057735 | ISBN 9781978818118 (paperback ; alk. paper) |
    ISBN 9781978818125 (hardcover ; alk. paper) | ISBN 9781978818132 (epub) |
    ISBN 9781978818149 (mobi) | ISBN 9781978818156 (pdf)
Subjects: LCSH: Caribbean fiction (English)—20th century—History and
criticism. | Heterosexism in literature. | Gender nonconformity in literature. |
    Group identity in literature.
Classification: LCC PR9205.4 .D66 2022 | DDC 810.9/353—dc23
LC record available at https://lccn.loc.gov/2020057735

A British Cataloging-in-Publication record for this book is available from the British Library.

♾ The paper used in this publication meets the requirements of the American National
Standard for Information Sciences—Permanence of Paper for Printed Library Materials,
ANSI Z39.48-1992.

www.rutgersuniversitypress.org

Manufactured in the United States of America

For my darling boys—Max, Asher, Charlie, and George—who have all grown up in the considerable time it has taken me to finish this book.

I am eternally thankful to you for reminding me that dancing in the kitchen, competitive quizzing via Zoom, laughter so intense it forces carrots down your nose, top trumps, bottomless appetites, and arthouse films with giant cinema popcorn are the happy and compelling stuff of which life is made.

I trust you to know that I love you beyond all possible description.

Contents

Creolized Sexualities

Introduction

• •

Undoing Heteronormativity
and the Erotics of Creolization

> There are no limits to what literature
> can do.
> —Omise'eke Natasha Tinsley

What does it mean to talk about the Caribbean as a place where heteronormativity is undone, as a constitutively queer place? In one sense, this proposition is clearly a provocation, a brushing against the grain of the Anglo-Caribbean's dominant cultural framing as a homophobic region, even "the" homophobic region. In another sense, it is the logical conclusion to a line of reasoning that has persistently and persuasively positioned the Caribbean as a creolized place that undoes the usefulness of thinking about identities in terms of origins, binaries, guaranteed lineages, and culturally discreet groupings. This potentially powerful conjunction framing the relationship between creolized Caribbeanness and erotic fluidity beyond heteronormativity animates my thinking throughout this book. My argument is that literary depictions of creolized sexualities offer a distinct expressive modality in which sexual autonomy and fluidity overlap kaleidoscopically to unfasten the categories of hetero- and homosexuality and bring forward a plurality of possible desires and attachments embedded in Caribbeanness.

This argument emerges from the confluence of two long-standing beliefs. The first is in the ongoing potential of Caribbean places and peoples to put pressure on the bounded categories commonly used to do the work of human

1

description. The second is in the privileged role of the literary that allows readers to occupy spaces where meaning is undone as well as done, sometimes simultaneously. *Creolized Sexualities* brings these two convictions together to show the extended, non-normalizing possibilities for erotic connections and attachments that emerge in a comprehensive range of literary depictions of Caribbean lives written in English across the twentieth century. I work with a consciously eclectic selection of Caribbean literary fictions in English in order to bring into view a range of fictional worlds where Caribbeanness, both at home and in the diaspora, and the undoing or undermining of heteronormativity can be read as mutually informing. This supple repertoire of creolized sexualities is discussed through a series of close readings of literary works, each energized by theoretical or historical interventions concerning or contesting the mapping of erotic norms within the "heterocolonial order" (Valens 2016, 66).[1] With a focus on the specifically Caribbean possibilities of creolized sexualities that share a non-normalizing and pluralizing expression of the erotic, I argue that these literary works represent ways of being Caribbean, and belonging to the Caribbean, that are already in existence and that continue to reach toward a differently possible Caribbean, even as or when they are unrecognized or disavowed.

From Contesting Homophobia to Undoing Heteronormativity

At the beginning of Lyndon Gill's book *Erotic Islands: Art and Activism in the Queer Caribbean* (2018a), which discusses "the long history of sophisticated strategies same-sex desiring artists and activists have used to make cultural interventions" (1), he asks "to what extent do overemphasizing exclusions prematurely blind us to various kinds of queer *embeddedness* seldom remarked upon in a scholarly literature racing to demonstrate and document systemic homophobia in the region?" (1). This question also sits behind my work here, which similarly seeks to pay attention to Caribbean forms of embedded queerness, although through engagement with literary works. In choosing this emphasis on the localized undoing of heteronormativity, I locate my discussion of creolized sexualities within what might be seen as a second wave of Caribbean queer studies, advanced by Tinsley (2018) and Gill (2018b), among others, which foregrounds the historical and ongoing undoing of sexual norms and categories in a Caribbean context. This mode of inquiry follows, but also overlaps with, a vital first wave of work that contests homophobia and the denial of and violence toward erotic ways of being and signatures of sexual identity positioned as incompatible with Caribbeanness according to (Anglophone) state, religious, and popular cultural discourses. Whereas the first wave may be broadly characterized as asserting the presence, identities, and rights of non-heteronormative subjects against the hostilities of both official discourses and everyday acts of violence, this second wave is motivated to explore the ways in which Caribbean creolized sexual practices are transformative in refusing the distinctions and boundaries between straight and gay/queer as meaningful to the expression and self-knowledge of erotic subjectivity. Other notable work in this vein includes Ronald Cummings's discussion of Jamaican female masculinities in relation to Nanny of the Maroons and the figure of the man royal. Building on Makeda Silvera's 1992 essay "Man Royals and Sodomites," Cummings discusses how the man royal "helps to diversify and extend the sites through which we have read constructions and performances of Caribbean masculinities . . . and to think about the ways in which cultural markers of masculinity have been produced and distributed across both male and female bodies" (2012/13, 150). Yolanda Martínez-San Miguel's 2011 article, "Female Sexiles? Toward an Archeology of Displacement of Sexual Minorities in the Caribbean," is likewise significant for addressing the destabilization, resistance, and "interrogation of heteronormative discourses" (822) in works by Caribbean writers Pedro Juan Soto, Mayotte Capécia and Michelle Cliff. "Broadening the meaning of sexile" (831), Martínez-San Miguel's article helpfully reads displacement from and unsettling of heteronormative national communities as potentially both dislocation and relocation, as the sexual outcast across these works provokes a recognition of desire as unfixed, an "unruly pulsion making possible other forms of identification that unsettle the confines of traditional definitions of postcoloniality while constantly questioning the co-opting forces of normativity" (832).

At the same time, paying attention to local situations, expressions, and practices that are neither queer nor straight in the orthodox sense need not downplay resistance to and refusal of queer Caribbean lives. In *Island Bodies: Transgressive Sexualities in the Caribbean Imagination,* Rosamond S. King (2014) points out how "the challenge for those of us who study non-heteronormative sexualities in the Caribbean is determining how to acknowledge real . . . homophobia without endorsing the idea that the Caribbean is uniquely and exceptionally homophobic" (83).[2] In 2008, in the introduction to his landmark anthology *Our Caribbean: A Gathering of Lesbian and Gay Writing from the Antilles,* Thomas Glave addressed the continued need to affirm multiple sexual desires and attachments as a Caribbean reality in the face of hostility and silence:

> It is no way an exaggeration to say that this gathering originated as an idea born out of the most extreme longing: the desire to know finally, and with complete certainty, that a book such as this one actually existed and could exist. Could exist in spite of thundering condemnation from Christian fundamentalist ministers and, from those in churches, mosques, and other places, sidelong disapproving—and sometimes baleful—glances. Could exist despite

proscriptions, banishments, ostracisms, and, in more than a few cases, extreme violence. Could exist: a book like this that, though some—including a number of our most renowned, if not always generous, Caribbean minds—might wish to ignore or dismiss it, none would ultimately be able to deny or wish away. (Glave 2008a, 1)

The anthology itself speaks out in essays, testimonials, and creative works that confirm and affirm a Caribbean queer past, present, and future, while still recognizing the realities of living in homophobic cultures.

Mindful of Maria Lugones's (2007) argument in "Heterosexualism and the Colonial/Modern Gender System," in which she illustrates how "heterosexuality, capitalism, and racial classification are impossible to understand apart from each other" (187), I recognize that my argument for the Anglo-Caribbean as a place in which invented and imposed norms of heterosexuality are inevitably (rather than impossibly) undone needs to be set within this recognition of the region as a homophobic place.[3] In most territories, the British colonial 1864 buggery laws remain intact, and everyday stories of harassment, violence, and fear are reported by non-heteronormative subjects, alongside more recent stories of public pride and legal challenge.[4] In the context of such urgent questions around the decriminalization of same-sex relations and equal access to justice, constitutional recognition, and citizenship, it is not surprising that attention to questions of sexual diversity often necessarily focus on contesting homophobia—politically, legally, culturally, and theoretically.

Within the literary context, creative works have been calling attention to the urgent challenge of confronting the asserted incompatibility between non-heteronormativity and Caribbeanness for a number of decades. Michelle Cliff's (1980) poetry collection *Claiming an Identity They Taught Me To Despise* and her 1982 (2008) essay "If I Could Write This in Fire I Would Write It in Fire" are landmark works, alongside Trinidadian Canadian Dionne Brand's 1990 prose poem *No Language Is Neutral*. A much larger body of literature in English has engaged with rendering the hostile realities faced by non-heteronormative Caribbean subjects and the multidimensionality of queer lives, including novels by Dionne Brand (1996), David Chariandy (2018), Michelle Cliff (1996), Ramabai Espinet (2003), Oonya Kempadoo (2013), Clem Maharaj (1992), Kei Miller (2016), Shani Mootoo (1996, 2008b, 2014), Patricia Powell (1994), Lawrence Scott ([1998] 2014), and H. Nigel Thomas (1993), as well as memoirs by Staceyann Chin (2009) and Faizal Deen (1999). These texts have helped to contest Caribbean homophobias in a variety of ways. Patricia Powell's (1994) *A Small Gathering of Bones*, Lawrence Scott's ([1998] 2014) *Aelred's Sin*, and Dionne Brand's (1996) *In Another Place, Not Here*, respectively, expose and erode homophobia by forging structures of empathy, depicting the injuries inflicted by hatred, and rendering same-sex relations as emotionally meaningful, unremarkable, and part of a larger sexual ecology of consenting and rewarding human relations.

These works and approaches have been immensely influential in terms of establishing what critical theorist Nancy Fraser would call an "affirmative" approach to recognition of non-heteronormative peoples that "seeks to enhance the standing of an existing sexual orientation" (Fraser and Honneth 2003, 75) in their collective promotion of same-sex erotics and defiance of homophobia. My readings in this book focus on the undoing of heteronormativity, rather than homophobia, as part of the second wave of queer studies mentioned earlier that follows what Fraser calls the "transformative" approach of destabilizing "the current grid of mutually exclusive sexual statuses" (2003, 75). My discussion of a fluid continuum of sexual identifications and practices across different Caribbean islands and diasporic geographies, as well as across the historical period from the 1950s to the present, is consistently attentive to creolized sexualities that are both off the grid and also refusing its coordinates.

Developing an appropriate vocabulary and methodology for this work has been an importantly unresolved task as the work of transformation and undoing demands thinking outside the embedded, identity-defining categories of sexuality and the vocabularies attached to these. Moreover, in a decolonial context, it is vital to recognize that the terms *straight* and *gay*, *heterosexual* and *homosexual*, *lesbian*, and *bisexual* all have their own cultural histories and meanings. As these terms have come into conceptualization and into usage within Western metropolitan cultures, they often appear to be, at best, inadequate and, at worst, reductive to the task of retexturizing a literary history of Caribbean people's erotic lives and orientations. While the term *queer* may also be viewed as an interruption and an imposition within this regional context, Caribbean scholars, such as Agard-Jones, Cummings, Deen, Gill, Tinsley, and R. Walcott, have established the Caribbean relevance of *queer* by deploying this term judiciously within their localizing approaches, as I will come to discuss. Moreover, the ubiquity of *queer* within global mass social media, television, and film means that this term has permeated the region and is now used domestically, becoming Caribbeanized at the same time. As Jafari S. Allen notes: "notwithstanding the understandable protests of those who reject *queer* as a name for black subjects on the grounds that it extends a white patronym: *queer* does also uniquely capture the sense of the nonnormative status of men, women, and others who identify with or are identified as homosexual or bisexual, and those whose gender self-identification is not resonant with the sex assigned to them at birth" (Allen 2012, 222). For this study, I am interested in the way in which *queer* can signify the disruption of normativities and suggest a conceptual bridge between creolized sexualities and global queerness in their underdoing of heteronormativity.

Indeed, the theoretical bearings of my inquiry lie in methodologies that show how Caribbeanness and the undoing of sexual norms are already close relations. Following Jafari S. Allen's call to meet the "challenge of these queer times by claiming intellectual kin where we find them" (Allen 2012, 215), I argue for creolized and queer as intellectual kin in their mutual repudiation of inadequate binarisms (black/white, female/male, homo/hetero) through which difference is contained and normalized. By bringing together creolized and queer sensibilities and mapping them within the same epistemological and ontological kinship networks, my aim is to provoke a critical reconsideration of the purchase and hold of sexual categorization within the Caribbean region, where the logics of classification, labeling, and static normalization have long been proven insufficient with regard to ethnic, cultural, and national belongings. Following the model adopted by Mae G. Henderson and E. Patrick Johnson in their notable 2005 edited collection *Black Queer Studies: A Critical Anthology*, I seek "to enlist the strategies, methodologies, and insights of black [Caribbean] studies into the service of queer studies and vice versa" (6), with a particular focus on Caribbean creolization as paradigmatic for the constitution of non-normalizing sexualities in and of the region. An emphasis on the region's unraveling of (hetero)normativity is something that Faizal Deen has noted as strangely absent from conversations: "People don't talk about the ways in which the Caribbean has always been queer or the ways in which decolonization and Caribbean responses to colonization have always been queer because they were always working against the normative" (Cummings and Deen 2021, 18).

In the twenty-first century, a flourishing of black queer studies and Caribbean queer studies has given expression to Caribbean peoples' disruption of heterocolonial sexual and gender binaries, as well as their multiple and mobile forms of erotic agency. My study builds on and is in dialogue with this body of work, and with Caribbean queer literary studies in particular. Alongside close attention to my selected literary works, I engage with critical studies by Nadia Ellis (2011, 2015a, 2015b), Rosamond King (2014), Kei Miller (2013, 2014), David Murray (2002), Omise'eke Natasha Tinsley (2008, 2010, 2018), Keja Valens (2013, 2016), and Gloria Wekker (1999, 2006, 2008), all of which have laid the foundations for my amplification of creolized sexualities in their explorations of a localized continuum of creolized relations and of an ingenious and cherished plasticity in terms of expressions of sex and sexuality. Important work on the reconceptualization of sexual citizenship by M. Jacqui Alexander (1994, 1997), Thomas Glave (2008a), Kamala Kempadoo (2009), Mimi Sheller (2012) and Faith Smith (2011), helps me to think through the connections between representations, rights, and freedoms. My interest in the intersecting character of creolized and queer also leads me to work with theories of cultural pluralism and newness presented by Édouard Glissant (1995), Sydney Mintz (1996),

Shalini Puri (2004), and Sylvia Wynter (1968, 1970, 2006), which I read as over-lapping with an epistemology of erotic expansiveness as framed by Lyndon Gill (2018b). The joint work of Yolanda Martinez-San Miguel and Sarah Tobias (2016), and of Keja Valens (2013, 2016), is important to my engagement with representations of Caribbean trans lives. While a localizing of Anglo-Caribbean erotics is the framing ethos for my work, I also refer to canonical works of queer theory situated within the global north, including work by Eve Kosofsky Sedg-wick and J. Halberstam, in order to read how Caribbean imaginative works both correspond with and extend their rubrics of queer imaginings that undo and denaturalize heteropatriarchal constructs.[5]

Creole Queer Kinship

My core argument is that bringing sexuality to the fore of creoleness offers an important opportunity to reconsider what the notable anthropologist Sidney Mintz (1996) characterizes as the "openness of the Caribbean" (295) in his essay "Enduring Substances, Trying Theories: The Caribbean Region as Oikou-menê." Mintz's description of a "a learned openness to cultural variety, an openness not so much relativistic as non-valuative—an openness which includes the expectation of cultural differences, and is not shocked by them" (295) offers creolization as a distinctive historical and ethical process. This same framing of creolized culture as predisposed toward an acceptance of variety is echoed in Glissant's 1995 essay "Creolization in the Making of the Americas," wherein he evokes the Caribbean as "a place of passage, of transience rather than exclusion. . . . It does not tend toward the One, but opens onto diversity" (268). What currently prevents a rewarding and rightful recognition of creolization as a consistent cultural and social process that also operates across the erotic dimensions of Caribbean life is an entrenched resistance to the nonvaluative openness that Mintz and Glissant describe when it comes to sexual prefer-ences and behaviors. Sexual lives and desires that diverge from the asserted norms of the heterocolonial order have become so value laden that they seem-ingly cannot be accepted as distinct but equable in the same way as creolized Caribbean languages, religions, musics, and even cuisines.

H. Adlai Murdoch ends his comprehensive discussion of Glissant's theories of creolization, particularly those following *Poetics of Relation* (1997), that model the conditions for "non-hierarchival coexistence" to offer "a vision [that] maintains and affirms the diversity and pluralities of peoples and places . . . the possibilities of inclusion" (2013, 888). Yet, while this amplified potential for inclusion and the embrace of diversity lies at the heart of creolization, which in turn is acknowledged to lie at the heart of Caribbeanness, it is notable that the space for critical rapport between creolization and queer studies remains virtually unbridged. Articulating the conjunction between creolization and non-heteronormativity much more strongly, I argue for erotic practices and identities as integral to a Caribbean creolized model of "infinite possibilities within these distinctions and many ways of asserting identity" (Brathwaite 1971, 310). Bringing the complicating dynamics of creolization and the unfastening of heteronormativity more firmly into each other's orbits allows for a recognition of the already-existing creolized texture of sexual lives as part of the fundamental character of Caribbeanness and not as a violation of it.

This intervention is therefore also a response to the virtual silence within creolization studies in relation to the possibilities of creolized sexuality. Major edited collections that look to map the concerns and contours of creolization—such as *Caribbean Creolization: Reflections on the Cultural Dynamics of Language, Literature, and Identity*, edited by Kathleen Balutansky and Marie-Agnes Sourieau (1998); *Creolization as Cultural Creativity* edited by Robert Baron and Ana C. Cara (2011); and *A Pepper-Pot of Cultures: Aspects of Creolization in the Caribbean* edited by Gordon Collier and Ulrich Fleischmann (2003)—pay virtually no attention to sexuality studies. Indeed, while the grounds for intellectual and ethical rapport between creolized and queer are strong, at present Caribbean creolization studies has not taken opportunities to challenge the anomalous closed and fixed attitudes toward non-heteronormativity. Rather, as Omise'eke Natasha Tinsley argues, following her critique of Glissant's seeming unreceptiveness to gender and sexuality, "The most renowned theorists of inclusive Creoleness often do not recognize how their very neocolonial rootedness in binary gender and sexual identities undercuts the complexity that they express as fundamental to their project" (2010, 25). While most queer studies of the Caribbean have mobilized critical inquiries separate from, or on the margins of, studies of creolization/creoleness, in her 2019 book *Queer Times, Black Futures*, Kara Keeling proposes an affinity between queer expansiveness and creoleness in a brilliant reading of Glissant's *Poetics of Relation* against the grain that styles Caribbean creolization as "a new and original dimension allowing each person to be there and elsewhere, rooted and open, lost in the mountains and free beneath the sea, in harmony and errantry" (Glissant 1997, 34). In her study of Black American culture and history, Keeling emphasizes the worldliness of creolization at the present time and the suggestiveness of Glissant's insights into ongoing and unpredictable processes of change as they relate to her own queer counterimagining of a "World Galaxy." I share an interest in the non-normalizing character of Glissant's formulation of creolization as a thoroughgoing challenge to conscripting norms, despite its absent referencing to sexuality. The constant disturbance and creative rearrangement rendered by creolization in Glissant's work remain highly suggestive for erotic formations that often both unravel and complicate norms in dynamic ways that are transformative, even though often unobserved at the macrolevel: "plowing up of phenomena that acquire significance when put together, and in the domain of the unseen of which we represent the constantly shifting background. The accumulation of the commonplace and the clarification of related obscurity, creolization is the unceasing process of transformation" (Glissant 1989, 142).

Another suggestive example of how creole and queer echo in a Caribbean context can be noted in the corresponding elucidation of both by canonical thinkers. In his highly influential study of Caribbean cultural formations, *The Repeating Island: The Caribbean and the Postmodern Perspective*, Antonio Benítez-Rojo (1996) argues for this dynamic elusiveness as fundamental to conceptualizations of Caribbean subjectivity: "Caribbeanness will always remain beyond the horizon" (xi). This same expression of the value of being positioned just beyond the vista of the known and knowable is echoed by Cuban American José Esteban Muñoz's (2006) in his formation of queerness: "Queerness is always on the horizon. Indeed, for queerness to have any value whatsoever, it must be considered visible only on the horizon" (825). My work here seeks to draw out and to amplify the overlapping character of creolized non-normalizing sexualities as they are glimpsed and often indirectly articulated across theoretical and literary works and thereby to make visible the particular contours and complexities of Caribbean cultures as they relate to erotic expression and behavior.

As well as pointing out the shared fluid and pluralizing ontologies of creolized and non-heteronormative subjects, I foreground how queer theory's investment in the points of rupture and limit within established identity narratives and categories, and in identity as stylization and performance rather than biological discovery or determination, is importantly correspondent with what is already cherished and theorized as Caribbeanness. Theories of creolization describe and affirm a process of cultural encounter and exchange emerging from the Caribbean's extraordinarily dense and multilayered social and cultural fabric that gives visibility and value to ways of being, acting, relating, speaking, and feeling that exceeded and exploded the established ontological rubrics that defined the so-called categories of African, Indian, and European. Likewise, queer theory puts pressure on the sexual categories straight, lesbian, and homosexual and attempts to speak to—although, as with creole, not to offer a definitive outline of—sexualities that are both surplus to and inassimilable to prevailing categories.

Creolized sexualities as a concept draws attention to the significant complementarity and overlap between the undoing of erotic normalization and Caribbeanness on which the arguments of this book build. Just as the intense diversity of the Caribbean, where people may claim many ancestries and be multiply creolized, puts pressure on received ideas of national, ethnic, and cultural identity, so too the analytical and political strength of queerness lies in its undoing of the seeming naturalization of identity categories and its investment in points of rupture and indeterminacy. Certainly, inasmuch as it is marked by a proliferation of cultural overlaps and ethnic heterogeneities that not only undoes the possibility for singular normativities or deterministic signatures of being but also dismisses the epistemological moorings that uphold such regimes of the normal, the creolized Caribbean is a queer place.

In his brilliant early work "The Schooner Flight" (1979), Derek Walcott's poetic protagonist Shabine declares: "I had no nation now but the imagination" (8). The Caribbean is an invented place, remade by the ragged and ruptured history of colonialism and the plantation economy. The differently marked arrivals of African, Indian, Chinese, Irish, Syrian, and other European migrants, who were brought to the region in forced, misled, and opportunist migrations, considered alongside the decimation of the majority of the indwelling populations by disease or violence, means that the relationship between people and place is discontinuous, layered, and precarious in this region, in a way that is more pronounced and extreme than almost anywhere else. As Omise'eke Natasha Tinsley foregrounds, this historically enforced confrontation with, and refusal of, received modalities of identity (cultural, national, and gendered) has generated a Caribbean plasticity of being, and of knowing that being, which can be read as a queer fluid ecology in which the "insistent pounding force of ocean waters . . . smash and wear away essentialist conceptions of race and nationality" (2008, 195). Yet, while the main provocation of this study lies in foregrounding creolized sexualities of the Caribbean, it is important to clarify that I am not proposing that the Caribbean is uniquely or exceptionally a queer place in this regard but rather that in the intensity of its unpredictable, overlapping instabilities, permeabilities, and fluidities it provides an exemplary place from which the inherent queerness of creolized, postcolonial, cross-cultural realities can be glimpsed and recognized.

Feeling Sideways

One of the methodological obstacles to be confronted in foregrounding this interface between queer studies and Caribbean studies where creolized sexualities can be apprehended and articulated is the fact that queer studies are organized diachronically. The idea of history is fundamental to the tradition of European theoretical thought, much of which informs queer theory and also underpins the trajectory of liberation movements that invest in the idea of a future in which the world will be a better place. There is a strong affirmation in global queer theory and politics that queerness is historically possible in a post-Stonewall global world.[6] In their introduction to *Queer Globalizations: Citizenship and the Afterlife of Colonialism*, Arnaldo Cruz-Malavé and Martin F. Manalansan IV open with the vision of an expanding horizon: "Queerness is now global. Whether in advertising, film, performance art, the Internet, or the political discourses of human rights in emerging democracies, images of queer sexualities and cultures now circulate around the globe . . . the increased global visibility of queer sexualities and cultures in the marketplace has also generated multiple opportunities for queer political intervention through an equally globalized coalition politics" (2002, 1). Although the plurality and specificities of located sexualities are explored in the collection, queerness is presented here as an established, even universal, phenomenon that can extend itself in encounters with other places: "Globalization then . . . has also provided the struggle for queer rights with an expanded terrain for intervention" (Cruz-Malavé and Manalansan 2002, 2). The implication here is that only certain areas mark the limits of a transformative sexual politics and that these "backward" places can eventually be queered and delivered into the dominant trajectory of sexual liberation. Not only does this vision of "expanded terrain" hardly denote a decolonizing perspective, but the idea of global "queer sexualities" fails to recognize significant context-specific differences within queer conceptual and lived repertoires. As Ronald Cummings and Faizal Deen argue, Caribbean queer studies has crucially engaged with the history of the region and shaped interventions that are responsive to its located and intersecting struggles: "Widening the imaginative focus of Caribbean experience through a proliferation of sexual nomenclatures forges, along with earlier antiracist gains of colonial struggle, more complete portraits of decolonial intervention and more inclusive human futures" (Cummings and Deen 2021, 400).

In *Feeling Backwards: Loss and the Politics of Queer History*, Heather Love (2007) argues that queer studies needs to take account of loss, trauma, and difficulty—elements that have been downplayed or disavowed within its dominant historical narrative by the pressing demands to narrate rising political agency. As Love (2007) points out, this was an argument about the present state of queer theory and activism because those seemingly compromised subjects whose stories were previously eclipsed "indicate continuities between the bad gay past and the present; and they show up the inadequacy of queer narratives of progress. Most important, they teach us that we do not know what is good for politics" (27). It may also be that the current orientation of queer studies toward the Caribbean is not "good for politics" in its cultural assumptions of universality and its investment in the idea that queerness remains almost impossible in certain spaces.

To address this (mis)construction of impossible queer places, we might conceive of a parallel move to Love's that brings an often-unnoticed creolized queerness of Caribbean lives into view. Feeling sideways, rather than backwards, allows for an examination of what is excluded from, still haunts, and might provoke a useful rethinking of canonical queer theory's configuration of location, as well as of history. My own departure from the model of queer identity and self-realization that Love (2007) critiques follows the pull of place over time. If we accept the Caribbean as beside (another place) rather than as before or behind (as is often implied in the historical model of less "developed" or progressive areas), then we need to account for the possibility of a Creole queerness that is not erased by the absence of the historically and geographically specific touchstones of pride, assertion, display, outness, naming, and parade that have come to signify queerness under the global rubric. Feeling sideways allows space for understanding how Caribbean subjects might perform and constitute creolized sexualities in differently different ways that need to be considered on their own terms. Similarly wanting to "jettison [queer's] homogenizing tendencies," I am inspired by E. Patrick Johnson's conceptualization of "quare" (in turn inspired from his grandmother's African American vernacular) to propose a methodology that brings queer theory's disrupting drives into orbit with located Caribbean lives, "such that ways of knowing are viewed both as discursively mediated and as historically situated and materially conditioned" (Johnson 2005, 127).[7]

To work in this way is to challenge the assumption of privileged and progressive insights around liberated sexualities in the global north which, as Vanessa Agard-Jones (2009) explains, "increasingly inscribes a narrative whereby metropolitan queers are mobilized to 'save' local (Antillean) queers from local (Antillean) people" (9–10). Rinaldo Walcott (2009) has addressed how "this developmental understanding of the place of people of the global south in the modern lesbian and gay movement" (10) limits the possibilities for thinking about localized realities outside progress narratives: "Thus in book after book that chronicles the queer history of the movement over the last thirty years, people of the global south arrive at the literal end of the discussion as the last set of persons and bodies to come into their queerness. This enduring coloniality of queer life deliberately positions queers of the global south as needing a helping hand from the North Atlantic that is most times not about genuine struggle to build community but about as Spivak (2004) puts it in 'Righting Wrongs,' 'that they must be propped up (542)'" (R. Walcott 2009, 10). Agard-Jones (2012) makes a clear intervention against this powerful framing of same-sex impossibility in her attention to the queer presence on two beaches on Martinique's coast. Her "deeply local framing of these questions" (326) enables her "to refute the idea that queerness does not and cannot exist, or must somehow remain invisible, in the Caribbean, and that it is only through diasporic movement that people gain their capacity to be legible, visible, and politically viable subjects . . . to pay equal attention to the rooted, to those Caribbean people who build lives for themselves right where they are, under conditions of both intense contradiction and sometimes, too, intense joy" (327). It is a parallel sideways move to consider how the Caribbean may already be queer and has long been so that motivates my inquiry into literary works here.

Thinking of the Caribbean as an always already queer space on account of its multiply creolized sexualities is, in part, a strategic intervention that calls on the materiality of the region's past alongside the possibility of a radical rereading that directly contests the impossibility of fluid sexualities in the region. It is also a deliberate shift away from the "queering of the Caribbean," with its reliance on established representational and rights-bearing discourses to deliver "liberation" to the region, and toward a Caribbeanizing of the queer through recognizing creolizing erotics across the region. This move, which arguably sits at the cusp of a second wave of Caribbean queer studies work focusing on undoing erotic normalization, is not only theoretically suggestive but has a basis in lived realities across the region. As Caribbean critics before me have shown, a shift from categorizing toward comprehending erotic lives allows for creolized possibilities to be recognized and affirmed. Two anthropological studies based on close engagement with Caribbean communities offer useful precedence. David Murray's (2002) *Opacity: Gender, Sexuality, Race, and the "Problem" of Identity in Martinique*, which examines the complicated performances of masculinity in Martinique—both formal and everyday—draws attention to the "problems" of bringing identity-based constructions of sexuality to the much more fluid and unresolved set of behaviors prompted by varieties of male same-sex desire. Toward the end of his study, Murray (2002) makes the point that, in their unfinished and sometimes contradictory nature, expressions of sexuality are no less or more stable than those of race or gender (from which they are also not separate) in this Caribbean context: "I have argued that no structural paradigm—no one pair of opposites—can explain the social and cultural density of this or any Caribbean society" (159). Gloria Wekker's (2006) research on *mati* work in Suriname, *The Politics of Passion*, has been particularly influential in questioning the usefulness of the hetero/homo binary in modeling Caribbean societies. By showing how intimacies between Afro-Surinamese working-class women both elude incorporation into a hetero/homo schema and present versions of female sexual intimacy for which *lesbian* was an evidently unworkable term, Wekker's (2006) study points to the need to attend to cultural specificities and develop sexual literacies that do not translate the realities of one located world into the frameworks developed by and for another. She names her own conceptualization of a framework for the community of Surinamese women she writes about the "Creole Universe." This is a space and time that delegitimates attempts at establishing sexual norms and asserts the following: "The organization of the fulfilling passion in this Creole Universe shows that there is no one 'natural' way of going about one's sexual business" (Wekker 2006, 119). Both Murray's (2002) and Wekker's (2006) work advocates the need to feel sideways toward localized grammars and lexicons of Caribbean erotics, and to make space to think about sex with men or women, or both, as something that one *does* and not the person that one *is*.

Kamala Kempadoo (2009), a leading scholar in Caribbean sexuality studies, reaches similar conclusions around the inadequacy of binary, object-based paradigms in her comprehensive literature review, "Caribbean Sexuality: Mapping the Field." Kempadoo (2009) resolves that "for sexuality to be a vantage point for Caribbean research and study, the current complexities need to be acknowledged and the intricacies of a range of sexual arrangements and practices appreciated" (12). She hints that one of the obstacles is the insistence on sexuality as identity bearing and object-oriented, and she draws attention to how "the specification of sexual identity groups often elides the very varied sexual arrangements in the region" (2009, 2). Kempadoo calls rather for a focus on "how sexuality is expressed or practised, not the way in which sexed bodies or sexualities are constituted or determined" (Kempadoo 2009, 2). The impossibility of meeting the Caribbean on its own terms is also significant to Kempadoo's conclusions around the continued invisibility of the much more pluralistic, plastic, and positively experienced set of creolized sexual practices that occur in the Caribbean region, such as those described by Wekker (2006) and Murray (2002). Kempadoo (2009) suggests that many of these sexual practices are not commonly discussed or acknowledged because they are not experienced as the "primary basis for social identification" (2) and she thereby affirms Wekker's and Murray's call for a reorientation of Caribbean erotics away from an identitarian model.

Literary Criticism and Caribbean Queer Epistemologies

In the last decade a number of Caribbean literary scholars have crafted careful and intricate locally responsive acts of criticism that attend to the erotic texture of lived relations in Caribbean places. Their work has established an erotic lexicon of the Creole world that sets a foundation for my own work on creolized sexualities. Omise'eke Natasha Tinsley (2010) returns to Michelle Cliff's (2008) question—"What would it mean for a woman to love another woman in the Caribbean?" (69)—in order to reflect critically on the historically determined conjunctions between women, loving, and the Caribbean. Tinsley's (2010) *Thiefing Sugar: Eroticism between Women in Caribbean Literature* is a definitive critical intervention that restores unknown and overlooked narratives of women-loving-women from within the region. Clear that "when a woman loves a woman in the Caribbean, none of these words will mean the same as they do in the global north," Tinsley works with an alternative metaphorical schema to "focus on how enslaved women and their descendants use *sex with each other* to effect a different kind of erotic autonomy, on how same-sex eroticism enters into the history of sexual labor in the Caribbean as a practice by which women take control of sexuality as a resource they share with each other" (Tinsley 2010, 15, 20; italics in the original). It is through this conjunction of eroticism and labor that Tinsley (2010) develops the perspective—shared by Wekker (2006), Murray (2002), and Kempadoo (2009)—of "sexuality neither as a natural given nor as an identificatory marking . . . it emerges as a series of activities that these women can perform or refuse, accept or transform, enact or rescript" (21). Crucially, by grounding her own critical discourse in both the historical conditions of the Caribbean and the literary discourses that have emerged in the region for reimagining these, Tinsley (2010) maps the Caribbean as a place where "sweet transgressions" among women can be read as infusing cultures with moments and arrangements in which "black women [are] taking themselves for themselves" (299).

A related approach of working across canonical women's writings from a range of Caribbean locations according to a queer metaphorical grammar underpins Keja Valens's (2013) work, *Desire between Women in Caribbean Literature*. Similarly sensitive to the way in which "relations between women twist around, across, and within other relations, desires, loves; they do not overturn or exit other arrangements, but they pervade Caribbean letters in a way that exposes the insufficiency of heterosexual and homosexual paradigms" (23), Valens proposes an epistemology of the mangrove. She reroutes the Créolistes' "deep mangrove swamp of Creoleness" (Bernabé, Chamoiseau, and Confiant 1993, 111) to render a queer creolized ecology in which the knotty entanglements of desire between women can be read, without underplaying the extent to which the characteristic "clashes, intersections, and hybrid formations start to feel excessive and difficult to sort out" (Valens 2013, 66).[8] Her readings draw out the complicated and mangled erotic relations that defy categorization and trace rhizomatic patterns of survival "in a literary, theoretical, and political world dominated by gazes and structures that expect and want binary hetero/homo models" (154).

The entanglements of flesh in the theoretical and political world of the wider Caribbean are more explicitly addressed in Rosamond S. King's (2014) *Island Bodies: Transgressive Sexualities in the Caribbean Imagination*, which is focused on bringing attention to the particularities of Caribbean-located bodies and the ways in which these are sexualized as well as sexually expressive. As an interdisciplinary comparativist project, this study engages with Anglophone, Francophone, Hispanophone, Lusophone, and diasporic "Caribglobal" cultures in order to discuss a wide range of material from the 1970s onward, including literature, film, music, and popular cultural forms, such as festivals, calypso, and activism. The book congregates an extensive range of lived and cultural narratives through its focus on specific modes of transgression to gender and sexual norms as presented by trans people; *el secreto abierto* (the open secret) of known, but unacknowledged, sexual attachments between men; women-loving-women; women as sexual agents; and the dynamics of interracial sex. King's discussions of both real and imagined subjects are also attentive throughout to the deeply ingrained class and race hierarchies that infuse Caribbean regulations of gender and sexuality. Her work stresses the importance of resisting the homogenization or appropriation of diverse island bodies to an imported schema. For example, when elaborating on her choice to use *women who desire women* over *lesbian*, King explains, "It is important to note that the issue is not 'just' one of word choice. The lived experiences of nonheteronormative sexualities are often different in different places. And, in fact, it is because terms represent lived experiences in particular cultural, geographical, chronological, and social spaces that they make sense to us all. To use a term in an inappropriate context is to erase the specificity of that context and the agency of the individual, and to superimpose assumptions on them about what it means to inhabit their identity" (King 2014, 94). King's own investment in bringing the variety, specificity, and multidimensionality of Caribbean sexual subjectivities to visibility enables her to detail a rich and creolized continuum that has been inspiring for my work. Although King describes sexual norms and transgressions when structuring her arguments in order to expose social consequences, her book reveals patterns of fluidity and continuums of variety that confirm the queerness of the creolized Caribbean. My own readings seek to deepen King's line of inquiry in relation to literary works in English and to reorient "portrayals of transgressive sexualities" (King 2014, 195) as expressions of Caribbean creolized sexualities against, but also alongside which, narrower, official versions of sexual propriety and normalcy are asserted through legal, religious, and national discourses.

This project of reorientation toward fluidity is strikingly undertaken in Tinsley's 2018 *Ezili's Mirrors: Imagining Black Queer Genders*, which centers Ezili—"the name given to a pantheon of lwa who represent divine forces of love, sexuality, prosperity, pleasure, maternity, creativity, and fertility" (2018, 4)—as a black feminist assemblage through which "black queer artists can imagine love and possibility." Tinsley delivers Ezili's queer prismatic pantheon as a means of unlocking theoretical, spiritual, and ancestral archives in three differently fonted modes of address that unite memoir, analysis, and recovery to decolonize queer studies and its racialized constructs in favor of a recognition of creative black queer genders.

Collectively, these studies render Caribbean realities in which erotic fluidity, autonomy, and diversity come to be recognized as the commonplace of local, creolized social fabrics—even though they may be met with hostility and discrimination. The tropes, metaphors, and epistemologies grounded in Caribbean places that these critical studies propose create valuable footholds for localized erotic literacies to develop. Part of this literacy includes the place of unnaming within a schema of undoing. Within most of the literary works that I discuss, nonheteronormative attachments, desires, and orientations remain unnamed. It is important not to attribute this unnaming only to fearful recalcitrance in the context of the homophobic Caribbean as this elides the possibilities for recognizing unspoken and uncategorized ways of being. As Jafari S. Allen reminds us,

"Some [Caribbean people] eschew explicit naming, preferring to live their verbs, as for example, simply *am, is, are, been, being, be*—or *interrupt, invent, push, question, refuse, serve,* or *shade*" (2012, 213). In many ways, this unnaming of erotic subjectivity can be read as a mode of what Glissant terms the opacity found within creolized cultures, a term that describes a means by which to retain difference and recognition yet resist interpellation. As Murdoch argues, "Glissant puts it succinctly in *Traité du Tout-Monde*: 'I claim the right to opacity for everyone, which is not a withdrawal. . . . I do not have to "understand" anyone, an individual, a community, a people, to "take" them with me'" (2013, 886). Resisting Western enlightenment's project to specify the world and bring it into its reality, representations of sexual attachments and feelings that are socially apprehended and acknowledged without being reduced to the demands of definition often point to a tacit knowledge of fluid possibilities that circulates in cultures of everyday interaction. These tacit understandings are also a means of feeling sideways and structuring belongings that resist the social exclusions of narrow erotic normativities without explicit recourse to a named difference.

The Caribbean models of sexual arrangements and orientations discussed in scholarly work that I have outlined thus far implicitly call into light the erotic dimension of Sidney Mintz's proposition for the "openness of the Caribbean" (1996, 295) that I introduced at the opening of this chapter, and confirm the underlying energetics of creolization to all aspects of Caribbean lives. They affirm how Caribbean cultural logics, landscapes, and lived realities already provide the conceptual tools for thinking about erotics in more traversing and liquid terms. Why then not simply accept creolization as the methodology for moving outside the intractable logic of sexual norms and abnorms that feeds the dehumanizing culture of homophobia in the region? Denise deCaires Narain (2012) makes a very persuasive case for this theoretical move in her article "Naming Same-Sex Desire in Caribbean Women's Texts: Towards a Creolizing Hermeneutics." Arguing for creolization as "a more fluid calibration of differences that could/would recognize the mutability and endlessly shifting constellations of identity as they continuously unfold and refold," deCaires Narain (2012) calls attention to the inherent potential within creolization for a Caribbean-centered challenge to the anomalous sexual binarism: "Informed by queering strategies, a creolizing approach might also call into question the continued presumption of a heterosexual norm" (199). Her concluding call for a "persistently and patiently creolizing hermeneutics . . . that is already historically attuned to the complicated, contradictory cultural, racial, and sexual politics that inform Caribbean literary texts" (210) is endorsed by readings of creolized desires in works by women writers as diverse as Phyllis Shand Allfrey, Jamaica Kincaid, and Oonya Kempadoo.

While my own approach here follows this call for a creolizing hermeneutics, it is consciously impatient with the lack of rapport and dialogue to date between creolization studies and queer studies and seeks to accelerate the study of erotic creolization by emphasizing how a whole range of literary works already bridge this silence in their articulation of demonstrably creolized non-heteronormative sexualities. Drawing creolization firmly into the orbit of sexual non-normalization and nonfixity makes a calculated incitement that demands attention to the place of fluid erotics within the creole continuum. Creolized sexualities follow the Caribbean-centered epistemologies of the repeating island, the mangrove, and opacity that establish the queer principle of looking across and between established objects and forms of knowledge as a locally grounded way of knowing. Indeed, as Caribbean cultural critic Stuart Hall explains in his posthumously published memoir, *Familiar Stranger: A Life between Two Islands* (2017), approaching the world in multiple, oblique ways is a distinctly Caribbean mode of engagement. Generated by the historical dis-possessions of colonialism and from being "conscripted into modernity as peculiarly wayward soldiers," Hall (2017) describes what might be noted as a "queer" perspective as characteristic: "Our capacity to see the world askew, from below or backwards, or from below *and* backwards, free from the desire for domination which characterized the imperatives of the colonial order" (61; italics in the original). Indeed, Hall's configuration of Caribbeanness here inter-estingly echoes back to the definition of *queer* offered by Eve Kosofsky Sedgwick in her canonical work, *Tendencies* (1993): "The word 'queer' itself means across— it comes from the Indo-European root *-twerkw*, which also yields the German *quer* (transverse), Latin *torquere* (to twist), English *athwart*. . . . Keenly, it is rela-tional, and strange" (xii).

Affiliating the creolized structures of Caribbean cultural identities that draw on intersecting and parallel ancestral traditions to which individuals may belong multiply in a nonoriginary, nonhierarchical, and nonidentitarian fash-ion with a supple erotic repertoire purposefully creates a perspective from which the natural, rather than unnatural, place of non-heteronormative subjects within the creolized Caribbean can be imagined and recognized. To this end, my argument focuses on places and moments in which the assumptions, struc-tures, vocabularies, and bodies that support colonial and national versions of heteropatriarchy are rearranged, less available, and denaturalized, as well as actively resisted and repudiated, and reads these as integral to the region's cre-olizing dynamics. In this way, I follow what Lyndon Gill (2018a) calls "A Queer Cartography of Desire," that informs his own work traversing anthropology, queer and Caribbean studies, as it pays attention to "how . . . queer Caribbe-ans claim fertile spaces for themselves in places that have long had a queer rela-tionship to formal legal and moral dictates, in places where authority—colonial, postcolonial, neocolonial—has historically been and continues to be precari-ous and imperfect" (1).

Creolized Sexualities and the Literary Imagination

My core argument in the chapters to follow rests on how a range of Caribbean literary works in English demonstrate an integral capacity to world-build alternative affective and erotic relations that unfasten the hold of hetero- and homonormativities. I aim to show how, in their accounts of the multitude of the quieter, turbulent, understated, and undisciplined acts of living and loving, writers have already represented a much more supple, pluralistic, and disordered inventory of desire correspondent with the fluidity and multiplicity associated with the creolized Caribbean. I argue that literary works from different periods render sexual plasticity, indeterminacy, and pluralism as an integral part of Caribbeanness: not an imported, unnatural, or inauthentic threat to the region's identity, but as one of the most compelling if unacknowledged ways of resisting the disciplining regimes of colonial and neocolonial power. Focusing on the intersections of creolized and nonheteronormative lives is also significant to understand how the literary can represent different sexual subjects by crafting a rhetoric of human intimacies, desires, and subjectivities beyond the reach of those colonial and neocolonial conceptualizations that distort constructions of sexuality in the Caribbean through their exaggerated investments in and governance of sex.

The persuasiveness of this study lies in making visible the persistent literary disruption of normativities; therefore, the range of examples is significant. My argument holds to the idea that Caribbean creolized queer sexualities are not attendant on a group of writers and writings associated with an LGBTQI agenda or self-identity, but that querying sexual classification is an already present aspect of the complicated and entangled ecology of Caribbeanness that infuses its literary outputs. To this end, I present readings of so-called early works (Salkey's [2009] *Escape to an Autumn Pavement*, originally published in 1960) alongside contemporary ones (Mootoo's [2014] novel *Moving Forward Sideways Like a Crab*); critically acclaimed works (Marlon James's [2014] Booker Prize–winning novel *A Brief History of Seven Killings*) alongside those that have received almost no critical attention to date (Curdella Forbes's [2008] "A Permanent Freedom"); works by openly same-sex-desiring writers (Thomas Glave [2007, 2008b, 2012]) and so-called straight writers (Junot Díaz [2007]); works that clearly articulate a guiding preoccupation with questions of sexual identification (Glave's [2012] "Jamaican, Octopus") and those in which the words *gay*, *homosexual*, or *queer* are never mentioned, but nevertheless represent the social density of Caribbean queer lives in which non-heteronormativity unfolds in many contexts, variously, as part of a continuum of behaviors: as intimacy, relationality, desire, and physical expression (Naipaul's [1994] *A Way in the World*).

What emerges from reading these works alongside each other is their collective capacity to undo the intelligibility and sufficiency of invented, yet naturalized, sexual categories and binaries based on object-choice. They reveal a compelling correspondence between the cherished idea of belonging across different cultural worlds and histories modeled on a creolized structure, and the creative capacity within Caribbean cultures to host and accommodate fluid and overlapping erotic desire and arrangements consistent with the queering of sexual categorization. By showing that a wide, and possibly surprising, range of Caribbean writers have contributed to the crafting of a supple and inclusive repertoire of behaviors and attitudes relating to Caribbean erotics across the second half of the twentieth century, the readings in this book aim to demonstrate that a recognition of creolized and pluralized sexualities already exists within the literary imagination.

Chapter 1 examines both critical and creative writings that have sought to characterize the region's cultural distinctiveness and its long history of intensive and mainly unequal cultural encounters and exchanges. My argument here is that instead of thinking of Caribbean non-heteronormativity as a momentary possibility that erupts arrestingly from within, against the odds of the generally conservative and often homophobic character of contemporary social formations, we might rather look at the Caribbean as defined in and by the undoing of norms in its historical formations and cultural expressions. Reading outward from [Edward] Kamau Brathwaite's (1975) foundational essay, "Caribbean Man in Space and Time," which characterized the region's distinctive style of being and belonging as one that defies orthodox signatures, such as ancestral origins and customs, to embrace multiplicity and mutability, this chapter discusses how the work of historians, sociologists, and writers captures the overlaps and fusions that have transformed all transplanted cultures in the Caribbean into something distinctive and new. From Orlando Patterson (1982), Sylvia Wynter (1968, 1970, 2006), and Kei Miller's (2013, 2014) studies on African retentions, through Shani Mootoo's (2008a) meditation on South Indian indentured migrants, to Joseph J. Williams's (1932) attempts to trace the Irish in Jamaica, these very different accounts cohere in their gestures toward the Caribbean situation as one where the non-normative was the norm and where adaptive forms of belonging queered a wide variety of cultural formations, expressions, and attachments from different locations, times, and ancestries. By drawing attention to the intensity of cultural encounter, exchange, and entropy that characterizes the creolized queerness of the Caribbean region, I lay the foundations for an exploration of creolized sexualities and attachments that are all too often invisible or disavowed in the conventional modeling of creolized societies in later chapters.

In its second part, this chapter turns to a reading of Naipaul's fictional biography of the gender-creative figure of Leonard Side, which is delivered almost as a preface to his 1994 work, *A Way in the World*. I draw on the epistemologies of queer commentary to argue that it is through Naipaul's narration of and identification with this figure and a recognition of his own queer creolized identity that he comes closest to acknowledging his inexorable connection to his Caribbean people and a place that can be named, explicitly and without irony, as "home" (1). Moreover, I suggest that it is as a creolized queer figure who positions himself athwart the expectations of others in such a way as to surface the norms associated with their demands that Naipaul can be best understood as a Trinidadian and a Caribbean writer. Taking Edward Baugh (2011a, 2011b) and Lawrence Scott's (2011) readings of Leonard Side into account, I am most struck by the fact that Naipaul's rendering of Side as archetypally Trinidadian in his creolized queerness was first published in the same year as M. Jacqui Alexander's (1994) critical intervention "Not Just (Any) Body Can Be A Citizen: The Politics of Law, Sexuality, and Postcoloniality in Trinidad and Tobago and the Bahamas," which lays out the exclusion of certain bodies within the legal frameworks of citizenship and her status as a queer outlaw.

The four chapters that follow each focus on a particular mode of resistance to erotic containment and sexual normalization. Across these chapters, I argue that Caribbean literary works in English find imaginative ways to render erotic desires and attachments that not only undo heteronormativity, but also unfasten homonormalization, hypermasculinity, and ultimately the very idea of the human subject as imagined in colonial and heteropatriarchal terms. Sometimes the literary unsettling of erotic norms is strident, and sometimes it is tentative; sometimes it refuses any accommodation to existing social structures, but mainly it disquiets from within the structures of family, neighborhood, and nation in order to reveal and question the artifice and invention of the supposed natural status of an imposed norm. Taken cumulatively and read as inherent to the Caribbean's history of creolized formation and its cultural consciousness in which multiplicity and fluidity combine, these gestures within literary works provide an imaginative account of a category crisis around sexual norms and binaries in the region, and offer a meaningfully alternative account of erotic desires, tendencies, relations, and possibilities.

Chapter 2 turns attention to literary works that explore Caribbean heteronormativity as productively unstable and non–identity defining. In the face of repeated assumptions around the impossibility of non-heteronormative lives for citizens in the Anglo-Caribbean, this chapter reads Curdella Forbes's (2008) long short story, "A Permanent Freedom," and Shani Mootoo's (2008b) third novel, *Valmiki's Daughter*, as works that undermine heterosexual relationships as expressive of a natural and exclusive state of heteronormativity by revealing the inherent fragility and instability of heterosexuality. Both texts expand the horizon of erotic arrangements within which heterosex can be experienced and expressed in order to queer its social meanings and amplify its multiplicity and fluidity. I discuss how Cathy J. Cohen's (1997) article "Punks, Bulldaggers, and Welfare Queens" and Maria Lugones's (2007) essay "Heterosexualism and the Colonial/Modern Gender System" bring critical awareness to the ways in which heterosexuality and erotic ecologies are shaped by histories of colonialism and ongoing racialized power differentials.

Forbes's story affirms ways of being heterosexual that need not deny the right and the reality of same-sex eroticism. Here, a wife whose husband is dying from AIDS facilitates the reconciliation and embrace of desires between men. Narrated in turn by Alain, the lover; Denton, the husband; and Marsha, the wife, Forbes's formal inclusion of three people's voices in the non-normalizing marriage that she depicts mirrors the dynamics of their fuller story. Impelled by the queer temporality of imminent death, the multiple, consenting, affectionate, and inclusive relations that develop among these three individuals undo the claims of heteronormativity. In the diasporic ground of the U.S., this queer and inclusive marriage is able to exceed the disciplining boundaries of heteronormativity to imagine an alternative conception of queer belonging beyond conservative Caribbean iterations of national identity.

In Mootoo's novel, the commonplace cultural pluralism of Trinidad is framed with a focus on its sexual dimensions in order to give representation to a locally sensitive yet socially subversive erotic repertoire that undoes *straight* and *gay* in its multiple nonbinary manifestations. I read *Valmiki's Daughter* as a highly intricate, hyper-realist rendering of a queer creolized Trinidadian neighborhood that meets J. Halberstam's (2005) call for "describing in rich detail the practices and structures that both oppose and sustain conventional forms of association, belonging, and identification" (4). As a postcolonial writer, Mootoo's imaginative focus is set on the yawning expanse between individual desires and historically and socially sanctioned possibilities for sexual and emotional fulfilment. The novel unfolds the stories of the Krishnu family and the erotic lives that cannot be contained by their respectable, middle-class home in San Fernando. Valmiki is a successful, married doctor with two daughters: Viveka and Vashti. He is also a man of unfulfilled yearnings whose queer life is characterized by regret and recalcitrance. His daughter, Viveka, boldly resists gender constraints, but only slowly comes to experience her sexual passion for women. Although the novel ends with its queer characters in heterosexual marriages, it offers no sense of sexual closure or normalization. Rather, the narrative spotlights the ideal of erotic liberation yet to come. It explores the constrained, but real possibilities for erotic lives that both allow for the social continuation of heterosexuality and at the same time contribute to its demise as the explanatory narrative of natural and rewarding human attachment. Both Forbes and Mootoo's literary works are interested in the ethical possibilities for living together in difference, as well as for living fully. They represent heterosexuality as a sometimes porous, creolized, and queer arrangement that can accommodate the very same-sex erotics against which a heteropatriarchally organized society draws its definitional and sanctioning power.

Chapter 3 centers on a reading of Andrew Salkey's (2009) *Escape to an Autumn Pavement*, originally published in 1960, and its abrasive insistence on queering the progressive politics of homonormalization emerging in Britain in the late 1950s from a distinctly Caribbean perspective. In many ways, this novel sits adjacent to its literary peers of the Windrush generation as a narrative of a Caribbean person reaching for cultural belonging in a landscape imprinted by colonialism. However, its sustained and direct engagement with erotic undecidability and freedom markedly distinguishes its engagement with the thematic of accommodation dominant during its era. Engaging with Kate Houlden's (2013) article, "Andrew Salkey, the British Home and the Intimacies In-Between," which focuses on how Johnnie, the protagonist, challenges the normalizing expectations of the English domestic space, I am interested in Johnnie's creolized Caribbean erotic subjectivity. Salkey's literary depiction of a distinctly Caribbean encounter with the horizons and limits of belonging works to critique and unsettle emerging, so-called progressive, discourses of sexual citizenship instantiated by the Wolfenden Report of 1957 and its defense of the respectable homosexual. The chapter discusses protagonist Johnnie Sobert's refusal of identity categories and identitarian politics that extends from race and class to sexuality, and how his rebuttal emerges clearly as a decolonizing impulse inspired by the fluid identity resources of being a creolized Caribbean person. I situate this reading alongside Nadia Ellis's (2015b) study, *Territories of the Soul: Queered Belonging in the Black Diaspora*, which takes Johnnie to exemplify the queer diasporic subject whose migrant status "lends to the queer refusal of lineage, futurity, and community" (99). Also attending to the novel's critical reception at the time of its publication, I argue that the correlation that this novel implies between creolized Caribbeanness and sexual non-normalization remains an open provocation and invites a meaningful engagement that continues today around the terms on which sexual desire and identification can be socially expressed and recognized.

Chapter 4 explores the queer character of hypermasculinity and the overlapping nature of extreme and extravagant performances of normative Caribbean gendered identity with queer desires. With a focus on Marlon James's (2014) *A Brief History of Seven Killings* and Junot Díaz's (2007) *The Brief Wondrous Life of Oscar Wao*, I explore how the strenuous and extreme performances of macho masculinity in these extended and excessive narratives expose the continuous and extraordinary effort necessary for maintaining the precarious fiction of a hypermasculine nature, rather than confirming the norm of masculinity that they insistently seek to present. Kei Miller's (2013, 2014) creative nonfictions are discussed for their shrewd engagement with the overlaps between Caribbean hypermasculinity and queerness. Indeed, the insights shared in these creative and critical works serve to complicate sociologist Linden Lewis's (2003a) own call for an extension and nuancing of the narrative of Caribbean masculinity, which is still based around an assumed hetero/homo binarism.

Given that Díaz's (2007) novel spins around and toward the expectation of its protagonist Oscar's lost virginity and his attendant acquisition of Dominican manhood, with its extreme heteropatriarchal calling in the mythic masculinity of *el tiguere dominicano*, the non-normalizing character of Oscar and of his decisive heterosexual encounter is compelling. Throughout the narrative there is a mismatch, an unsettling asymmetry, between Oscar's erotomania and his virginity as he becomes an unreadable figure in the Caribbean diasporic world into which he is born. Oscar's queerness is both highly visible and utterly unrecognizable without recourse to the novel's footnote-freighted context of the Dominican Republic's historic bond between state violence and hypermasculinity, which I discuss with reference to Maja Horn's 2014 *Masculinity after Trujillo* and Dixa Ramírez's 2018 *Colonial Phantoms: Belonging and Refusal in the Dominican Americas, from the 19th Century to the Present*. I offer a reading against the grain of Elena Machado Sáez's (2011) claim that Oscar's queerness is silenced, in favor of the novel's articulation of cosseted yearnings toward distinctly other possibilities for erotic and emotional connection and attachment. James's (2014) novel similarly surfaces attention to the demands that political struggles place on muscular masculinity in the different Caribbean context of the political unrest of 1970s Jamaica. *A Brief History of Seven Killings* can likewise be read as a novel that critiques the corrosive performance of the hardcore masculinity that accrues and exudes its power across the novel's 700 pages. The hypermasculinity of gangsters and drug dons is an unremarkable state in the ferocious places that the novel narrates and the "bad man" who has sex with men, such as Weeper and John-John K., is no less bad in this regard. Reading between Nadia Ellis's (2015a) critique of the novel's excess and her refusal "that understanding Jamaica requires quite this much of everything: pages, characters, violence, sex" (n.p.) and Sheri-Marie Harrison's (2015) spirited defense of the novel as "redefining the political stakes of the Anglophone novel" (n.p.), I focus on the extravagant erotic politics of James's novel and the complicated identity performances and solidarities that queer both hypermasculinity and homophobia without denying their social power.

In reading creolized and non-heteronormative hypermasculinity across two narratives that speak to the social complexity of American Dominican and Jamaican lives, respectively, I am aware of the discrete national histories shaping these distinctively excessive scripts of gendered and erotic performance (the Dominican diasporic *tiguere* and the Jamaican don), as well as the role played by the U.S. in shaping both these Caribbean masculinities at home and in the diaspora.[9] With the inclusion of Díaz's *The Brief Wondrous Life of Oscar Wao*,

I am also stretching beyond the Anglo-Caribbean world to explore work that is written into the diasporic Americas in English—although importantly an English that is pushed to "the edge of disintegration" (Díaz in Celayo and Shook 2008, 14) in its code-switching collisions with Spanish, African American vernacular, and "nerdish." Díaz's depiction of language, belonging, ancestry, and identity as intensely creolized in the Caribbean American, American Caribbean world the novel navigates, queers normative borders as its imaginative promiscuity unsettles linguistic, territorial, cultural, gender, and sexual norms. Indeed, including Díaz's novel and its exploration of Dominican American lives within a Caribbean enclave in the United States draws attention to the ongoing creolization process associated with the dynamics of the diaspora and the resultant transitions and expansions of Caribbean literature in English as a corpus that is happening through writers from the Hispanophone or Francophone Caribbean writing in English in the U.S., and the new directions for critical and cultural inquiry this allows.

Chapter 5 turns toward two more imaginings of Caribbean bodies and lives that are not determined by configurations of sexuality and gender as identity bearing and thereby undo the claims of heteropatriarchy. Reading Shani Mootoo's novel *Moving Forward Sideways Like a Crab* (2014) alongside Thomas Glave's shorter works "Whose Caribbean? An Allegory, in Part" (2008b), "He Who Would Have Become 'Joshua,' 1791" (2007), and "Jamaican, Octopus" (2012), this chapter explores the potential of creative works to re-engage discourses of the natural in such a way as to disrupt historically imposed sexual categorizations that support the heteropatriarchal biopolitics of church and state. Mootoo's novel takes the form of a fictionalized memoir to consciously address what it means to tell and to know a life—both another's and one's own. The novel explores the relationship between Jonathan Lewis-Adey, a Canadian writer in his forties whose career is faltering, and Sid Mahale, whom Jonathan first knew as Siddhani, the Indian Trinidadian female partner of his white English biological mother, who left their home and Jonathan when he was ten years old. When Jonathan finally finds Sid in Trinidad—decades later—she has transitioned to Sydney. The novel embeds this reunion story in a wider Trinidadian context, and, while it seeks to pluralize the possibilities for sexual being, it also reveals the limited categories through which sexual subjectivity is permitted to articulate itself. Through Jonathan's final acceptance of Syd and of Trinidad, this text reveals how creolized realities open an alternative approach to sexual and gender differences that may exceed identities altogether in its focus on being. Responding to Rosamond King's (2014) critical observation in *Island Bodies* of the "backhanded" (25) inclusion of trans characters in Caribbean literary works, and Keja Valens's (2016) approach to "the trans relations in *The Pagoda* as offering ways around, through, and under heterocolonial patriarchy" (80), I read the consciously digressive narrative of *Moving Forward*

Sideways Like a Crab as a deliberate means by which to frustrate the ready-made identity stories that give bodies meaning in order to feel sideways toward a possible Caribbean creolized erotic agency.

Glave's "Whose Caribbean? An Allegory, in Part" (2008b) and "Jamaican, Octopus" (2012) issue a distinctive challenge to sexual intolerance by imagining a posthuman queer ecology. Glave's (2012) vision of trans-species embodiment resurfaces—through a creatively queer state of mind—an agency that allows him "to swim, sentence by sentence, toward a language that might in some way capture, represent, even directly (or at least figuratively) illustrate, the ways and hows of becoming the varying and occasionally connected whos whom I wish (and sometimes, depending on the day and environment, do not wish) to be" (91–92). These works vividly shift the expected thresholds of ontological experience beyond what might be seen as normal human variation and toward seemingly unrecognizable and unassimilable difference in such a way as to agitate understandings of gendered and sexed embodiment as they have come to be naturalized within the social imperatives of anthropocentric heteropatriarchy. Reading Glave's writings in the historical context of the criminalization and dehumanization of same-sex acts in Jamaica, which date back to the postemancipation period, highlights the representational and anatomical grammars of colonial discipline contested by his radically reimagined discourses of the natural and the erotic. Aligned with the work of erotic restitution Audre Lorde (1984a, 1984b) made so significant and urgent in her essay "The Uses of Erotic: The Erotic as Power," Glave's writings affirm a queer way of being on its own terms. Indeed, rather than making space for the accommodation of different sexual subjectivities, these texts render a submerged paradigm of experience where bodies are released from all accepted reasoning around the configurations of sexual encounters and claims to sexual citizenship.

In keeping with the other imaginative works discussed in this book, these writings by Mootoo and Glave are transformative in unsettling norms and rearranging understandings of sexuality and identity. Through this series of close readings, I aim to highlight the particular potential of the literary to help imagine who Caribbean erotic subjects want to be, how they want to be known, and what kinds of freedom they desire in fresh and surprising ways. My claim is that the varied Caribbean literary works in English with which I engage collectively question the configurations of attachments, the movements of desire, and the thresholds of erotic intelligibility to bring to light a radical rethinking of creolized sexualities and undoing heteronormativity as a means of extending and embedding queer belongings.

1

The Queer Creolized Caribbean

● ●

> Caribbean peoples seem to have fewer problems than most in recognizing the fuzziness and overlap of categories.
> —Michel-Rolph Trouillot, *Silencing the Past*

> Its fragmentation; its instability; its reciprocal isolation; its uprootedness; its cultural heterogeneity; its lack of historiography and historical continuity; its contingency and impermanence; its syncretism, etc.
> —Antonio Benítez-Rojo, *The Repeating Island*

This chapter continues to dispute the anomalous imposition of a heteropatri-archal norm for regulating and describing erotic desires and attachments in the Anglo-Caribbean by arguing for creolized sexualities as intrinsic to the region's historical formation. The Caribbean is widely acknowledged as a region that has made possible new ways of experiencing culture and new ways of theorizing identities as syncretic and hyphenated, as hybrid and cre-ole. Indeed, the region's creative cross-cultural interactions have long been proposed as its defining character. In his celebrated edition of *The Repeating Island*, originally published in 1992, Antonio Benítez-Rojo (1996) elaborates on the Caribbean's "sociocultural fluidity," positing that this is the fundamental design "that the Caribbean archipelago presents, with its historiographic turbulence and its ethnological and linguistic clamor, with its generalized instability of vertigo and hurricane" (3). This characterization is immediately followed by Benítez-Rojo's call for creative methodologies equal to the "multidisciplinary maps of unexpected designs" (3) that this region inspires. Reflecting on this established account of the intrinsic variability of the Caribbean and the demand its complexity and mutability issues for inventive ways of theorizing cultures and identities, it is striking how, to date, sexual fluidity has not been addressed as an integral part of the Caribbean's cultural mix. As Kamala Kempadoo (2009) concludes in "Caribbean Sexuality: Mapping the Field," her critical overview of sexuality studies in the region, "Common to many of the studies is that sexual practices and arrangements are held to be operational around a gender binary that firmly attaches the biological to the social, and where heterosexuality is seen as the only form of legitimate sexuality" (9).

In order to make my wider claim about the correspondences between Caribbeanness and non-heteronormativity, in this chapter I walk through the existing bridges that Caribbean writers and intellectuals offer between what is already accepted as the character of the Caribbean in terms of its sociocultural fluidity and that which is not yet accommodated within discussions or models of creolization—the diversity of sexual desires and attachments. In making this connection, my work also looks back to Shalini Puri's (2004) argument in her important book, *The Caribbean Postcolonial: Social Equality, Postnationalism, and Cultural Hybridity*, and in particular, her core objective "to connect a poetics of hybridity to a politics of equality" (1). Although Puri (2004) does not explicitly connect hybridity to the equal status of queer subjects, she makes it clear that "'equality' is a necessarily open-ended term, the meanings, reach, and sites of which may continually expand through social struggles" (1–2). The timeliness of a critical conjunction between Caribbean hybridity and Caribbean sexual pluralism is certainly highlighted by the struggles facing non-heteronormative subjects in the Anglo-Caribbean today. Moreover, while Puri (2004) warns us not to take any innate congruence between cultural hybridity and social equality for granted, as "discourses of hybridity may be harnessed to quite different political projects (from bourgeois nationalism and dependent capitalism to socialism or fascism)" (5), her own readings ably demonstrate the potential that the poetics and politics of cultural hybridity hold to challenge and renegotiate dominant discourses of cultural nationalism.[1] Working in this vein, my effort here is to explore how this same discourse of cultural hybridity and creolization, that is accepted to characterize

Caribbeanness, can offer ways to animate and renegotiate understandings of Caribbean sexualities such as to bring a model of diversity and one of equality into closer kinship.

When Nadia Ellis (2011) draws her article "Out and Bad: Toward a Queer Performance Hermeneutic in Jamaican Dancehall" toward a close, she focalizes on the intimate bodily rapport between two Trinidadian women engaged in the participatory carnival rituals of Jouvert, and offers this to the reader as a moment "when the culture itself produces or enables the [Caribbean] queer" (21):

> A poetics that caused these women to dance with each other with a fluidity that it is impossible to describe here, their bodies equal in size and scale, welded together as if they were matching halves, spiritual twins—one light, one dark—creating a synthesis of race and gender through linked and coordinated body movements that seemed memorized in another time and invoked here by the music, the rum, the crowds, the sun. Evoked by the license provided by a centuries-old tradition that named the carnivalesque—the parodic, the subversive, the topsy-turvy inversion of all that is normative and status quo. These women were the most arresting images of Jouvert that morning because their pleasure instantiated a queer performance that was wholly of its place and time, consecrated by the popular traditions at the very heart of the nation. (Ellis 2011, 23)

While Ellis points to the particular license of carnival as creating a breach in the "normative" cultural order, my aim in this chapter is to think differently about the holds of the "normative" within Caribbean societies and cultures. I want to propose thinking of Caribbeanness as a mode of cultural agitation as well as formation that persistently disavows and undoes the predicted uniformity of identities and relationalities implied in and imposed by the idea of normative culture.

Through a discussion of a range of accounts focusing on different ancestral groups brought to the Caribbean region and the violent crucible of plantation culture, I venture that normative cultural orders were never fully established as a way of living even though strict social norms were (and continue to be) politically enshrined and legally enforced. My argument is that instead of thinking of creolized, non-normalizing sexualities in the Caribbean as a momentary possibility that erupts arrestingly from within, against the odds of the generally conservative and often homophobic character of contemporary social formations, we might rather look at the creolized Caribbean as already queer in its historical formations, lived realities, sensibilities, and cultural expressions. In many ways, this is an act of feeling sideways around what is already recognized about Caribbean identities.

In his essay "Caribbean Man in Space and Time," [Edward] Kamau Brath-waite (1975) outlines the way in which the tensions between the administered norms and social hierarchies of the plantation society operated multiply and contingently within its lived contexts to establish a dynamic, complicated, and renewing set of possibilities in which the variance from the imposed norm would itself vary and differ among different groups and across different times:

> The rigid classificatory orders (culture, class, color, money, status) set up as the result of colonialism and slavery, developed into caste-like structures mainly because of the massive importation of African slaves and Asiatic labor between the xvii and xix centuries. These peoples brought with them into the region a non-European culture, which under the extensive and multiform conditions of the plantation, developed into a kind of negative pole to the white European orientated patterns of the elite, reacting with these to create a *creole* personality. *But this "creole," as a result, no doubt, of its origin and manner/circumstances of evolution, did not become a single/whole norm; but itself a product of the fragmentation syndrome of the entire region, divided itself into multi-variate orientations, reflecting its complex ancestry.* (Brathwaite 1975, 5; italics added)

Brathwaite's work on the formation of creole societies remains well regarded and influential for its description of the creolization process over forty years after its first publication. My argument for the normal story of the Caribbe-an's undoing of heteronormativity draws on Brathwaite's foundational descrip-tion of the region's distinctive style of being and belonging as one that defies orthodox signatures, such as ancestral origins and customs, to embrace multi-plicity and mutability. As Brathwaite makes clear, this creolized fashioning results from the material histories of forced migrations, contested colonialisms, and multiple diasporas. The deconstructive force of the Caribbean's historical situation informed by an unrivaled velocity and violence of global compression resulted in the rupture of national and continental belongings, and its planta-tion cultures became a crucible where cultural encounter and exchange occurred with accelerated intensity and astounding multiplicity. In this context, the very idea of stable and shared normativities became unsustainable. My aim in this chapter is to explore how the uncontroversial porosity and plurality of Carib-bean cultural identities have already been described and celebrated by a range of writers and thinkers and offer an important conduit for recognizing sexual pluralism and plasticity as an integral part of composite Caribbeanness.

Queer Ethnicities: Performing Identities after Origins

Historical sources relating to slavery and indenture are notoriously incomplete and often so biased toward the colonial worldview as to be irrelevant in terms of restoring or recognizing enslaved and indentured lives. The varying degrees of agency and powerlessness that enslaved Africans and indentured Indian, Chinese, and Irish populations encountered when they arrived in the Caribbean alongside a small European planter class remain the subject of historical inquiry and debate. However, what most extended histories do reveal (and the phenotypical variety of the Caribbean instantly confirms) is that the mixing and exchanging among these groups and others that took place over generations made the possibility of restoring natal identities increasingly difficult, if not impossible. While certain recitals of and claims to ethnic clarity, such as the Afrocentric Rastafari movement, have a durable presence in the Caribbean, theirs is a demonstrably performative gesture of inherited belonging that must consciously and creatively style the signatures of ancestral cohesion to forge affective pathways of historical continuity. What is more interesting perhaps than the difficulty of restoring originary identities is the way in which such identities became simply redundant or irrelevant in terms of shaping Caribbean identifications. Indeed, it is this reorientation away from origins that Derek Walcott claims as integral to Caribbeanness in his 1974 essay "The Caribbean: Culture or Mimicry?": "In the Caribbean history is irrelevant, not because it is not being created, or because it was sordid; but because it has never mattered. What has mattered is the loss of history, the amnesia of the races" (6).

In his landmark study *Slavery and Social Death*, the Jamaican historical and cultural sociologist Orlando Patterson (1982) speaks about the enslaved as "alienated from all rights or claims of birth, he ceased to belong in his own way to any social order" (6). The consequences of this brutal alienation from ancestral modes of belonging and the impossibility of such belonging as a future assurance of self-knowledge and transgenerational identification enacted a monumental transformation in terms of identity-making norms. As Patterson (1982) describes: "What is critical in the slave's forced alienation, [is] the loss of ties of birth in both ascending and descending generations. It also has the important nuance of a loss of native status, of deracination" (7). Elaborating Patterson's "notions of freedom, politics, and world-making activity," Greg Beckett (2017), highlights how the creolized cultural formations that developed from the historical trauma and compulsion of the Caribbean situation became constitutive of what he calls "Freedom from a Caribbean Point of View":

> After all, Caribbean societies were born on slave plantations designed to prevent the continuation or emergence of cultural and social forms of collective life. Slaves were violently torn from African societies; most, if not all, ties of kinship, affiliation, language, culture and religion were severed. In the midst of this natal alienation and social death, Caribbean slaves forged new ties, created new languages and religions, and gave birth to new cultural formations. In short, the Caribbean case shows how freedom—as world-making activity—can

emerge from even the most radical forms of discontinuity and domination. (Beckett 2017, 187)[2]

Arguably, even for those population groups who came to the Caribbean and who were not enslaved, such as the Indians who arrived postemancipation on indentured contracts and were able to retain their religions and languages, the devastating conditions and exploitative practices of the plantation made their right to return practically impossible and their ability to retain their cultural wholeness and integrity untenable. They too participated in these particular modes of creative freedoms.

The lived realities of these histories were devastating, and the colossal violence and injury that colonialism inflicted on the enslaved and the indentured should not be understated in any account of the cultural outcomes of the Caribbean's historical formation. As Derek Walcott (1998) again captures in his later essay "The Muse of History," the colonial project in the Caribbean was an extraordinary world-building exercise, and the result of its violent welding of continents and peoples and its monumental displacements was nothing less than a shift in the terms of belonging: "I give the strange and bitter and yet ennobling thanks for the monumental groaning and soldering of two great worlds, like the halves of a fruit seamed by its own bitter juice, that exiled from your own Edens you have placed me in the wonder of another, and that was my inheritance and your gift" (64). Walcott's expression of the Caribbean's disorientation to ancestral identities has infused his poetry too, and his works gently but insistently render realities that shift assumptions about subjectivity and the claims of colonial history. In Shabine's famous declaration in "The Schooner Flight,"—"I have Dutch, English and nigger in me / Either I'm nobody or I'm a nation" (D. Walcott 1979, 4)—Walcott recenters human experience away from the Cartesian choices and racial categories that shaped the enlightenment subject of colonial discourse to chronicle and validate what the Caribbean experience made possible that was not otherwise in existence.

In other works of fiction and of scholarship, this alternative grammar of Caribbeanness that exists alongside the official norm-imposing orders of colonial and then national institutions is similarly articulated as a subjugated knowledge. Reading across works of sociology, anthropology, and autobiography that focus on the African, Indian, and Irish experience in the Caribbean, I aim to draw out the correspondence between the distinctive cultural improvisations and intersections that these works describe as fashioning Caribbean lives and sensibilities and the non-normalizing, or queer, cultural expressions and identities that emerge. Collectively, these accounts reveal vibrant lived alternatives to the authorized, official versions of self and sovereignty enshrined in colonial education, law, and the church. They chronicle the mobility and multilayering of the social and cultural influences by which Caribbean peoples came to know, express, and legitimize themselves. Again, this is not to claim that the Caribbean is uniquely informed by heterodox cultural influences. As Glissant reminds us, "All societies undergo acculturation" (1989, 141). It is rather to follow Glissant's idea of cross-cultural poetics and to amplify the importance of his observation that the Caribbean is distinguished by not wishing "to deny or disguise" its composite nature in relation to gender and erotic relations (141).

In her article, "Jonkonnu in Jamaica: Towards the Interpretation of Folk Dance as a Cultural Process," the Jamaican scholar and writer Sylvia Wynter (1970) addresses an important fissure in colonial historiographies through which the alternative grammar of the "little traditions" of Caribbean folk culture can be mined: "History has mainly been about European super structures of civilization. Yet, in the interstices of history, we see, in glimpses, evidence of a powerful and pervasive cultural process which has largely determined the unconscious springs of our beings: a process that we shall identify and explore as the process of '*indigenization*' a process whose agent and product was Jamaican folklore, folksong, folk-tales, folk-dance" (35). Like Brathwaite (1971), who referenced Robert Redfield's model of a distributed, but interdependent civilization in which "there is a great tradition of the reflective few, and there is a little tradition of the largely unreflective many" (Redfield's 1956 *Peasant Society in Culture* quoted in Brathwaite 1971, 213), Wynter (1970) also draws on this term to argue for the continued significance and value of submerged vernacular folk cultures in the Caribbean.

For Wynter, restoring the meanings of these folk rituals through historical account and sociological analysis provides an important critical intervention that restores the worth and legacy of African survivals. Wynter (1970) focuses on the "Jonkonnu or John Canoe festival [which] had its beginning in a cultural process that Sloane witnessed and described in the seventeenth century" (37). Establishing the connection of this festival to the African yam festival and associated religious practices with drum and dance, Wynter traces how the historical sources also point to the name Horsehead—an acculturation with English Morris dance. She accounts for this cultural exchange and fusion within the ethnically diverse and socially compacted enclaves of eighteenth-century sugar production: "Each estate was an enclosed world and although the refusal of the Jamaican planters to Christianize their slaves (for economic motives) prevented the latter acculturation that would take place, there were points of contact between the English, Scotch and Irish indentured servants, and particularly the bookkeeper class. It was through this class, poor, cut off from much contact with their fellow-whites, living in concubinage with African, creole, and mulatto women, that some sort of cultural fusion must have occurred" (38). Despite her rigorous examination of sources that help to discriminate possible origins, the fact of these cultural exchanges gradually becomes more significant than their individual ancestries in this work.

Referring to the "Sword dance-cum-Play" that Edward Long describes in his three-volume 1774 *History of Jamaica*, Wynter (1970) comments on how the sword "may suggest the influence of the English Sword-dance-cum-Play. The sword is also important in Ashanti rituals, however" (38). She later discusses another element of the dance that further implies the unsteadiness of historical origin as explanation, and expresses the fluidity of cultural exchange and identity performance: "The *numerous crowd of drunken women* who follow him and refresh him with aniseed water finds a replica in the band of women who escorts [sic] the chief masquerade Egungun-Oya. Oya, the river goddess, is here supposed to assume the form of man and so the women are her escort. Could the aniseed water be an offering to the river goddess?" (38; italics in the original). Wynter's argument is driven by the significant and timely postindependence task of recognizing and appreciating African cultural retentions in a Jamaica where they were still routinely denied and reviled. Her careful scrutiny of numerous sources proves that "Africa would *not* be denied" (44). Yet, while Wynter seems to associate the Jonkonnu dance's "true" meaning with its original meaning, her essay as a whole moves against this logic. The giddiness of loose and multiple cultural signifiers declares itself, and the queerness of the performance might also suggest that origins are no longer relevant in this creolizing context.[3]

Wynter also identifies the dance's character as an embodiment of cultural encounter and exchange as key to its social function. Indicative of the nascent Caribbeanness that folk culture expressed and enabled, Jonkonnu's supple, multiple, and indistinguishable ancestral signatures enable a cultural incorporation open and meaningful to all: "The society—with its numerous and bitter divisions—found a precarious integration in a festival whose framework and function was African in origin. The framework and function was [sic] able to fuse with the Haitian-Catholic Carnival influences, since, in spite of its overlay of civilization and Christianity, the European Catholic Carnival was itself a reinterpretation of pagan folk rite. It was with this ritual remnant that the Jonkonnu, in its indigenous aspect, found culture contact points; thereby absorbing elements into its own structure" (Wynter 1970, 43). The African origin is the substantial point to Wynter given her objective to establish a critical alternative to a colonial historiography tilted toward European cultural legacies. I wish rather to highlight the heterodox character of Jonkonnu and the way in which recognizable African gestures, such as masks and dances, evolve over time through cultural exchanges such that they can no longer be tied back definitively to any one place of origin. This is not an argument to diminish African survivals, which, as Wynter demonstrates, were integral to the "indigenization' process [which] represents the more secretive process by which the dominated culture survives; and resists" (39). Rather, it is an argument in favor of recognizing how early Caribbean cultures evolved from encounters and exchanges between ethnic groupings, which may have been densely differenti-ated in terms of social and economic hierarchies but which were also often inti-mate and overlapping in the proximities of the plantation. In Wynter's own terms, the continual renewal of Jonkonnu to accommodate new elements and new festivals—including in the Hussay Festival of Indian Muslims—demonstrates how "the little traditions of Africa, England, Scotland, and India fused" (45). It is arguably then in these creolized expressions that result from proximate relations and inclusive, participatory festivals that different ancestral groups can trace their cultural survivals in which, distinctively, the whole becomes more significant than its parts. The little tradition of Caribbe-anness emerges and evolves in the vernacular, creolized fluidity that leaves behind the authority of discrete ancestry. As Glissant (1989) notes, "Composite peoples, that is, those who could not deny or mask their hybrid composition, nor sublimate it in the notion of a mythical pedigree, do not 'need' the idea of Genesis, because they do not need the myth of pure lineage" (141).

The final Jonkonnu parade dance that Wynter (1970) discusses continued until at least as late as 1969 and was known as Sailor and a Whore Girl *"who dance[d] vulgar all the time"* (43; italics in the original). Her account draws attention to the burlesque of sexual acts and identities: "Apart from Whore Girl, there was another character called the Wild Indian. In this dance, both these principals are men, but Whore Girl is dressed as a woman. He/she lifts his/her dress, holding it at both sides to show the underwear, bends back with knees open and bent forward, and does a dance, which is an exaggerated form of the hipsway and pelvic roll" (43). Wynter also details another possible vari-ation of this dance that multiplies its capacity for obscenity: "The movement of the Whore Girl, as she leans backwards with legs open and upper portion of her body steady as she *"hipsaws and winds and twists*," is a parodied and more explicit motion of the original African courtship dance.... But, at the same time, the fusion of the original African pattern and the European individual couple context, causes the dance to seem indecent both in its Christian/Euro-pean context, and in its African religious context" (44). These descriptions catch the traces of different histories appearing in simultaneous presents to attest not only to the discontinuities of ancestral time and place, but also to the joyful contravention of gender and sexual norms that moves within and across different traditions and that plays up the transcultural meeting. Cross-dressings and the same-sex play they license are overlayered here too by extrav-agant performances of cross-cultural scripts. While these exaggerated and exceptional acts of disobedience to gender conformity, if not to gender bina-rism, can be read as warnings and assertions of the norm, they still make visi-ble the performativity and thereby creative possibility of gender.

Perhaps then it is not surprising that when the contemporary Jamaican writer and essayist Kei Miller (2013) addresses the subject of "queer and mythological beings" in "Maybe Bellywoman Was on 'Di Tape (2011)'" it is to the manifold undecidability of Jonkanoo that he also turns:

> Jonkanoo is a word of disputed etymology. Some say it is Malinke, where jonkanoo would translate to "the sound of the slaves." Others say it is a festival named after a mythical slave called "John Canoe" who perhaps, if we are [to] take his last name as a sign, sailed all the way back to Africa. Others root it in other West African tribes and celebrations, but no one knows for sure. . . . It is a parade featuring a strange and nightmarish cast of characters from the skeletal Hobby Horse, to the Pitchy Patchy figure in all its rags from the Great House (yes, a character with the actual effigy of a house on his head), to the Policeman with his baton, and the Devil with his fork. And finally—here it is— Bellywoman—with a ridiculously sized ass, and a ridiculously sized belly in front. These two things jiggle the more that Bellywoman dances. And what makes this performance all the more ridiculous/odd/queer is that Bellywoman is always played by a man. (Miller 2013, 105)

In Miller's account, the origins are unclear, possibly irrelevant, but what is striking is how the festival surfaces the subjugated knowledge of fluid sexualities. As Miller observes, "looking at queer or gay identities in postcolonial countries like Jamaica; they seem to live more comfortably in mythical rather than in actual spaces" (100).

Miller does not seek to translate the meaning of Bellywoman to any fixed sexual identity or singular sense, but he does point to the way in which it is in this "little tradition" of folklore that accommodation of Caribbean-specific non-heteronormative gender and sexual expressions can take place: "I don't think the word 'queer' nor, again, am I immediately aware of some kind of 'gaydar' going off. It is simply of interest to me the ways in which Jamaican culture makes space for transgendered performances, but always in these almost mythical characters" (Miller 2013, 105). This point is elaborated when Miller refers to other figures within the fabric of folklore who challenge how enforced norms and expectations around sex and gender are performed: "River Mumma—that great cock-tease, always trying to tempt men into her depths, but when it comes to it, absolutely impenetrable. Or . . . the orisha, Guede, that dandy of a man with his cigars, and famously bisexual. Or . . . the trickster spider, Anansi, with his high-pitched voice, the ease with which he leaves his web in full drag—rouge and lipstick and his wife's high-heeled [shoes] on all eight legs—" (100). In Miller's contemporary observation, the cultural meanings of these folk performances are released from their ancestral origins as they come to resonate with and magnify possibilities for expressing the subjugated knowledge of Caribbean non-heteronormativities. His reading of these mythical creatures suggests that the queerness of the creole mix already allows for a recognition of the multiplicity of sexual and gendered ways of being just as it allows for the recognition of multiple origins.

A similar recognition of non-heteronormative possibilities within a Caribbean history that eschews the claims of "pure lineage" is articulated by the Trinidadian Canadian writer Shani Mootoo (2008a) in her autobiographical account, "On Becoming an Indian Starboy," which opens with a striking declaration of creolized queerness: "Given my own coordinates, transnationalism seems to have been bred in the marrow. It and various forms of queerness swing hand in hand" (83). When giving an account of her ancestral story of Indian Trinidadians who crossed the kali pani and changed their names to shed caste and possibly religion, Mootoo concludes "why not?—in a new land they might as well become whatsoever and whosoever they fancied" (83). Significantly, Mootoo draws here on queerness as the term that can make intelligible the particular Caribbeanness of the possibility for reinventing and reimagining identity stories away from ancestral norms:

> I suspect that once an Indian from India stepped foot on one of those boats in the nineteenth century, bound for the islands of the British Empire, in leaving behind language, family ties, community, the village, tradition in general, very specific religious rites, he or she was transitioning into a *queerness* of no return. Those of us in more recent times, responding to a restlessness no doubt provoked by that earlier rupture, have migrated elsewhere again. And now, far from Trinidad, we continue to invent entirely new ways of being. Yet by dint of the original displacement, we seem destined to limp along in a limbo of continuously changing and challenging queerness. (Mootoo 2008a, 83–84; italics added)

This same call on queerness as a feature of a Caribbean history is made by Sean Lokaisingh-Meighoo (2000) in his article "Jahaji Bhai: Notes on the Masculine Subject and Homoerotic Subtext of Indo-Caribbean Identity," which argues outward from the profound compression of homosociality of the boat brotherhood to come to something of the same conclusion, "that jahaji bhai already contains a queer quality, and always has" (89).

Mootoo's own family's contribution to this cultural mutability—her birth in Ireland and her pulls to the African-centered carnival and steel pan in her youth—did not however prevent a repeated familial insistence on her becoming "a good Indian girl." While these admonitions were directed at ethnic conformity, it was the assumed norms within the implied gender script of an "Indian girl" that Mootoo privately queered (Mootoo 2008a, 87). Appearing to herself as the Indian starboy of Hindi movies in her "own performance of female masculinity," Mootoo crafted herself as the object of female desire "admiring my cream-colored scarf, my tall cowboy boots, and accepting me fully for all that I was and was not" (90). However, as her narrative relates, aware of the barriers to social acceptance of this styled "me," Mootoo's public performances of the star-boy were muted. They were, however, still resistant enough to those of "a good Indian girl" to allow her to escape being appropriated by the family's heteropa-triarchal narrative: "I wouldn't be—and didn't want to be—as competent as they were in the ways of courting and being courted by boys, or be the object of potential mother-in-law's interests and inquiries. To quietly underscore and ensure all of this I adopted a dress code that all but made me invisible" (92). Con-sciously narrating this choice within the logics of a "queer time and place," that queer theorist Halberstam (2005) posits as an alternative to a heteronormative temporality based around successive generations, Mootoo (2008a) describes her conscious refusal to conform: "While [my sisters and other girls at my school] dressed for the male-female, heterosexual schedule of time, where boyfriends, marriage, babies, etc. were points along their route that told them how well they were doing, I dressed not to be noticed at all" (92–93).

Importantly though, Mootoo does not render her refusal of Indian Trini-dadian and Trinidadian gender and sexual norms as a condition of individual dissidence. Rather she sees herself as "a person in a country and in communi-ties that are constantly transitioning" (Mootoo 2008a, 94) and concludes her essay by suggesting that her story is a very Caribbean story, confirmed by and consistent with the region's histories. In Mootoo's account both the Caribbean and queerness mark a place where the disappearing acts of identity and the inventions of being can be acknowledged: "As my queer Indo-Trin-Can stories suggest, transnationalism is not an entirely new story. It is an old, complicated, and on-going one" (94). In this way, Mootoo deliberately accommodates the vocabulary of sexuality studies—queer, transitioning, trans—into her account of Trinidadianness, to foreground the affiliations and associations between sex-ual and cultural fluidity, as well as the inherent non-normalizing tendencies of her creolized place across time.

Interestingly, Montserratian poet E. A. Markham (2002) echoes Mootoo's imagined response of "why not?" to the question of reinvented ancestry in his autobiographical poetic work "Lines Composed to Test the Idea of Montser-rat." Like Mootoo, Markham refuses a linear organization of space, time, and ethnic markers as a way to know and tell his Caribbean self.

I'm writing an autobiography,
was born there, grew up here, etc.
Somewhere I'll lay claim to heritage, why not Irish;
so, to get there I won't start from here, sort of thing.
Here, you see, is the wrong place. (Markham 2002, 34)

Markham's interrogative "why not" points, as in Mootoo's work, to Caribbe-anness as an openness to possibility rather than a measure of genetic or geographical predictability. His orientation to ethnicity is not straight—genetic or ancestral—but rather an expression of the possibility of multiple directions that exceed geographical belonging.[4] The poem refuses the predetermined compulsion of bloodline in favor of affiliation, of assent, of craft. Markham's temporal and spatial grammar of an autobiography is consciously queered by the celebrated imprecision of a creolized inheritance and a diasporic life, here made into a virtue and subject-making practice by the will to allow imagination to act as memory.

As these examples across the twentieth century show, in the contemporary period the positive framing of Caribbeanness as an identity in which categorical stability is both an impossible and an undesired social objective has become more obvious. I have already alluded to how this focus on Caribbeanness openness generated by the overlapping intensities of multiplicity and hybridity underpins Benítez-Rojo's (1996) *The Repeating Island*, originally published in 1992, and Édouard Glissant's (1989) *Caribbean Discourse*—two of the most influential works to theorize global Caribbeanness. This same emphasis is also articulated within an Anglophone tradition of critical-creative thought. Indeed, Glissant's conceptualization of "subterranean convergence" and transversality (66) was an inspired response to Brathwaite's (1974) evocative imagining of a Caribbeanness in *Contradictory Omens* in which "the unity is submarine," and offers a compelling means by which to "see the fragments/whole" (64, 7):

And so transversality, and not the universal transcendence of the sublime, has come to light. It took us a long time to learn this. We are the roots of a cross-cultural relationship.

Submarine roots: that is floating free, not fixed in one position in some primordial spot, but extending in all directions in our world through its network of branches.

We, thereby, live, we have the good fortune of living, this shared process of cultural mutation, this convergence that frees us from uniformity. (Glissant 1989, 67)

George Lamming (1960), in his classic analysis of colonial relations, *The Pleasures of Exile,* had also earlier highlighted the exceptional suppleness and resilience of West Indian subjects as their historical advantage in an increasingly cross-cultural world: "We in the West Indies can meet the twentieth century without fear; for we began with colossal advantages. The West Indian, though provincial, is perhaps the most cosmopolitan man in the world. No Indian from India, no European, no African can adjust with greater ease and naturalness to new situations than the West Indian" (37). A portrait of this pluralistic Caribbean situation is sketched beautifully in Derek Walcott's (1993) Nobel Prize acceptance speech, *The Antilles: Fragments of Epic Memory* and his subjunctive rendering of the Trinidadian capital city, Port of Spain: "Above all, it would be so racially various that the cultures of the world—the Asiatic, the Mediterranean, the European, the African—would be represented in it, its humane variety more exciting than Joyce's *Dublin*. Its citizens would intermarry as they chose, from instinct, not tradition, until their children find it increasingly futile to trace their genealogy" (74). What Walcott catches here is the Caribbean as a cultural location that incarnates the possibility of a future in which ancestral and ethnic motivations are no longer in play. The lateral solidarities imagined in the place of originary bonds emerge from the freedom of human desires unregulated by regimes of the normal that inherited traditions seek to impose.[5]

Within Caribbean studies most attention has been placed on recovering and re-evaluating the origins and survivals of an African ancestral world violently denied by enslavement and disciplined by colonial culture, as well as South Asian and Chinese histories lost to their Caribbean descendants through the brutal conditions of indentureship. The defining lines of racial power between White and non-White in the region have made the study of White ethnic minorities less compelling but the particularly paradoxical situation of the Irish—both victims and perpetrators of the colonial system—makes for an interesting study in terms of creolized queerness. Although traces and signs of Irish lives in the Caribbean are now scant, and proofs of cultural encounter and exchange among the Irish and different ethnic groups are principally momentary, fragmented, and incomplete, there is still enough to suggest an intriguing and complicated history of lived experience in intimacy with one another, if never quite in equivalence. Since their arrival in the region in the seventeenth century, the Irish have occupied an ambiguous role: White but mainly unfree; of Europe but also a cultural and faith minority; sometimes the victims of colonialism, sometimes the beneficiaries, and sometimes transitioning from one to the other on account of their Whiteness. This is a Caribbean situation that the Irish share to some degree with the Portuguese who were brought to Guyana as an alternative labor sources following the abolition of slavery in 1834.

For Irishness, an ethnicity that is so celebrated and championed as an identity with ethnic stability and continuity (especially in the American diaspora), the relationship to the Caribbean is especially controversial and vexed because it dissolves into the creole solution with its queering of ancestral claims. The first book-length study on the subject of the Irish in the Caribbean—*Whence the "Black Irish" of Jamaica?*—was written by Jesuit priest Joseph J. Williams (1932). The book's title poses a question about origins, and Williams is keen and earnest in his attempts to present a genealogy that discriminates historical fact from the competing versions of events his sources commonly present. Yet, despite Williams's attempts to discipline his sources, his account inevitably becomes entangled in a matrix of historical possibility that exceeds a reliable accounting of actuality.[6] While Williams's fourteen-page bibliography evidences his commitment to recovering this history in detail and exactness, he continually infers the difficulty of overcoming national, faith, and class bias within his sources as well as the exaggerations of hearsay. Finally acknowledging the incomplete and uncertain knowledge of Irish origins and lines of ancestry, he declares: "Whatever, then, may be the final conclusion about the fate of the Irish 'wenches' and boys who were ordered by Cromwell to be shipped to Jamaica, a question which, for the present at least, must be left as an open one, this much is certain, that from the earliest days of the English occupation of the Island, there was a large proportion of Irish, both Catholic and non-Catholic, in the make-up of the population, and that not only Irish names but Irish blood as well is widely diffused throughout the island today" (J. Williams 1932, 74–5). Offering an alternative to the impossibility of an official history of the Irish in the Caribbean, Williams moves closer to a Caribbeanized creolized history of the Irish in which the markers of their distinctiveness are eroded by the accelerated cultural and ethnic mixing and intermixing that characterize the region.[7]

Like Wynter, Williams's (1932) encounter with historical sources finally yields a narrative of contradictory calls upon identity that helps make more meaning of the fluid, noncategorical Caribbean present and future than it does of any individual group's discrete past. What makes Williams's understanding of the history of the Irish in the Caribbean so demonstrably one of queer relations are the images that accompany his text. The book opens with the title page framed on the left-hand side by a remarkable figure, named as "Typical of the 'Black Irish' in Jamaica."

For Williams, having worked through the fragments of historical record and all its contradictions and twists, such "typical" black Irish are unproblematic and unremarkable—a consequence of a characteristically queer Caribbean history in which phenotype no longer functions as a guarantee or even a sign of origin. This seemingly conventional studio portrait of a man of African descent who is also Irish also provides a characteristically Caribbean response to Markham's earlier call of "why not?"

Belonging to Each Other through Queer Relations:
V. S. Naipaul's *A Way in the World*

Across these different accounts, the Caribbeanness of the Caribbean is consistently characterized as emerging from an overlapping of different cultural influences, survivals, and narratives that queer both singular ancestral and genealogical claims, as well as the imposed colonial codes of being. Collectively, these accounts of creolization point to how—partly from historical necessity and partly from creative determination—the Caribbean situation became one

FIG. 1. "Typical of the 'Black Irish' in Jamaica," in Joseph J. Williams, *Whence the "Black Irish" of Jamaica?* (New York: Dial Press Inc, 1932).

where the non-normative was the norm and where adaptive forms of belonging queered a wide variety of cultural formations, expressions, and attachments from different locations, times, and ancestries. They also confirm contemporary sociologist Linden Lewis's (2003b) observation that "it is in the interstices of negotiating issues of blood and belonging, location and identity, that considerations of gender and sexuality in the Caribbean must be located" (2). These diverse accounts collectively offer glimpses of supple identities, not organized around a hetero-originary norm, as an integral part of the creolized Caribbean.

My argument that a wide range of Caribbean writings reveal the inherent undoing of heteronormativities in Anglo-Caribbean societies means that it is important to be able to show this in relation to writers and writings that are not ordinarily considered to be aligned to queer agendas. The late Nobel Prize–winning Trinidadian novelist V. S. Naipaul certainly fits into this category. In an interview with Farukh Dhondy (2001), Naipaul accused E. M. Forster of homosexual predation with a colonial twist. In another interview at the Royal Geographic Society (2011),[8] he claimed that not a single woman writer was his equal. Indeed, it would seem Naipaul provided plenty of evidence to support Trinidadian writer Lawrence Scott's (2011) observation in "The Novelist and History" that "Naipaul is old-fashioned, old-fashioned about race, about women, about sexuality; an isolated figure, unaware of how the world around him is changing, with regard to these issues, or, if aware, untouched, unmoved, isolated in a kind of 'conservatism' pursuing now the fictional writer-self in these later days" (180). Scott is not alone in condemning Naipaul's attention-seeking refusal of the defining contract brokered between anticolonial politics and the obligation of the writer to represent the lives of their people through a humanizing lens. Acclaimed writers and critics, including Chinua Achebe (1997), Edward Said (1986, 2001), and Timothy Brennan (1989), have commented on how Naipaul's politics and prejudice cannot and should not be a mere aside in affirmations of his obvious literary prestige.[9]

Importantly though, despite the seemingly compelling grounds for Naipaul's dismissal and his notorious self-exile, the impulse to respond to and engage with his work remains strong in the Caribbean. According to one of Caribbean literature's founding critics, Edward Baugh (2011a), "Running through this continuing attention is the conviction that Naipaul has not lost, cannot lose his West Indian connection" (6). Or, as Trinidadian writer and critic Jennifer Rahim (2007) expresses it, "Naipaul's voice is irresistible, even as it can disturb and exasperate, illuminate and vex us" (xxv). A fascinating focus for this paradoxical notion that Naipaul might actually illuminate the very place and people he has often been perceived to distance himself from emerges in his fictional portrayal of Leonard Side, a consciously minor and marginal figure in Naipaul's (1995) *A Way in the World*, first published in 1994.

I want to read Naipaul's Side as a queer figure who brings pressure to bear on assumed normativities by living between genders and mixing cultural, ethnic, and religious codes and in whom, remarkably, Naipaul apprehends the possibility of his own belonging in and to Trinidad. For those who see Naipaul as terminally estranged from Trinidad, it is usually his first work of nonfiction, *The Middle Passage* (1962), that is invoked as evidence. It was for this work that Naipaul returned to Trinidad from Britain, where he had initially migrated to study at Oxford University, on a scholarship offered by the then chief minister Eric Williams. Published in 1962, the year of Trinidad's independence, Naipaul's account could hardly be described as a celebration of a nation. It was, rather, an unfolding of the overlapping wounds that sliced through the society and its aspirations—the past of slavery and indenture, the present of corrupting nationalism, and the future of American cultural imperialism. As Patrick French (2008) observes in *The World Is What It Is*, "Vidia's caustic presentation of the Caribbean would mark him as a writer at odds with his society and the conventional nationalism of the 1960s" (207).

More than any other remark, Naipaul's (1962) comment in *The Middle Passage* that "history is built around achievement and creation; and nothing was created in the West Indies" (20) remains his most quoted denouncement. It is taken to crystallize his choice to "side" with the West, viewing Trinidad through a gaze that Selwyn Cudjoe (1988) characterizes as "intense disdain" (120) in *V. S. Naipaul: A Materialist Reading*. While this infamous declaration has become an inescapable refrain commonly portrayed as Naipaul's last word on the subject of his home, it is not. Indeed, just sentences before this seemingly conclusive denouncement, Naipaul (1962) writes, "The history of the islands can never be satisfactorily told" (20). It is to this issue of the satisfactions perpetually unmet by the telling of partial histories (nationalist, heroic, religious) that Naipaul returns in an altogether more intimate register in *A Way in the World* ([1994] 1995), Naipaul's "summing up" book, "the magnum opus of my maturity" (Gussow 1994, n.p.). In it, he returns to some of the figures and historiographical problems addressed in his (1969) work *The Loss of El Dorado—a Colonial History*. Here, though, there is a heightened concern with his own legacy as a chronicler of the island and his career-long quest to come to terms with its history—or what might exist in the absence of the "properly historical." Rhonda Cobham-Sander (2011) comments that "Naipaul knows that his work will outlive him, and in this later writing he is fighting for the right to influence the way in which that legacy will be read" (54) in her essay "Consuming the Self: V.S. Naipaul, C.L.R. James and *A Way in the World*." Like most other readers of *A Way in the World*, Cobham-Sander is most interested in Naipaul's portrayal of his legacy in comparison to that of C.L.R. James, "a historical figure who many consider his nemesis" (59). Since this is a book in which Naipaul draws on the stories of other lives to position himself,

I want to argue that it is Leonard Side who plays the most transformative role in framing Naipaul's sense of belonging and legacy. Side has attracted little comment in the protracted critical conversation about Naipaul's allegiances. Yet it is arguably through his opening story in this work that Naipaul finds a way to address his lingering and painful relation with a past and a people who were never fully known or knowable to him and, thereby, to face what is at stake in his own frustrated satisfactions.

In his essay on the "The Making and Self-Making of V.S. Naipaul," Edward Baugh (2011a) locates Side's story as an opener to the "central concerns of the book" (13). He argues that Side's eccentric occupations and surprising tastes present "the sort of bizarre juxtaposition that Naipaul delights in" and that "ultimately the sense of the incongruous, the bizarre, even the morbid, that attaches to Side is symptomatic of an incompleteness of self-knowledge, an incompleteness related to his loss of ancestral inheritance, his displacement, his loss of history" (14). In *Caribbean Autobiography: Cultural Identity and Self-Representation*, Sandra Pouchet Paquet (2002) also notes Side's function in this textual sequence as "prelude to a narrative quest for forms of identification with which to circumnavigate the enigma of racial and cultural inheritance" (198). I extend these readings here to explore how it is more precisely in Side's non-normalizing nature that Naipaul finds a way to make a nascent ethical gesture toward his Caribbean belonging via the shared loss of inheritance and of deterministic signatures of being.[10] I argue that it is through Naipaul's narration of and identification with a queer figure that he comes closest to acknowledging his inexorable connection to his people and a place that can be named, explicitly and without irony, as "home" (Naipaul 1995, 1). It is also as a queer figure who crosses and twists to position himself athwart the expected norms of others that Naipaul can be best understood as a Trinidadian and a Caribbean writer. Through Naipaul's alignment with Leonard Side's queerness, we can feel sideways across the established presumptions of Naipaul as someone who has changed sides to advocate for the global north, to a place where the insistence on taking sides can be abolished and his intimacy with the queerness of his Caribbean self can find expression.[11]

A Way in the World begins with Naipaul's childhood and works backward, telling stories of Columbus, Raleigh, and Francisco Miranda, a failed South American revolutionary, as well as of the other world-famous Trinidadian C.L.R. James (who appears under the fictitious name Lebrun). However, Naipaul (1995) opens this work of encounter with monumental historical figures with a prelude on Leonard Side, "a decorator of cakes and arranger of flowers," whose story is told to him by a woman schoolteacher (2). In the single page that prefaces Side's story, Naipaul (1995) speaks about how, on his return to Trinidad, "everything was strange and not strange" and how "to go back home was to play with impressions in this way" (1). Moving the narrative into the schoolteacher's voice, Naipaul's telling of her story recounts three encounters with Side as she first seeks him out at The Women's Auxiliary Association to judge a flower-arranging competition for her female students. The collision of Side's gender dissidence and her professional duty to deliver a mode of education that ensures normative gender socialization is narrated with as much ingenuousness as the word *home*. All the same, both this seeming contradiction and the intriguing mixed matrix implied in the promotion of a May Day fair (with pagan roots) by a Presbyterian teacher of Indian descent for the improvement of "girls from laboring families" (2) queers the narrative frame by twisting the transmission of social and cultural norms from the start. On each occasion that the teacher encounters Side, he is going about his everyday life. What she sees is unremarkable to him and those who live around him, yet she registers her shock and near disgust at the incongruities he presents.

On the first occasion, redirected from her initial destination, the teacher does not realize she is entering a funeral parlor and is so taken aback by the "dark Indian man . . . doing things with his fingers to a dead body on a table or slab in front of him" that she runs off (Naipaul 1995, 4). Called back by his "soft voice," incongruous with "the hairy fingers I had seen dressing the dead body on the table" (5), she makes the arrangement with Side for judging the girls' competition and accepts his suggestion of a posy of pink rosebuds as a prize. When she returns the following year, determined not to enter the funeral parlor, the teacher goes directly to The Women's Association.

> The little Spanish-style house was full of women, and inside the room Leonard Side was doing things with dough, using his hairy fingers to knead dough. . . .
>
> 'He was teaching the women how to make bread and cake. After he had finished doing the dough, he begun to teach them how to ice a cake, forcing with those hairy fingers colored icing out of the special cones or moulds he had. He pressed on and then into the moulds with his hairy fingers, and out came a pink or green rosebud or a flower which he then fixed with icing-flecked fingers on to the soft-iced cake. . . .
>
> 'But I didn't like seeing those fingers doing this kind of work, and I liked it even less when, at the end, with those same fingers he offered the women little things he had iced, to eat . . . (Naipaul 1995, 5)

The delicate, dexterous, and delicious workings of Side's hairy fingers provoke a recurring aversion. The promised rosebuds of the first encounter, now a sweet-tasting delicacy to be taken into the body, provoke a further turbulence in the strangely erotic and yet morbid risk they present to bodily containment.

On the third occasion the teacher visits Side at his home where, mistaken for the doctor, she is invited into Side's bedroom: "There I found Leonard

Side, very sick and trembling, but dressed for a meeting with the doctor. He was in a shiny brass fourposter bed with a flowered canopy, and he was in green silk pajamas. His little hairy fingers were resting on the satin or silk spread he was using as a coverlet. He had laid himself out with great care" (Naipaul 1995, 6). This time, dissonance is announced first by the sick body having laid itself out in silk pajamas in an uncanny echo of the funeral parlor. In this scene, the troubling incongruity that the teacher repeatedly registers between Side's physical body, his place, and his acts of being is extended outward to the cultural mélange presented by the bedroom setting—crepe paper flowers, bows, and a framed picture of a radiant, beautiful Christ even though she knows him to be Muslim. Although Side stirs feelings of pity as well as of fear, it is his blurring of boundaries that most disturbs the teacher: "It was his idea of beauty that upset me, I suppose. . . . That idea of beauty—mixing roses and flowers and nice things to eat with the idea of making the dead human body beautiful too. . . . The mixing of things upset me" (Naipaul 1995, 7). In the teacher's story, Side's hairy hands, crossing between the equally delicate work of mortician, flower arranger, and cake decorator, are agents of contamination and category confusion. Her narrative concludes: "He frightened me because I felt his feeling for beauty was like an illness; as though some unfamiliar, deforming virus had passed through his simple mother to him, and was even then—he was in his mid-thirties—something neither of them had begun to understand" (Naipaul 1995, 7–8).

In the only other close reading of this scene known to me, the Trinidadian writer Lawrence Scott (2011) draws attention to the single digression in the teacher's story, which punctuates this bedroom scene: "It was late afternoon, warm still, and through the open window came the smell of the cesspits of St James, the cesspits of those dirt yards with the separate little wood houses, two or three to a lot, with runnels of filth from latrines, runnels that ran green and shiny and then dried away in the dirt; with the discolored stones where people put out their washing to bleach; with irregular little areas where . . . fruit trees and little shrubs grew" (Naipaul 1995, 6–7). For Scott, the insinuation of a horizon between Side and the cesspit draws an explicitly homophobic frame. Naipaul's own toxic and discriminatory public remarks function as a powerful imprint for his reading of this scene.

> This is clearly a portrait of a gay man who is ill. The language and the pathetic fallacy of the "cesspit" and the "slimy" drains point to him and his world as dirty, even as the narrator conveys fears of his beauty. Why does Naipaul try to give the story of Leonard Side to his schoolteacher narrator? What is gained? Is this a mask of sorts? We know what he thought of E. M. Forster and Maynard Keynes from one of those recent outbursts . . . attacking them as homosexuals. The persuasive stylist tries to take us in, but the craft is serving some other

purpose. Is this the homophobia not of some fictional female schoolteacher, but the author himself, V. S. Naipaul? (Scott 2011, 180)

While the teacher's fluctuating gaze, inward at Side and outward at the cesspits, does create an unmistakable echo of her revulsion at the shared shiny green of the effluence and the pyjamas, her inside-out perspective constructs the scene as she averts her gaze from the disquieting sight of Side and his bedroom. For the teacher, this act of looking away is also a refusal of her own fixation on his body, specifically his fingers. Side's world intrudes into her senses—her sight, her taste—and she wants not to be "touched" by what she sees.

While I do not disagree with Scott's (2011) conclusion that "the question of sexuality seems deeply problematic in Naipaul's work" (180), I read the relations between Naipaul, the teacher, and Side differently by giving more weight to Naipaul's distancing of himself from the teacher in his subsequent reflections. After the schoolteacher's story and her expressions of fear and distaste, there is a clear pause in the narrative—registered by a line space, a new paragraph, and the words "This was what I heard" (Naipaul 1995, 8). Only after this do Naipaul's considerations take shape—mainly the shape of his own unknowing. Unlike the teacher, in telling his story Naipaul looks toward Side, rather than away from him, and narrates precisely how he is touched by him and by his connectedness to him.

Naipaul (1995) observes that he does not know what happened to Side, he does not know what Side would have known about his own family, history, or "nature": "All Leonard Side would have known of himself and his ancestors would have been what he had awakened to in his mother's house in St. James. *In that he was like the rest of us*" (8; italics added). Indeed, this is an affinity Naipaul (2001) seems to affirm in "Two Worlds," his Nobel acceptance speech: "We made no inquiries about India or about the families people had left behind. When our ways of thinking had changed, and we wished to know, it was too late. I know nothing of the people on my father's side" (n.p.). In the closing paragraphs of his prelude, Naipaul returns to what Edward Baugh (2011b) defined as the author's ongoing "quarrel with history," a dispute that has animated both Naipaul's writings and their reception. Acknowledging the failure of the conventional historical archive to yield knowledge that can satisfy the demands of originary belonging, Naipaul attaches his historical sensibility to the personal stakes of this absence:

> With learning I can tell you more or less how we all came to be where we were . . . While the documents last we can hunt up the story of every strip of occupied land.
>
> I can give you that historical bird's eye view. But I cannot really explain the mystery of Leonard Side's inheritance. Most of us know the parents or grandparents we come from. But we go back and back, forever; we go back all

of us to the very beginning; in our blood and bone and brain we carry the memories of thousands of beings. I might say that an ancestor of Leonard Side's came from the dancing groups of Lucknow, the lewd men who painted their faces and tried to live like women. But that would only be a fragment of his inheritance, a fragment of truth. We cannot understand all the traits we have inherited. Sometimes we can be strangers to ourselves. (Naipaul 1995, 8–9)

Forced to relinquish legacy, ancestry, heritage, and the heteronormative indicators of genealogy that also reproduce social norms and values, Naipaul prefaces his writing into, and of, Trinidad in this work of returning home by enlisting Leonard Side.

If, as Edward Baugh (2011a) argues, Naipaul's literary returns to Trinidad "dramatize his effort to understand himself as the product of his beginnings" (5), then the rhetorical shifts from *his* to *ours* and from *I* to *we* in this closing passage etch the psychological returns in those notoriously difficult navigations Naipaul makes between himself and other Trinidadians. The body insistently out of place becomes the body in place with his realization of Caribbeanness as the condition of being creolized and queer, both multitudinous and fragmented—or, as he expresses it, of being "strangers to ourselves" (Naipaul 1995, 9). Side's is a life barely known to him, a life with no official or even imagined Caribbean history to support it. Yet the queerness, the composite cultural attachments, and the creativity of this life speak most compellingly to the creolized, uncategorizable condition that Naipaul comes to recognize as his own and as Trinidadian. Strange as it may be, Side is the found subject, the historical explanation—by the very virtue of his queerness and his absence of history—of a Caribbeanness that allows Naipaul (1995) to conclude his prelude with a statement of belonging in and of estrangement: "Sometimes *we* can be strangers to *our*selves" (9; italics added). In *Finding the Center*, Naipaul (1984) confesses: "I grew up with two ideas of history, almost two ideas of time . . . there was the history with dates [that] affected people and places abroad. . . . But Chaguanas where I was born had no dates" (58). In recounting Side's history, Naipaul finds a way to reconcile conceived space and lived space and, as the outsider becomes the insider, his way in the world is made possible.

When Edward Said (2001) asks of Naipaul, "But does he write *for* and *to* them? Does he live among them?" (116; italics in the original), the critical consensus has been "no."[12] Naipaul is seen to have ensconced himself in the history and historical perspective of the West. Yet, in this episode, which he names "An Inheritance," Naipaul breaks from the ethnographic mode of the schoolteacher for whom Side is the phobic body, and moves into a narrative of self-fashioning. The rhetorically performed kinship in these lines is astonishing. In his brief mediated portrait of Side, all that Naipaul is alleged to disdain—impurity, the body, cultural confusion—is transformed into a zone of recognition. Side rouses Naipaul to identify the vanishing point of historically, ancestrally, genetically guaranteed ways of knowing that is also the horizon of the distinctive trauma and privilege of the creolized Caribbean subject. Naipaul reads himself, like Side, as marked both by incompleteness and estrangement and, simultaneously, by a queer excess of belonging.

If it is as a creolized, queer figure that Naipaul best knows himself to be a Caribbean subject, it is perhaps also as a creolized, queer subject that we can best understand Naipaul as a Trinidadian and Caribbean writer. His insistence on "freedom from people, from entanglements, from rivalries, from competition . . . [in which] one doesn't have a side, doesn't have a country, doesn't have a community; one is entirely an individual" has been scripted as his rejection of Caribbeanness (Rowe-Evans and Naipaul 1971, 31). In part it is. As he writes in *The Enigma of Arrival*, Naipaul (1987) wished to be distant from a divided society that seemed to demand singular allegiances and futures, a desire prompted by "the fear of being swallowed up or extinguished by the simplicity of one side or the other, my side or the side that wasn't mine" (140). Yet, in this same work he carries Side's Caribbean condition of feeling "unanchored and strange" to England (Naipaul 1987, 6). Naipaul's refusal to be placed is also the very assertion and declamation of his Caribbeanness, one which he is able to humanize through the misrecognition, the category confusion, and the lost origins of Leonard Side. Through his identification with Leonard Side, Naipaul narrates his sense of himself as a Trinidadian or Caribbean person most fully by acknowledging that his condition of creolized belonging will never be fully self-present, never available to interpretation through a singular framework.

Naipaul's reflection on Side as a figure for his own homing is all the more striking in that it was published in the very same year as Trinidadian M. Jacqui Alexander's (1994) searing critique of how non-heteronormativity marks the limit point of citizenship and belonger status within Anglo-Caribbean nations: "Not Just (Any) Body Can Be a Citizen: The Politics of Law, Sexuality and Postcoloniality in Trinidad and Tobago and the Bahamas." Alexander (1994), a leading feminist and anticolonial theorist, opens her analysis of sexual citizenship with the statement "I am an outlaw in the country of my birth" (5), and moves on to scrutinize how "naturalized heterosexuality shapes the definitions of respectability, Black masculinity, and nationalism" (7). She explains how "having refused the heterosexual imperative of citizenship, these [queer] bodies, according to the state, pose a profound threat to the very survival of the nation," also exploring the ways in which "as the state moves to reconfigure the nation it simultaneously resuscitates the nation as hetero*sexual*" (6, italics in the original).

In this context, Naipaul's narration of Leonard Side offers an extraordinary reversal of the heteronormative logic of the state that renders a shared queerness as both the lived condition and the conceptual space where human difference and relationality can take form. Yet, while the historical coincidence of Naipaul and Alexander's sketches of the outlaw citizen may be compelling, they are also meaningfully distinct in their modalities and their social stakes. To paraphrase Barbara Johnson (1987) speaking on Derrida, while Naipaul may narrate himself as philosophically positioned as a queer figure, he is not politically positioned as such. Being positioned as a queer figure is not something that is entirely voluntary (2–3). Naipaul's portrait of Side answers powerfully to the epistemological issues around Caribbean historical subjectivity that may offer important ground for thinking through possibilities for collectivity, but it does not respond to the ontological ones—how to live as a queer subject in the region. There is a substantive difference between Naipaul's exilic sensibility and the condition of being denied full citizenship on account of sexual orientation. The interior sense of Naipaul's estrangement is exteriorized for queer subjects, whose dislocation is marked by others as exclusion with a threat of literal exile.

All of the works I have discussed in this chapter demonstrate how across centuries of transition shaped by the exchanges and encounters of peoples from different, multiple, and amnesiac ancestries, the Anglo-Caribbean has come to understand itself, in Glissant's (1989) words, as a "'manifestly' composite" (141) place, "woven from enduring patience and irreducible accretions" (142). As a place that undoes the usefulness of thinking about identities in terms of discrete categories—whether based on shared origins, singular ancestries, guaranteed lineages, or culturally distinctive groupings—the Caribbean can be recognized as a queer place. Such a recognition makes tilting Glissant's claim that "it is now imperative that Diversity should 'pass' through whole communities and peoples. Sameness is sublimated difference; Diversity is accepted difference" toward the Caribbean's erotic ecology a persuasive move (1989, 98). Indeed, if we muster this observation around the constitutive queerness of the creolized Caribbean in the face of the region's homophobic statutes and theologies, a number of interesting observations emerge. The first is how much the insistence on sexual absolutes (a colonial legal legacy) stands out as anomalous and inflicted. The second is how, given the heightened awareness of, and sensitivity to, fluid identities as integral to Caribbeanness, it is only a small and consistent step to appreciate sexual attachments that queer norms as an extension of Caribbeanness and not a transgression of it. The third is how attention to queer attachments augments Brathwaite's (1971) emphasis on the "area of sexual relationships" (303) as one of the most potent facilitators of the "two-way process" of "intercultural creolization" (300) highlighted in his landmark study, *The Development of Creole Society in Jamaica, 1770–1820.* By attending to the ways in which same-sex and multiply configured erotics contributed to "a bridge, a kind of social cement, between the two main colors of the island's structure, thus further helping (despite the resulting class/color divisions) to integrate the society," this study is not constrained by reading the legacy of sexual intimacies only in "the large and growing colored population of the island" (305).

In the chapters that follow, I discuss examples of Caribbean literary imaginings in which the creative compression of cultural plasticity with sexual dissidence exemplifies the queerness of the creolized Caribbean and its established and anticipated possibilities for accommodation and co-belonging.

2

Creolizing Heterosexuality

• •

Curdella Forbes's "A Permanent
Freedom" and Shani Mootoo's
Valmiki's Daughter

> It is not our differences that divide us.
> It is our inability to recognize, accept,
> and celebrate those differences.
> —Audre Lorde, *Our Dead Behind
> Us: Poems*

> Borders are set up to define places that
> are safe and unsafe, to distinguish us
> from them. A border is a dividing line,
> a narrow strip along a steep edge.
> A borderland is a vague and undeter-
> mined place created by the emotional
> residue of an unnatural boundary.
> —Gloria Anzaldúa, *Borderlands/
> La frontera: The New Mestiza*

In this chapter, critical attention shifts to heterosexuality as a site of turbulence
and Caribbean queerness. In the face of repeated assumptions around the
impossibility of non-heteronormative lives for citizens in the Anglophone

region, Curdella Forbes's (2008) long short story, "A Permanent Freedom," and Shani Mootoo's (2008b) third novel, *Valmiki's Daughter*, are read here as literary works that open up heteronormativity to scrutiny at the level of lives lived under its rubric and yet against its presumptions and assertions of a natural and normal sexual orientation. This chapter explores how these literary works expand the horizon of creolized erotic arrangements, within which heterosex can be experienced and expressed by Caribbean subjects in such a way as to queer its social purchase and amplify its internal fluidity and inclusiveness.

As I do throughout this book, I argue here that literary works present an opportunity to read Caribbean lives outside and beyond the hegemonic explanatory categories around sexuality that too often speak over rather than for localized and located realities. The reasoning here builds on the core argument of this book—that Caribbean literary works can render worlds of human relations and desires that are as complicated and meaningfully descriptive as sociological or historical studies, or more so, and that such acts of imaginative representation participate in creating ethical possibilities for living together in difference, as well as for living fully. From this chapter onward, the book turns more directly to the task of arguing for the depth, breadth, and value of literary depictions of inclusive erotic ecologies in or of the Anglo-Caribbean that are the product of adaptations to local conditions—communities nestled within homo-hostile states. Often, like the social environments their representation imaginatively coordinates with, these ecologies are influenced by the strong imperatives for sexual coherence and normalization that exist at the level of state authority in many Anglophone nations, and by the asymmetric distributions of social power according to race, gender, and class. All the same, they are also—like lived Anglo-Caribbean spaces—constituted by and open to the uneven interfaces between social practices and diverse erotic desires that exist in and through everyday acts of living.

Literature's particular susceptibility for rendering these erotic ecologies and their fluctuating mediation of social forces and individual inclinations comes from its capacity to render interiority coterminous with social encounter and thereby to capture the density of human possibility against the surface relief of any single act or decision. Andrew Salkey's *Escape to an Autumn Pavement*, discussed in chapter 3, provides a superb example of a narrative in which an almost excessive subjective intensity opens up a queer sensibility in the diaspora. In this work, the protagonist, Johnnie, has an acutely Caribbean sensibility of creolizing multiple sexual scripts while complying with none, which cannot be mapped onto the social world of pre-Wolfendon London and its organization of erotic commitments within hetero-/homonormalizations.

Curdella Forbes's (2008) "A Permanent Freedom" shares this literary method of observing and recording microdynamics and emotional intensities at the level of the local to make queerness visible and intelligible. Indeed, she has stressed this witnessing as her creative approach in an interview, stating, "I tend to listen to the interiority, what goes on in the community" (Forbes and Gifford 2014, n.p.). In this long short story, Forbes brings the complicated interior of a marriage to literary scrutiny in order to radically resignify the heteronormativity that this institution is assumed to express, uphold, and normalize. Narrated in turn by Alain (the former lover of Denton), Denton, and Marsha (the wife of Denton), Forbes's formal inclusion of three voices in the queer, expanded marriage that she depicts mirrors the expanded capacity this story narrates for multiple, consenting, affectionate, and inclusive relations. The relationship between Alain and Denton is only briefly alluded to in flashbacks as Forbes's story narrates a queer coming together, based on a common love for Denton as he reaches the end of his life. In her article, "Reclaiming Sexual Identities in Patricia Powell's *A Small Gathering of Bones* and Curdella Forbes's *A Permanent Freedom*," Marie Sairsingh (2013) argues that Forbes's story "explores possibilities for reconciliation between two diametric and frequently polarized concepts of heterosexuality and homosexuality, and thus presents alternatives to hegemonic antagonisms often portrayed in fictional works on the subject" (65). What matters for my argument is how Forbes's highly specific scripting of entangled lives that bridge the interstices of two acknowledged erotic arrangements—the heterosexual marriage and the homosexual relationship—unfastens the claims of heteronormativity while affirming the possibility for ways of being heterosexual that need not deny the right to and value of same-sex eroticism.

In *Valmiki's Daughter*, Mootoo (2008b) frames the commonplace culturally plural (and commonly promiscuous) ecology of a Trinidadian neighborhood with a focus on its sexual dimensions in order to give representation to a locally sensitive yet socially subversive erotic repertoire that not only undoes *straight* and *gay* in its multiple queer manifestations but also erodes the conventional standing of heteropatriarchy. Mootoo sets her imaginative focus on the yawning expanse between individual desires in a colonial and postcolonial context and the historically—and socially—sanctioned possibilities for sexual and emotional fulfilment. This novel unfolds the stories of the Krishnu family and the erotic lives that cannot be contained by their respectable, middle-class home in San Fernando. At the family's head is Valmiki, a successful, married doctor with two daughters, Viveka and Vashti. While Valmiki's queer life is characterized by regret and recalcitrance, Viveka is swift to resist gender constraints and just a little slower to embrace her sexual passion for women. Although the novel ends with its queer-desiring characters in heterosexual marriages, remarkably and significantly Mootoo offers no sense of sexual closure or normalization. Rather, the sundry and varied erotic lives that populate this novel, while ostensibly allowing for the social lie of heteronormativity as a "natural and eternal given" (Duggan 2007, 193), powerfully contribute to its demise in their radical disorganization of its natural status.

In both of these fictional works, heterosexuality is creolized and queered as it takes on a capacious and volatile form. Importantly, this repositioning of heterosexuality as a fluid option within a continuum of arrangements rather than a fixed and exclusively legitimate orientation makes space for a reconceptualization of sexual normalization. In *Straight with a Twist*, Calvin Thomas (2000) frames such a gesture as "resistance to this normative interpretation of sexual difference as difference itself, a resistance in which straights could conceivably participate, not by surrendering or representing their desire for sexual objects of the opposite gender, but by questioning the dominance of the assumption that such interest constitutes the natural paradigm of interest in the Other, or in others per se" (14).[1]

Queering Heteronormativity

The body of secondary literature on queering heterosexuality remains relatively small but Cathy J. Cohen's (1997) "Punks, Bulldaggers, and Welfare Queens," makes an especially significant and relevant intervention. Cohen's article addresses how "the inability of queer politics to effectively challenge heteronormativity rests, in part, on the fact that despite a surrounding discourse which highlights the destabilization and even deconstruction of sexual categories, queer politics has often been built around a simple dichotomy between those deemed queer and those deemed heterosexual" (440). Paying attention to differential power relations informed by race, class, and gender, her work calls for an awareness of the distance between heteronormativity—"the privilege, power, and normative status invested in heterosexuality"—and the much more variegated realities and privileges of heterosexual lives (447). In critiquing how "much of the politics of queer activists has been structured around the dichotomy of straight versus everything else, assuming a monolithic experience of heterosexual privilege for all those identified publicly with heterosexuality" (452), Cohen focuses on the ways in which heterosexuality has historically been shaped by the racializing discourses of colonialism to position non-White sexualities outside of heteronormativity. Her discussion provides an important theoretical touchstone for the literary analysis undertaken in this chapter as her provocation to rethink how "heteronormativity works to support and reinforce institutional racism, patriarchy, and class exploitation" (455) is a project of decolonizing also explored in the imaginative worlds and lives crafted by Forbes and Mootoo.

In "Heterosexualism and the Colonial/Modern Gender System," Maria Lugones (2007) provides a theoretically determined exploration of the intersections and vectors of power that Cohen identifies in order "to understand the very meaning of heterosexualism as tied to a persistently violent domination that marks the flesh multiply by accessing the bodies of the unfree in differential patterns devised to constitute them as the tortured materiality of power?" (188). Tracing the colonial/modern organization of gender, Lugones (2007) illustrates how "biological dimorphism, heterosexualism, and patriarchy" are all characteristic of gender as a colonial concept the dominant institution of which erased various precolonial (non)conceptualizations of sex and gender (190). While it draws us back to a colonial epistemology, it is relevant to acknowledge how the historically and culturally constructed idea of heterosexuality came to be upheld and affirmed to such a degree that its currency as normal, healthy, and axiomatic now passes unnoticed. The definitional codependency of the categories of heterosexual and homosexual, seemingly undetectable in their common contemporary currency as essentialized identities, dates back to 1860s Europe and the flourishing new discipline of sexology. The term *Homosexualität* was first used by the German Hungarian Karl-Maria Kertbeny in 1868 in a letter to Karl Heinrich Ulrichs, whose 1864 *Researches on the Riddle of Male–Male [Man-to-Man] Love* had sought to explain same-sex attraction as a natural part of human development (Katz 2007). For Kertbeny, this term was a tool in his wider argument that same-sex desire was natural, and as such should be a matter of private behavior beyond the interference of the law (not dissimilar to the argument made by Wolfenden in 1950s England, which I address in chapter 3). In order to categorize sexual preferences for the opposite sex as part of the broader schema, Kertbeny also put forward his complementary term to *homosexuality*: *heterosexuality* (Katz [1996] 2007).[2] By the end of the nineteenth century, *heterosexual* and *homosexual* were no longer neutral, legal, scientific terms specific to Europe, but the signs under which sexual behaviors were understood, in modern terms, as identity bearing. As Lugones (2007) persuasively argues, the colonial project operated as the definitional and differentiating driver, and "as global, eurocentered capitalism was constituted through colonization, gender differentials were introduced where there were none" (196). Indeed, Lugones points to scholars whose work provides insights into cultural ecologies free of gender binarism, including Oyèrónké Oyěwùmí's 1997 research on Yorùbá peoples of the contemporary Nigerian, Benin, and Togo states. This may well be directly relevant for Caribbean ecologies given Yorùbá linguistic and religious survivals in the region, and such survivals may also help explain why and how the invented and imposed disciplining structures of homosexuality and heterosexuality never fully accounted for more porous social worlds of the creolized Caribbean toward which we can "feel sideways" through these literary works.[3]

The Caribbean literary works in focus here queer heterosexuality in ways that undo the hold of heteronormativity, specifically by representing expansive, multiple, and nonexclusive relations and intimacies hosted under its unforgiving exterior, and by depicting heterosexuality as just one element within a fluid sexual repertoire that neither guarantees nor precludes social normalization. Other recent studies interested in the diversity of sexual orientations within Caribbean societies have also pointed out how heterosexuality is often adaptable and lived in varied and fluid terms. In *Island Bodies*, Rosamond S. King (2014) draws attention to a range of sexual behaviors among women across the Caribbean region that do not correspond to any conventional definition of heterosexuality and yet are often practiced under this rubric: "Furthermore, the diversity of individual sexualities means that women that are married to or have sex with men *and* have sex with other women, women who have sex with other women but profess not to fall in love with them, and women who only engage in particular sex acts with women may not label themselves as lesbians or as anything other than heterosexual" (94). Similarly, accounting for his research on gender identities and sexual tendencies among men in Martinique, David Murray observes a capacious understanding around object choice and sexual identities in *Opacity: Gender, Sexuality, Race and the "Problem" of Identity in Martinique*: "I met men who engaged in same-gender sexual relations but did not in any way perceive themselves to be 'macoumé' or anything other than a 'normal' (i.e., heterosexual) man who occasionally engaged in sex with other men and, in doing so, would often explain that they didn't have a girlfriend at that particular moment. Yet I also met men who engaged in these kinds of sexual relations who identified themselves as 'branché' or 'gai' (but never 'macoumé'), terms which communicated self-recognition and ascription as (not effeminate) men who have sex with other men" (Murray 2002, 110–111). In these Caribbeans, sexual behaviors loosen their ties from oppositional sex-object identities to become part of porous queer arrangements that are not defined by or as same-sex erotics but can readily accommodate these.

Turning now to the literary work of Forbes and Mootoo, I shall draw attention to how the alternative erotic ecologies presented in their fictions become a powerful means by which to expose "the constructedness of the heterosexual matrix, the chinks in its ideological armor . . . seriously attempting to work the weaknesses in its machinery, imagining ways in which we might bring about system failure" (O'Rourke 2005, 112). Interestingly both works explore how the Caribbean heteropatriarchal family may surreptitiously sabotage what Jafari S. Allen (2012) names the "projects of respectability," even as this familial structure outwardly supports "the notion of citizenship, with its obvious rules of exclusion and exception . . . [in which] nonstate actors such as families, and religious and cultural organizations, often *think like a state*" (220; italics in the original).

Heterosexual Undoings of Heteronormativity

In her tripartite story, "A Permanent Freedom," Forbes (2008) creates narrative space for a self-authorizing version of a heterosexual marriage that nevertheless undermines heteronormativity: "the institutions, structures of understanding and practical orientations that make heterosexuality seem not only coherent—that is, organized as a sexuality—but also privileged" (Berlant and Warner 1998, 548). The story surfaces an embedded queerness within a Caribbean marriage that circulates as a strongly expressed but quietly articulated possibility for inclusion and co-belonging. In many ways, this story is a strenuous defense of same-sex loving, yet it validates and celebrates the erotic and emotional connection between Denton and Alain without promoting the sexual binarism of homosexual/heterosexual or denying the meaning and value of the marriage between Denton and Marsha.

As we piece together the stories that emerge across their three accounts, we understand that Alain, a New Zealander, had met Denton, a Jamaican living in Grenada, in Portland, Maine, while Denton was on sabbatical from his home university. The two men had quickly become involved in a passionate sexual relationship. Alain acknowledges that he "knew from the beginning that it was a holiday because it was too intense to last. Parts of [Denton] were tightening up more every day, and [Alain] could feel that it wouldn't be long before he was unable to continue making himself forget the things he had put aside on shelves" (Forbes 2008, 83). Yet Alain is still scorched by Denton's words when they are reunited in the final weeks of his life, "'There was no us, Alain. I never gave consent to it—not with my will, not—'" (91). Counterintuitively, and against both of their own intimations of impossibility, it is Marsha who both recognizes and restores their need for each other by ventriloquizing each one reaching toward the other. This act of loyalty to which she knows her husband to be at the end of his life is both surprising and profoundly rearranging to all three. In some sense, it is the queer temporality of death, which—against the *longue durée* of traditions, conventions, and generations—"creates a new emphasis on the here, the present, the now" and unleashes "the potentiality of a life unscripted by the conventions of family, inheritance, and child rearing" (Halberstam 2005, 2). For Marsha, both this acute sense of compressed temporality and the sideways place of the diaspora extend the horizon of imaginable life beyond the narrow parameters of heteropatriarchal nationalism.

Alain's account is the first to be narrated and with it his shock at how everything that happens to him at Marsha's invitation is so astounding to his assumed sense of what is expected, that it seems almost unimaginable as well as painfully real. Initially he is shocked just at hearing from Denton:

> Behind my eyelids I wondered what the hell I was doing, what was wrong with me, getting on a plane in answer to a cryptic email from a guy I hadn't seen in years, who had torn my guts out, pretty near massacred me. What the hell was this all about, what was *I* all about? Was he really ill, how ill was he, what

exactly was wrong with him, or was it just a ploy to get me to turn up, to start something all over again? But why? Maybe his wife had left him or something, the bastard. (Forbes 2008, 70)

As it emerges that it is Marsha who has orchestrated their reunion because her husband is dying from AIDS, Alain finds his bearings unmoored. When she quietly makes them both a coffee and leaves them alone, he finds it "too bizarre for words" (Forbes 2008, 81). Eventually, he challenges Marsha directly:

"Denton told me about you—about your part of the world. You don't approve—you think men like us are wrong—wrongly made. Anathema."
"I am sure Denton didn't tell you that I considered men like you—anathema."
"OK, maybe not. That's my interpretation then, if you like."
"I see. So why did *you* come, and why did you stay, having come?"
It was a reasonable question. I shrugged. "I have done stranger things. It's the way I grew up." Her eyebrows raised a little so I explained, "I didn't have a very orthodox upbringing."
"I see. And yet you have very . . . orthodox views—about people." (Forbes 2008, 88)

Refusing a straight alignment of Marsha's seemingly conventionally lived sexuality with conventionally conceived sexuality, Forbes's story reveals the heterosexual wife to be the most non-heteronormative voice in this work. Alain's sense that Marsha's act of reconnection is almost beyond words surfaces his own suppositions about heterosexuality, but also primes the reader for an expressive reality in which acts and feelings take precedence over the definitions promoted by the linguistic categories he relies on. For Alain, the unanticipated afterlife of his relationship to Denton is not only to become uncle to Denton's son with Marsha, but also to engage in a deep inquiry into how relationships are meaningfully understood and experienced. He reflects, "Even later still, what I thought I understood then, about them, about us, about why any of us is here, came up for question and turned out to be only a small part of the truth" (Forbes 2008, 90).

Denton's account, which follows Alain's, mirrors his end-of-life shifts between memory and hallucination. Flashes of intense being shared with Alain, *"He had never dreamed the question at the base of his belly all these years would have been answered in this way, so fluently and so long"* (Forbes 2008, 100; italics in the original), are set against equally intense feelings of "the tyranny of life lived among expectations" to stave off those "questions that had made of his entire being one large unspeakable question sign" (97, 104). His memories of the freedom experienced in his time in the U.S. are filtered through those of his always present and acute sense of how living such freedom would be understood back home in the Caribbean: "He tries to touch this pending freedom, but is unable, because he cannot imagine it. He imagines its consequences, the whisperings, the speculations, the questions" (97). What he also can barely imagine outside of a heteronormative frame is his wife's compassion and concern for him given her knowledge of his same-sex desires.

Marsha's account comes last and is by far the shortest. It is also the most provocative and explicit in terms of its undoing heteronormativity. Aware of the unintelligibility of her actions in a heteronormative world, Marsha's narration seems to be the strongest, the most centered, in contesting normative expectations: "I am not crazy, neither am I a fool, but I know I do things that people think don't make any sense at all" (Forbes 2008, 108). When she later confesses "I don't want to be doing any of this, not here, not now, manufacturing a guilt I do not feel" (109), the logic of her sentence gently overthrows social convention. Her refusal is not related to her role in bringing Alain and Denton together, but rather to the social framework in which she is positioned as the wife of a same-sex-loving man. Her understanding of her motivation for reuniting Alain and Denton is not only unconstrained by the normative bearings of social expectation, but deeply transgressive to an Anglo-Caribbean rendering of heteronormativity as rooted in religious authority: "Either I don't know my own heart, or something else, bigger than the sum total of who we are, demanded it . . . If I said I was led in this, everybody would say I was mad. But God knows" (109).[4]

It is Marsha, whose heterosexuality and religious commitment are unquestioned in the story, who most powerfully queers sexual categories and undoes homophobia. Her choice to enable Denton to share his last weeks of life with a man he loved and desired most fully, alongside her decision to remain at his side, reveals how heterosexual subjects can queer heteronormativity. While the story draws its attention to the demanding situation of present care and anticipated grief, its unforced gathering of same-sex lover and devoted wife sets into crisis the "the mutually reinforcing relationship between [heterosexuals'] culturally sanctioned sexual practices and their privileged and valorized social identities" (Thomas 2000, 89). Indeed, in Cohen's (1997) terms, Marsha is a queer figure (a queer activist) who "might construct a new political identity that is truly liberating, transformative, and inclusive of all who stand on the outside of the dominant constructed norm of state-sanctioned white middle- and upper-class heterosexuality" (441).

Marie Sairsingh (2013) draws attention to how Forbes's story "fractures what Timothy Chin refers to as 'the us/them, native/foreign, natural/unnatural' dichotomies that often complicate and obstruct the broad view of human relations," stating, "Forbes's text ruptures the notion of a master narrative of normativized heterosexuality and explores multiple possibilities within the discourse of human sexuality" (75). Importantly, this literary exploration of multiple possibilities not only extends beyond heteronormativity but also encompasses it. Through a determined focus on the intricate emotional character of lived lives, which complicate the social practices and positions assumed to be socially normative, Forbes's fictional world of intimate connections renders the uneven and often unexpected terrain of an erotic ecology in which heterosexual marriage—sanctioned as the expression of the natural desire of men and women for each other—is queered to become a consensual arrangement that can accommodate same-sex-desiring men. The permanent freedom that Denton has sought in exile and beyond the confines of his marriage is paradoxically finally realized in this relationship and through what can be seen as a characteristically creolized Caribbean sensibility of trusting in spiritual guidance to do right by others. Forbes's story implicitly draws on the cultural expansiveness of Caribbeanness, well recognized for its diasporic dimension, as it stretches out categories that are narrowly perceived to contain and constrain sexual identities—most powerfully those of heterosexual and homosexual. Challenging the purported natural precedence of home and heterosexuality, Marsha and Denton's relationship, with its recognition and engagement of multiple attachments and orientations, might be queerly figured as diasporic in kind as well as in location.

Commonplace Pluralism and Unremarkable Queers

In Shani Mootoo's (2008b) novel, *Valmiki's Daughter*, the queering of heteronormativity is more explicitly linked to the creolized cultural fabric of the Trinidadian urban milieu in which tendencies toward the fluidity and multiplicity of attachments are narrated as the established norm of everyday creolized realities: "A downtown babel of shop signs and streets, mongrelized, polyglot, a ferment without a history, like heaven" (Walcott 1993, 11). As a whole, the novel renders the porosity and openness of gender and cultural identities that characterize this place—even as some of its characters still voice conservative, orthodox versions of being a girl, or a wife, or an Indian, that seek to uphold the idea of natural identities somehow existing without strenuous, if often stealthy, processes of social normalization. Indeed, *Valmiki's Daughter*, Mootoo's third novel, issues an impressive challenge to the normalization and stabilization of heterosexuality as an arrangement that describes and convenes the natural pattern of human desires and attachments. By rendering the commonplace sexual pluralism of Trinidad through a predominance of queer realities that can also sometimes be described as heterosexual, the novel unfastens heteronormativity as it gives representation to a locally sensitive yet socially subversive erotic repertoire that exceeds identitarian categories and binaries.

Since the publication of *Cereus Blooms at Night* (1996), Mootoo's writing has come to be associated most strongly with a breaking of Caribbean literary silence around sexuality and non-normalizing desire. This novel brought to fiction some of the most sensitive issues around sexuality in the Caribbean—transgender identities, same-sex desire, incest, rape, and queer subjects. Yet its setting in a fictionalized, but recognizably Caribbean island, considered alongside the diasporic identity of its author and the spectacular retreat from the world of the social enacted by its protagonist, Mala, has meant that this novel is often critically appreciated for its lyricism, magical realism, and harrowing emotional themes rather than for its forceful social critique of the limits of Caribbean sexual citizenship.[5] While in many regards *Valmiki's Daughter* continues the project of representing the lives of Caribbean queer subjects, what is so distinctive and dissimilar about the style of this novel is its acute realism and attention to a precision rendering of place. In the more recent novel, readers are not permitted any escape from the Trinidadian world of the narrative, and Mootoo's commitment to realism becomes a means by which to insist on the recognition of desiring lives in a specifically Caribbean place that might otherwise be denied or overlooked. Realism, in this sense, as Pam Morris (2003) argues, "participates in the democratic impulse of modernity" (3) and specifically operates here as a means of democratizing sexuality by emphasizing the social praxis of desire.

Mootoo's novel is set very firmly in Trinidad's San Fernando. Indeed, after a brief, but telling prologue that frames a father's regret at his inability to empower his daughter to live a life unconstrained by the same compulsory norms of gender and sexual socialization that compromised his own happiness, the narrative opens by quite literally positioning the reader where they can see the inclusive realities of a local neighborhood:

> If you stand on one of the triangular traffic islands at the top of Chancery Lane just in front of the San Fernando General Hospital (where the southern arm of the lane becomes Broadway Avenue, and Harris Promenade, with its official and public buildings, and commemorative statues, shoots eastward), you would get the best, most all-encompassing, views of the town. You would see that narrower secondary streets emanate from the central hub. Not one is ever straight for long. They angle, curve this way and that, dip or rise, and off them shoot a maze of smaller side streets. (Mootoo 2008b, 7)

This description of place continues for a full thirteen pages before the narrative lens re-focuses on the activities of Vashti Krishnu, the other daughter of Valmiki Krishnu and sister to Viveka, to whom the book gives its title. In these opening pages, the novel summons a multisensory literary navigation screen that plots "your journey" through place—street by street, sound by sound, smell by smell. The narrative style is consistently marked by an excess of materiality and detail consistent with the early promise of an all-encompassing vantage point. This is demonstrably a novel committed to describing life as it is. This is not, however, a conservative commitment given that the life it describes in scrupulous, almost feverish, detail is a life thick with commonly unimagined possibilities in terms of what it might mean to love and to live in the creolized Caribbean.

It may be the well-established role of the novel to narrate for us what it is like to be somebody else, but *Valmiki's Daughter* sets its lens at a panoramic angle to catch snapshots and close-ups of a whole range of lives along a continuum of sexual arrangements that not only represent the queerness of non-heteronormative subjects but also begin to unsettle and undo the idea of straightness, as well as to question what lies beneath the smug social serenity of marriage and the heteropatriarchal nuclear family. It is no coincidence that our initial orientation as a reader is to Trinidadian streets that refuse a straight journey and lead, rather, to a maze of entangled routes, for this knotting also patterns the human landscape of the novel once we venture beyond the facades of its seemingly socially well-coordinated lives. In the extended orientation exercise that opens the novel, the narrator cannot help but document the ubiquitous signifiers of heterogeneity and porosity that crowd the vista. The seamless parade of Anglican and Catholic churches, civic buildings, shops, a convent, and an Indian movie theater effortlessly represents the cultural mélange of Trinidad that, significantly, takes the shape of an unbounded overlapping: "The convent, oddly, shares a wall with the cinema next door and if you listen just now, you will hear the lunchtime programming begin. The cinema's walls are not soundproof, and in every direction the soundtrack of movie trailers can be heard above traffic sounds, and the laughter and chatter of students, vendors and passersby" (Mootoo 2008b, 24). This busy and motley congregation of the secular and the religious, East Indian popular culture and Catholic pedagogy mixed with the roar of roads, offers a glimpse of the cultural liquidity of Trinidad, "a place that is so miraculously varied geographically, environmentally, socially, linguistically. It sounds like a hodge-podge of a place, but it's more like a well-seasoned, long-simmering stew" (25). With a linguistic nod to the idea of the callaloo nation that Mootoo (2008a) invokes in her essay on queer belonging, discussed in chapter 1, this novel is also at pains to register the seepage and correspondence between seemingly distinct ways of living that Trinidad's creolized cultural environment both obliges and promotes.

In drawing attention to the creolized queerness of this place, Mootoo's novel offers a literary depiction of what is already well recognized within sociological and ethnographic discourses. The fictional mapping of the opening journey in this novel is, however, distinctive in its unexceptional inclusion of diverse and multiple sexual arrangements. Navigating the neighborhood for the reader, the narrator describes the motley acoustics of street culture where the nut seller's call and the church organ clamor alongside "the theater of a spurned lovers' quarrel, all the better when not two but three are involved" (Mootoo 2008b, 8). Slightly farther down the road there is a pause to consider the inhabitants of a house divided into apartments: "An ageless man who lives by himself and wears dresses (he had ambitions to be a fashion designer and dressmaker but was unable to find clients and sews only for himself now)" lives alongside a piano teacher and midwife (Mootoo 2008b, 14). A little later still, we have the mapping of doubled lives that often characterize the inside of marriage in this novel: "The hotel is mostly used by visitors to the island, but it is known to be available on occasion to certain businessmen and professionals who are willing to pay the daily double-room rate for the privacy of their illicit pleasures" (18). Soon after, we discover that Valmiki conducts his own "illicit" pleasures with a host of different White women in his doctor's surgery and with Saul in a cabin in the Maraval Hills. By rendering a local geography where sexual desires are represented as porous, proximate, and plural, Mootoo embeds sexual diversity as an unremarkable part of the fabric of this place, commensurate with and simply part of its pervasive creolized configurations. In this literary reorientation exercise, what might be marked as sexual deviancy in official national discourses—transvestism, adultery, prostitution, homosexuality—becomes the commonplace actuality of heterogeneous Trinidadian lives. In this world where object choices overlap, the meaning and consequences of heterosexuality are no longer guaranteed by marriage, and the usefulness of thinking about sexuality in binary terms begins to give way to new conceptions grounded in local lifestyles more than in socially assigned identities.

The novel's meticulous representation of the social and sexual density of everyday lives that directs attention toward the messy, contingent, and indeterminate relations and attachments through which sexual desires and associations flow, shows how often queer arrangements overlap with and infuse the structures of assumed "normativity." J. Halberstam's (2005) study, *In a Queer Time and Place*, was highly influential in extending the discussion around queerness as a "nonnormative logic" that shapes alternative lifestyles and temporalities to enable imagined futures outside of the heteropatriarchal logics of "family, inheritance, and child rearing" (2). Halberstam argues that contemporary critical languages that aim to identify "the obstacles to social change have become adept . . . at talking about 'normativity,' are far less adept at describing in rich detail the practices and structures that both oppose and sustain conventional forms of association, belonging, and identification" (4). *Valmiki's Daughter* offers that which Halberstam sees as lacking in current theorizations of social transformation. The novel is acutely watchful of and unforgivingly alert to "the practices and structures that both oppose and sustain conventional forms of association, belonging, and identification" (4) as they play out in the disappointed and disappointing lives of the middle-class and middle-brow families of Luminada Heights, with their entrenched prejudices, self-interests, and deceits. In this way, the acute geospecificity of the narrative corresponds with Halberstam's conception of queer place, refusing to elevate the global as the proper plane of investigation and instead validating the local, "with its associations with the concrete, the specific, the narrow, the empirical and even the bodily" (11).

As the creolized and syncretic horizon laid out in the first part of the reader's journey reveals, the locale of San Fernando, Trinidad, is a place of intensified and multiple cultural exchanges, a vibrant hub of cross-continental encounters, where the ooze and flow between different, even seemingly competing, acts of identity and belonging cannot be stemmed. There is nothing unusual or surprising in this depiction of Port of Spain as a queer place. As outlined in chapter 1, the Caribbean is widely acknowledged as an exceptionally diverse and animated (as well as historically violent) crucible of human encounter from which new thinking on the modeling of culture, race, and ethnicity has emerged. What is particularly interesting and valuable about Mootoo's novelistic depiction of Trinidad's creolized sexualities in *Valmiki's Daughter* is that in its meticulous representation of what is already real, the novel reveals the blurring and blending of so-called heterosexual and homosexual lives so as to queer both. Making the inadequacy of these modes of human description evident in the Caribbean world she renders, this novel takes up the project that Mootoo (2008a) calls for in her essay "On Becoming an Indian Starboy" to "beg for longer notions of all that we are" (94). Interestingly, this call connects in its expansive yearning to Alain's queer sensibility of living "*so fluently and so long*" (100; italics in the original) in Forbes's (2008) "A Permanent Freedom" and suggests an alternative temporality and spatiality that calls into imagination a differently Caribbean queer future, family, and inheritance that is, as I will discuss later, also ethically at odds with canonical White queer theory's sense of an after.

Caribbean Queerness and "Longer Notions of All That We Are"

Valmiki's Daughter centers on the Krishnu family whose lives spill out from their comfortable home in the elevated middle-class neighborhood of Luminada Heights. Valmiki, whose story comes first, is a seemingly socially successful and sexually assured doctor, married to a socially ambitious woman, Devika, with whom he has two daughters, Viveka and Vashti. He is also a man of unfulfilled yearnings whose sexual transgression in the form of liaisons with local White women sit in complicated relation to his same-sex desire for a local working-class man of African descent, Saul, and his twenty-year longings for his fellow medical student, Tony, who still lives in India where they studied together. Despite the fact that in all his life-defining decisions Valmiki has chosen the socially endorsed and expected path, his sense of sexual restlessness, compromise, and self-deceit vibrates through the narrative. His yearnings for sexual and social accommodation pull him in opposite directions, and Mootoo's writing ensures that we feel the tug of both.

As a young man, Valmiki had the opportunity to build a future with his lover Tony. Yet when Tony wanted to announce their relationship to his family, Valmiki rushed back to Trinidad and arranged his engagement to Devika, unwittingly sealing his contract with a heteroreproductive culture by making his fiancé pregnant during his first heterosexual encounter. The force of his attachment to social approval was such then that "even when he heard that Tony had tried to kill himself, he felt there was nothing he could have done differently . . . he congratulated himself again and again on his astuteness in making sure that he had had sex with that girl back home" (Mootoo 2008b, 69). Decades later, as an established professional and family man, the conflicting pulls of social and sexual fulfilment continue to torment him. Still, his imaginings of potential futures cannot surface without a sense of their social consequences: "How he sometimes wished, though, that stories of his philandering would leak—no, rather explode—throughout the town, and cause such a scandal that his family would toss him out like a piece of used tissue or flush him from their lives, and he would be forced to leave the country. He would be freed. He revised his thought: perhaps he, forever concerned about appearances and doing the praiseworthy thing, would never really be free" (Mootoo 2008b, 42). Yet, when Valmiki dreams of a different future, it is not a life that negates the emotional bonds of his marriage or the codependency he has with Devika, but rather a life that stretches his marriage to accommodate these relations. He dreams of a "longer notion" of himself that would allow his love for men to develop too: "He imagined a time when the two girls would be married off—hopefully not to a man like him. He would not leave Devika. But he imagined coming and going as he wished. Falling in love even. Maintaining his obligation to Devika—there was no question about that, he would do that for her—but loving someone, a man, a man from his own world with whom he would share another life" (71–72). In fact, this queer marriage he dreams of is his present life, although he is the least able to recognize and embrace it as such. His wife Devika, like Valmiki himself, is glad of his affairs with other women as they provide a camouflage of heterosexual dissent and thereby protect their secure social position. But her compliance with this arrangement is based on a tacit knowledge of her husband's sexual attraction to men: "Devika seemed content with the respectability and comfort of being Dr. Valmiki Krishnu's wife. She and he slept in the same bed, shared children, a bedroom, a house, a life. She was not an unfeeling woman, and she was not unaware" (70).

The conditions of social acceptance to the world of Luminada Heights demand silent conformity and, correspondent with Halberstam's (2005) conception of queer time, the narrative foregrounds "how respectability, may be upheld by a middle-class logic of reproductive temporality" (4–5). Yet, in a novel where the intersections of class, ethnic, and erotic ecology are sharply registered, it is the wife of Valmiki's male working-class African Caribbean lover Saul who breaks the covenant of respectable silence: "I know about him and you, you know, Doc. I know he real take to you" (Mootoo 2008b, 74). Her elaboration of their marriage reveals that, for her, security and loyalty are "better than *that*" (75; italics added). The de-privileging of heterosex here, as in Marsha's marriage to Denton, underlines the possible opening between heterosexuality and heteronormativity in which marriages offering social cohesion or approval are lived alongside same-sex erotic attachments: "Doc, we are not rich people. I can't get up and leave just so. Leave and go where? I have to stay and make do. Saul happy, and I happy for him. It might be a strange thing, but I will say it, I happy for him because he happy and he my husband" (75).

As in all the marriages that this novel depicts, and in Forbes's story too, individuals' erotic and emotional intent is rarely aligned with their adopted social norms. The sexually disheveled and yet seemingly secure marriages that these texts render present a queer heterosexuality that is experienced as unexceptional. As Saul's wife explains, "Is only strange if you not in the situation yourself and you watching—judging from outside" (Mootoo 2008b, 75). Indeed, while Valmiki remains distressed by the threat his queer desires and marriage present to his respectability, status, and privilege, the novel represents a wider Caribbean world in which sexual multiplicity is unremarkable to many. His receptionist, Zoraida, whose coded gestures communicate the different needs of certain women who visit his surgery, as well as the arrival of his wife, remains unmoved by his complicated sexual arrangements. And "Saul's accepting male friends would come up and meet them, and they would all head deep into the northern range to hunt. Hardly anyone minded or wondered about that" (43).

Yet Valmiki is not alone in seeking to preserve a veneer of heterosexual accord, and the novel consistently exposes renewed social investments in gender and class conformity that sustain the idea of heteronormativity and repress its inadequacy as a descriptor of creolized, local erotic ecologies. While Anick, the sophisticated French wife of Nayan (Viveka's childhood friend), who is newly arrived in Trinidad, has been open about her sexual relations with other women, as soon as they are married and settled in Trinidad, Nayan "[tells] Anick he hated that part of her life, that he was appalled, even tormented, by the idea that she once loved women" (Mootoo 2008b, 233). Unable to accept the surplus of Anick's desire to the structures that he wishes her to occupy in this place, Nayan's unhappiness with Anick increases as she fails to fulfill "everything he had been taught was proper in a woman and a wife" (250). Yet, in the queer, creolized location of the novel it is Nayan's words and not Anick's desires that appear unjust and unfitting.

Queering Heterosexuality: Social Imperatives and Non-normalizing Affections

The many complicated lives the novel represents suggest that sexual desires and encounters are not organized around the given primacy of heterosexuality, but rather that this is a socially enforced practice, both historically and culturally situated, with which subjects collude in order to protect their fragile status inside the barely holding framework of the socially expected. What Valmiki and Nayan cannot see, but Mootoo is concerned to make visible to us as readers, is how many of those they live alongside have equally unresolved, concessional, and queer lives. The novel shows how it is "respectability" or "how things are expected to be" (Mootoo 2008b, 3), as much as direct homophobia, that damages expressions and fulfilments of desire.

The combination of respectability and abuse told, through the story of Merle Bedi, indicates the timeliness of Viveka's petition for erotic freedom: "In exchange for honesty, integrity, a lifetime of service, she prayed that she and all people like her be granted the freedom, so long as it did not hurt anyone, to love whomever they chose, to love well, and to have that love returned without judgment" (Mootoo 2008b, 360). Merle Bedi, a young woman of Viveka's age and an old school friend of hers, represents the brutal alternative world outside the heteronormative family—poverty, social isolation, and the wreck of desire. We catch sight of Merle early on our journey, as Vashti encounters her while she waits for lunch at the doubles stand:

> She wears what was once a white shirt, a school shirt from not too long ago, but it is yellowed and soiled, and the trousers she wears, men's trousers, are covered in dirt, dust, urine. They are several sizes too big for her, held high above her waist with a belt and, as if that were not enough, a length of heavy rope. She is barefoot.
>
> . . . But she does not want her friends, anyone on the promenade, even people who are strangers, to see that she knows this woman about whom rumors have spread far and wide. . . . She is said to give her body to men, right here on the promenade, behind statues at night and in the bushes in the day, in exchange for a cigarette or money to buy a flask of rum. (Mootoo 2008b, 22)

Merle's public reputation is as a woman who has announced her desire for other women, a desire that became both subject defining and impossible for her at the point of social articulation. Merle's vagrant life and her denial as a desiring subject is the penalty she suffers for insisting that her desire be recognized on the exterior of her social being: "Merle Bedi told Viveka about wanting to kiss Miss Seukeran. Saying those words out loud was craziness. But Viveka understood something of it. That kind of talk, she felt, could get them both in trouble. A clash of thoughts, incomplete ones, incomplete-able ones, resounded in her head" (Mootoo 2008b, 94–5).

Merle's wretched presence breaks the surface of the narrative on several occasions, thwarting any idealized reading that in a creolized queer place like Port of Spain, not conforming to heterosexual normativity is an easy possibility. Within the ethical framework of the novel, Merle's forced prostitution is one of many instances where right and wrong cannot be mapped onto a hetero-/homosexuality divide. Yet, for Vashti waiting in the lunch queue, the talk of Merle's "other" sexual life as a prostitute seems at first a contradiction and then a solution in the perverse logic of heteronormativity: "But if she is doing this sort of thing, what they say about her can't be true then. It can't be that she is a buller. If is woman she like, how come she doing it with man? Well maybe is not a bad thing, then? That might cure her. And from such a family, too. It is killing her parents. No wonder they put she out the house" (23). Transactional heterosex is seen as bringing Merle back into a socially normative reality, regardless of her evident exploitation. It also exposes the public impossibility of queer lives not sheltered within a marriage. For Vashti and the community, Merle's autonomous erotic subjectivity remains both inconsequential and invisible—another way in which she mirrors the extremity of queer life.

Navigating between its social and emotional realism, Mootoo's narrative depicts many passionate subjects acting with caution.[6] It is also notable that the possibilities for same-sex desire are realized in the novel only when socially defined lives can be temporarily suspended: Valmiki and Saul, and Viveka and Anick meet in the forest beyond the hold of social reputation and respectability. At the same time, the novel demonstrably invests throughout in the frisson and rewards of imagined and recollected same-sex desires, as well as in moments of physical encounter. The opening page of the first narrative section devoted to Valmiki focuses on his ineffaceable sensual remembrance and yearning for Tony that reaches both across twenty years and the almost mythical expanse of the kala pani: "That was a long time ago, and much had happened for both of them since, and still every minute of their time together was indelibly etched in Valmiki's body and mind—even though they hadn't seen each other in twenty-something years. . . . Still, whenever Valmiki felt disoriented as he did just now, it was Tony, not his wife or any of their friends on the island, he reached for" (Mootoo 2008b, 26–27). For Valmiki, that queer place and time, beyond the restraints of his family and Trinidadian middle-class society, is the past present of connection and belonging, even if it can only be accessed through memory.

The novel's description of a queer community whose ostensibly orthodox social body is deeply veined with moments and memories of same-sex sensual pleasure repudiates the claims of a heteropatriarchal national discourse to proscribe natural and normal lifestyles. In this way, while Viveka's ideal of freedom remains an entreaty its ethical force cannot be denied. For Viveka herself, sexual queerness is part of a general "disloyalty against identity" (Butler 1993, 220) as it shapes itself into the constraints of feminine gender/ Indianness/wife. Early on in the narrative, when she is campaigning for her right to play basketball, Viveka contests the feminine and Indian-centered ideal of her mother's world. While her imagined boy-self Vince is a trans sensibility not shared with others, Viveka is vocal about contesting her mother's assertions of ethnic purity. Devika voices these first in relation to Viveka's friend: "Helen is not even Indian. At least, not *properly* Indian. Her father is white," and later in relation to what can be seen as her own people, "Those town Indians have no respect for their origins, they forget their place, they ooh and they aah over curry as if they never had curry before, and they give their children names like Helen" (Mootoo 2008b, 47, 48). Viveka's challenge to her mother's narrow version of ethnicity and gender is shaped by her understanding of Caribbeanness as a lateral solidarity. Viveka imagines human relations following the same horizontal plane of multiple convergences that opens the novel, and her call aligns with the novel's investment in the socially transformative potential of creolized place: "I mean, after all, we are a small island, and rather than form cliques we should indeed be learning from and about one another, helping another one upward, you know what I am saying?" (46).[7]

In terms of her sexual "disloyalty," Viveka's early tepid sexual encounters with the persistent and eligible male Elliot, and tingling attractions toward her female gym teacher, are transformed in the heady passion of her encounters with Anick. The narrative blushes with sexual anticipation on the subject of Viveka's almost and imagined kisses with Anick, creating an immense erotic charge with barely any sexual content. In their first physical encounter, the mere touching of a knee leads to an "earthquake" (Mootoo 2008b, 260) on the inside: "Now Viveka relived the touch of cheek and hand, and each time without fail felt a rush of dizzying desire. It was weakness, daunting and wonderful, that began in her toes and washed quickly upwards, to land between her legs, gripping her there in ecstasy . . . Over and over. She put the back of the hand that had held Anick's to her mouth, and with her lips closed, brushed it" (260). At moments when Viveka's social and erotic inclinations collide, it is the erotic that the narrative invests in: "Viveka oscillated between two poles. She decided one minute to still whatever thoughts and feelings Anick Prakash had stirred in her. Such thoughts and feelings were dangerous tricksters out to trip her up and land her, like Merle, out on her own, family-less. . . . But there was always the other pole: the desire to see, speak with, touch Anick Prakash was like the pull of a tidal wave against which Viveka decidedly did *not* want any cautioning or power" (261). And while her interior struggle to negotiate socially consoling identities and compelling, but disruptive, desires continues, her persuasions toward the erotic also endure: "If her parents were to find out that she had such feeling for a woman. If Nayan were to know that his wife made her dizzy like this. . . . But most of all, she imagined Anick and herself in the house in Rio Claro, with doors and windows closed and no prying eyes around. They would lower themselves onto the floor of the kitchen, and she would lie there with Anick, holding her face, stroking her hair, and kissing her mouth" (297). Here, and throughout the novel, the force of the erotic is felt as real when it is nostalgic, unrequited, or fantasized. In this way, the novel reminds us how erotic desires and subjectivities are composed of flutters, imaginings, and longings, as well as acts, practices, and identities.

For Viveka, the moments when living and loving do come together are cherished, charged with anticipation and longing, and marked by the expression of excess: "Viveka and Anick kissed lightly at first, but their passion grew and they pushed and pulled each other, their mouths locking, tongues probing, tasting, hands searching frantically, bodies taking turns turning, lying one on top of the other. . . . Viveka's body was an electric current of pleasure, but she was spurred on more by her desire to give Anick all that she so clearly wanted than by any need of her own. Then it was as if Anick's pleasure opened as wide as it could, and she burst, and burst and burst" (Mootoo 2008b, 322). Such moments summon a different meeting point of place and the possible, as the narrator describes Trinidad from a queer perspective. It is in these moments that the possible itself changes form and where apprehensions are rearranged in such a way that the seeming historical and cultural guarantees of the impossible (same sex attachment, multiple lovers) can never be fully persuasive or adequate again.

Caribbean Queer Futures and Families

In its hyper-realist narration of Trinidadian outer and inner lives *Valmiki's Daughter* works toward a locally sensitive idea of creolized erotic being and sexual relations that accounts for the complex and distinctive matrix of human relations that guarantee a rewarding life. In this way the narrative asks us to acknowledge how such imaginings—often inscribed around ideas of an individual subject with absolute rights and entitlements—can be negotiated around the happiness and emotional security of significant others, such as family. The focus here is not on what it means to have any particular erotic orientation but rather on how varied and complex the sexual choices and practices are that inform what it means to have a Caribbean life that feels possible.

Despite her contempt for the societal norms that underpin the ideology of the family, Viveka's attachment to her own family is incontrovertible and an important consideration in her thoughts on possible futures: "Which was greater she wondered—to be all that you were, to be true to yourself, or to honor one's family, one's society, one's country? Her family, despite everything, was her life. She could never be without them. She could never do to them what Merle Bedi had done to her family" (Mootoo 2008b, 326). Her appreciation of the substantial bonds of family are also an immediate consideration shaping possible futures when Anick proposes "you and me and the baby can go away together," to which Viveka replies, "You think you can take Nayan's chile, Ram Prakash's grandchild, and go your own way?" (357). While Mootoo clearly reveals the repressive features of patriarchal familial expectation and reproductive heteronormativity, she also does not deny the security, comfort, and belonging of family. While in Halberstam's version of a queer time and place (2005) "quests for community are always nostalgic attempts to return to some fantasized moment of union and unity [that] reveals the conservative stakes in community for all kinds of political projects" (154), Mootoo's Trinidadian postcolonial community is one in which the experience of belonging to each other is more fraught and complex as it looks back to a traumatic history in which familial and community bonds were severed and denied. In its engagement with what Jafari S. Allen calls "liberatory models from the past, and project[ing] our imaginations forward, to possible futures" (Allen 2016, 38), *Valmiki's Daughter* surfaces a tension that also exists within Black queer studies' rejection of canonical White queer theory's stance on an antireproductive futurism.[8] As Omise'eke Tinsley affirms in conversation with Allen, "Crying out for 'no future' just isn't for people of African descent; we've been slated for no future since the door of no return. So we need alternatives to that painful, slaveheld past that colonial and plantation records so precisely and soul-crushingly document for us, in order to create alternatives to the living deaths that are supposed to be our future" (Allen and Tinsley 2012, 258). In the context of Mootoo's Trinidad, where the failures of those of Indian and African descent to build community have consistently undermined the quality of postindependence life for all, the post- and anticolonial future community that Mootoo invites us to imagine, one in which Valmiki and Saul can be lovers, offers a particularly, powerfully Caribbean queer ecology.

Queered Conjugality

By simply paying more attention to inner lives, Mootoo's novel renders the turbulence within heteronormativity as an already lived dimension. In its detailing of the intricate internal folds of so many differently desiring lives the novel represents a range of creolized Caribbean sexualities that undo heteronormativity. Indeed, while the novel ends with Viveka, like her father before her, consenting to marry, her "compliance" to a heterosexual marriage with Trevor may be read as a betrayal of self, but it is also a betrayal of marriage and on both their parts. Trevor is attracted to what is nonconforming about Viveka, including her evident and eventually confessed intimacy with Anick: "It's hard to pin you down, isn't it? I like that. You're pretty complicated" (Mootoo 2008b, 373). Trevor accepts Viveka's desire for women and, like Viveka herself, acknowledges that who we are is always in excess of how we can be named. What makes their future marriage queer is also what queers the marriage of Marsha and Denton: an awareness that to deny the complexity and difficulty of desire is to deny what might make us most fully responsive to each other, as well as most complete in ourselves.

While the surface tension of gender, class, and ethnic cohesion is held in place by Viveka's adherence to the marriage script, for Mootoo's readers everything has changed. Mootoo's thick description of the lives of Valmiki, Viveka, Devika, Saul, Saul's wife, Anika, Merle, and Tony gives representation to "multiple queer desires that were not identity-based or identity-forging" (Howard 1999, 29) and that often also exist alongside heterofamiliar desires.[9] In this continuum of desiring subjects, the novel renders an already queer Trinidad through which our understandings of erotic attachments are creolized. It demands a recognition of how the heterosexual and the queer often occupy the same spaces, live the same lives, have the same unruly and multiple desires. By focusing on lives that are messy, compromised, and incomplete, yet vibrant, pleasurable, and rewarding, *Valmiki's Daughter* reaches beyond an imagined extension of sexual normalization (in which subjects identified as homosexual enter into marriage, child-rearing, and so on). Her rendering of a shared queerness more radically questions the identity-making necessity of erotic desire and the social power attached to object choice. It is also an erotic ecology entirely congruent with the multiply creolized milieu of San Fernando.

Conclusion

By representing heterosexuality as a sometimes porous, queer arrangement that may undermine rather than endorse heteronormativity, both Forbes's story and Mootoo's novel render social realities that contribute to tacit forms of knowledge around which more inclusive queered communities come into being. Both destabilize heteronormativity by revealing how non- heterosexual subjects can be heteronormative (Valmiki), and heterosexual subjects can be non-heteronormative (Marsha). Importantly, they also show how heteronormativity not only leads to the marginalization of those who do not conform to its hegemonic type but also to a general diminishment of the possibilities of human connection, of emotional fulfilment, and of erotic realization for all. As Cohen (1997) argues, "In narrowly positing a dichotomy of heterosexual privilege and queer oppression under which we all exist, are we negating a basis of political unity that could serve to strengthen many communities and movements seeking justice and societal transformation?" (453). Forbes's and Mootoo's fashionings of social and sexual arrangements complicate and challenge this divide to imagine solidarities and coalitional struggles not possible without an interrogation of how creolized sexualities undo heteronormativity.

3

Caribbean Freedoms and Queering Homonormativity

• •

Andrew Salkey's *Escape to an Autumn Pavement*

To live in the Black Diaspora is I think to live as a fiction—a creation of empires, and also self-creation. It is to be a being living inside and outside of herself. It is to apprehend the sign one makes yet to be unable to escape it except in radiant moments of ordinariness made like art.
—Dionne Brand, *A Map to the Door of No Return*

London was an imperial metropolis, and its queer cultures reflected the influence of immigration and racial difference upon metropolitan life. National newspapers reported metropolitan vice more frequently than any other urban center, establishing an axiomatic connection between "homosexuality" and the capital.
—Matt Houlbrook, *Queer London*

This chapter returns to the core question of this book—how does Caribbeanness promote an undoing of heteronormativity—by offering a reading of Andrew Salkey's second novel, *Escape to an Autumn Pavement*, first published in 1960. Salkey had migrated from Jamaica to London in 1952 in order to study for an English degree at the University of London. His novels, too seldom noted in critical accounts of either Caribbean or Black British fiction, record lives in both places. His first, *A Quality of Violence* ([1959] 1978), is set in rural Jamaica in 1900 and his third, *The Late Emancipation of Jerry Stover* ([1968] 1982), returns to Jamaica for its damning indictment of the nihilism of middle-class Caribbean life. *The Adventures of Catullus Kelly* (1969b) is set back in London, and Salkey's last major fiction, *Come Home, Malcolm Heartland* (1976) has as its theme the revolutionary pursuits of exiles in London.

Salkey is probably now better known for his role in the development of literary culture than for his own writings. His contribution to Caribbean literary history was both significant and characteristically multilocational. He played a foundational role in two of the most influential developments for Anglo-Caribbean literature during its boom decades of the 1950s and 1960s. In the 1950s, he served as a presenter and an editor on the BBC *Caribbean Voices* program (1943–1958), the now legendary platform for West Indian literary visibility that offered both a vital venue for creative works to be broadcast across the region and a metropolitan gathering point and employment opportunity for budding young migrant writers, such as George Lamming, Edgar Mittelholzer, and V. S. Naipaul. However, while Salkey was at the center of a West Indian literary community, he also had his finger on the pulse of literary London. He was a prolific reviewer and a generous networker, introducing both Naipaul and Wilson Harris to their U.K. publishers. In 1966, when it was believed that the prominent profile afforded West Indian writing in the 1950s was waning, Salkey, along with Kamau Brathwaite and John La Rose, formed the Caribbean Artists Movement (CAM) to organize cultural events and raise its profile. The movement's associated journal, *Savacou*, published some of the earliest experimental works in nation language and built a crucial creative pathway for ideas and voices to travel between London and the Caribbean. Salkey was also important for gathering West Indian writers together in publication form, and his four short-story anthologies were decisive tools of communicating a (male) tradition in the making: *West Indian Stories* ([1960] 1969a); *Stories from the Caribbean* (1965); *Caribbean Prose* (1967); and *Island Voices: Stories for the West Indies* (1970). Arguably then, Salkey helped to curate and to calibrate what we now know and understand as Caribbean literature, but if his own writings are called on today, it is usually his powerful works for children, including *Hurricane* ([1964] 1979a) and *The River That Disappeared* (1979) or his playful and irreverent collections of Anancy tales, *Anancy's Score* (1973) and *Anancy Traveller* (1992), that spin this Jamaican African–inspired local genre across global justice agendas from the exploitation of women, poverty, and dispossession, to the Vietnam war.

It is this sense of Salkey's creative work as a nodal point for cross-articulating local and global concerns, and its potential to speak across and beyond national audiences, that I want to draw on in my reading of *Escape* as a narrative that queers a progressive politics of sexual identity in Britain in the late 1950s from a Caribbean perspective. In many respects, *Escape* is in keeping with its Windrush literary peers as a narrative of a Caribbean person reaching for cultural belonging and place in a landscape strongly marked by the imprint of colonialism. However, its setting in the urban motherland and its sustained and direct engagement with issues around sexual accommodation distinguish it markedly. The landmark Anglo-Caribbean novels of this period, all of which were published when their authors were based in England, are commonly cited as Wilson Harris's *Palace of the Peacock* (1960), V. S. Naipaul's *A House for Mr. Biswas* ([1961] 1983), and George Lamming's *In the Castle of My Skin* ([1963] 1991). Like *Escape*, all three focus on the journey of a Caribbean man toward self-knowledge and an understanding of his own Caribbeanness. Each inflects this journey differently, although they all trace the pathways that cut across exterior and interior realities to deliver narratives that focus on spiritual, political, and social awakening. Collectively, as Supriya Nair asserts, these works were able to reshape ideas of both Caribbean lives and Caribbean literature: "Their anxiety over claiming a specific space and their determination to build their own literary tradition responsive to Caribbean realities, however entangled with their mixed colonial heritage and overwhelmed in many cases by physical exile, mark the literally groundbreaking creative fiction of this period" (Nair 2011, 173). Although *Escape* can certainly claim the accolade of being groundbreaking, it has seldom been attended to within the same context as these formative canonical narratives or read as "responsive to Caribbean realities." Both the urban diasporic setting and the direct, often abrasive, discussion of race and sexual politics in Salkey's work strike a departure from the cherished nucleus of Caribbean stories of self-determination. The novel was reissued in 2009 as a Peepal Tree Caribbean Classic, with an introduction by Thomas Glave, the Jamaican American writer-activist probably best known for his work with J-FLAG, an organization advocating for Jamaica's All-Sexuals.[1] Glave's (2009) recommendation of this work "as a bold journey into explorations of sexuality" clearly foregrounds the alternative direction of its cultural footsteps (5).

Two recent critical engagements with this novel that discuss its expressions and vectors of non-normalizing erotic belonging lead in very different directions, indicative of the open weave of the narrative's style. Kate Houlden's (2013) article "Andrew Salkey, the British Home and the Intimacies In-Between" focuses on how the protagonist Johnnie's intimacies with his neighbor/friend/lover Dick, disturb and thereby challenge the normalizing expectations of the English domestic space. Houlden reads the novel as "making the claim for home being haunted and unsettled by unacknowledged racial and sexual desires" (107) in its "literary exploration of queer and migrant lives conducted in the intimate space if the British home" (106). Although initially interested in how the "settled domesticity" (101) of Johnnie and Dick's relationship seems to mirror the homonormalization of its time and place, Houlden also acknowledges allusions to a world beyond the home that open this novel outward toward the possibility of encounter with "the city's homosexual underworld" (105). Nadia Ellis's (2015b) reading in *Territories of the Soul: Queered Belonging in the Black Diaspora*, approaches Salkey's novel from a very different angle, as an exploration of "how it can be possible to belong while rejecting the strictures of conventional relationality" (98). For Ellis, Johnnie in *Escape* exemplifies the queer diasporic subject whose migrant status "lends to the queer refusal of lineage, futurity, and community" (99). In an illuminating reading of the novel as a story of postwar migration in which the intersecting tensions of class and race politics infuse and inflame Johnnie's relationships with his fellow West Indians, aspiring White working-class Britons and his sexual partners, Ellis shows Johnnie to be a "figure eluding identity" (130). Aspects of both readings are relevant to my own interest in Salkey's transnational novel exploring colonial and sexual citizenship in the 1950s and my focus on how these two charters for negotiating and resisting social identities collide in the rendering of erotic subjectivity. In particular, I am interested in how Salkey's literary depiction of a distinctly Caribbean encounter with the horizons and limits of belonging to London in the 1950s works to critique, unsettle, and creolize emerging, so-called progressive, discourses of sexual citizenship.

I begin by considering where we might look to for a literary context for *Escape*'s exploration of same-sex sociality and intimacy within the Caribbean literary tradition of its day. I then turn to the cultural history of debates relating to sexual freedoms and identities prominent in 1950s London. I read the novel's depiction of queer London with its assemblage of sexual terrains and behaviors, and the protagonist's stylization of a creolized queer subjectivity that insists on remaining open to the possibilities such a place offers, alongside the Wolfenden Report of 1957. The historical record rightly recognizes Wolfenden for his report's recommendation of the decriminalization of homosexual acts between consenting adults in private—a recommendation that would not become law for another decade.[2] Wolfenden's report was also deeply invested, though, in the relationship between sexual behaviors and identities, and in this way it established certain conditions for the expression of same-sex male desire. By inscribing the identity of the "respectable homosexual" that traded private legitimacy for public regulation, the Wolfenden Report arguably began the process of homonormalization.[3] My close reading of the novel's narration of overlapping cultural and sexual nonconformities that follows, looks in particular at its protagonist's—Johnnie Sobert's—repeated and emphatic assertion of his entitlement to complete self-determination and freedom from categorization and containment (an interesting echo of Naipaul's similar insistence discussed in chapter 1). I explore the ways in which Salkey draws on the liquidity and autonomy of a decolonized, creolized Caribbeanness, albeit in anticipation rather than actuality, as a mode of resistance to the stabilization and contraction of identity scripts, including the script around homosexual identity that was emerging at this time.

Same-Sex Male Intimacy and the Postwar Caribbean Novel

There is much to be said for returning to canonical works of Anglo-Caribbean literature and rereading their blatant, often strident, heteronormativity as a necessary carapace that protected vulnerable gender categories (especially a fragile and embattled masculinity) wherein latent same-sex intimacies and desires remained concealed or differently coded. Indeed, I take this critical approach of scrutinizing inflated accounts of heteronormative sexual desire and their role as camouflage strategies for erotic identities in crisis in chapter 4 to read Junot Díaz's (2007) hyperbolic depiction of Dominican hypermasculinity in *The Brief Wondrous Life of Oscar Wao* and Marlon James's (2014) brutalizing account of Jamaican heteropatriarchal erotics in *A Brief History of Seven Killings*.

Ian Smith's (1999) "Critics in the Dark" is a pioneering essay in this line of thinking and one especially relevant to the consideration of the 1950s and 1960s writings. Smith prefaces his reading of H. Nigel Thomas's (1993) *Spirits in the Dark* with a discussion of the tensions between the narrative affirmation of compulsory heterosexuality that was seemingly integral to earlier Caribbean migration narratives and the encounter with homosexual lives in England that nevertheless creates a turbulence not quite contained by the narrative's efforts. In his article, I. Smith (1999) discusses Sam Selvon's iconic 1956 novel of metropolitan migration, *The Lonely Londoners* ([1956] 1979), alongside V. S. Naipaul's equally classic 1987 work, *The Enigma of Arrival*, to which I referred in chapter 1. Reading *The Lonely Londoners*, a work on masculinity in the metropolis that has far outshadowed Salkey's in reputation, Smith draws attention to the ballad section when Cap both simultaneously confesses and denies his sexual encounter with a transvestite man.[4] His reading alerts us to the subsequent attempts at narrative containment of this erotic risk in a novel full of the animated urban encounters between West Indian men:

> Replete with textual denials from Moses, "at the time he didn't know nothing" (39) and from Cap, "He tell Moses he didn't know anything until he begin,

when he find the going difficult and realize that something wrong" (40). Delivered with the typical self-inoculating humor of the group of friends, this narrative of homoerotic misadventure is immediately, without transition, followed in the text by the sudden announcement of Cap's marriage: "Who can tell what was the vap that hit Cap and make him get married?" (40). The textual question, inviting speculation on the unstated cause by virtue of its structural relation to the homoerotic narrative, suggests a deep psychological crisis in Cap, a self-regulatory response to compulsory heterosexuality, a social paranoia within which he can fix his sexual identity. The homoerotic "ballad" is rendered incomplete. (I. Smith 1999, 2–3)

I. Smith also points out how the narrator's own sexual curiosity is revealed later in the novel as Moses "engages a "pansy" in a protracted, elaborate sexual rendezvous, urging the man to "tell him what and what they wouldn't do" (92)" (I. Smith 1999, 3).

While I agree with I. Smith (1999) that Selvon's novel offers glimpses into "a writerly consciousness struggling to articulate the place of the homoerotic in the social life of the double diaspora of London" (3), I am not so sure of his conclusion that "the homoerotic life of the Londoner generates an extreme loneliness" (3). Moses does clearly insist on heteronormative narrative closure in his parting line, "It was the sort of night that if you wasn't making love to a woman you feel you was the only person in the world like that" (Selvon [1956] 1979, 141). However, in addition to the passages of encounter with openly non-heteronormative subjects that I. Smith (1999) alludes to, *The Lonely Londoners* is brimming with West Indian male-male intimacies. These do not figure explicitly as part of the erotic energetics of the novel, which retains a focus on "white pussy" (Selvon [1956] 1979, 90) that is inflated to the point of irony. Nevertheless, the novel does render a world abundant in the density of homosocial bonds and the physical proximity of men undertaking everyday living in crowded bedsits and basements, even hot-bedding in shifts. As a whole, *The Lonely Londoners* creates a compelling world of male-male embodied and affective attachments. It could also be argued that Selvon's novel, published while the Wolfenden enquiry into sexual offences was taking its evidence from London homosexuals, renders visible the risk associated with public encounters. The two encounters of Cap and Moses that I. Smith (1999) discusses seem to register the public curiosity around emergent discourses on homosexual lifestyle choices that had been as loudly stigmatized and more widely reported in the "vice-ridden" metropolis of London than in Caribbean societies. However, the novel also signifies, in its concentration of male-male exchanges and encounters, a world in which homoerotic possibility is never fully erased by stories of heterosexual conquest or homosexual disavowal.

The fact that I. Smith's (1999) framing argument turns to Selvon's work and its "anxious disavowals of the homoerotic" (2) is particularly interesting given this novel's historical and content-based proximity to Salkey's *Escape to an Autumn Pavement*, which approaches questions of sexuality in an intriguingly different mode and in which it is far more evident how "sexuality and language intersect to produce a revised geography of the self" (8). Indeed, although I. Smith's article makes the historical leap to 1993 in order to find a literary work that defies the sexual disavowal that he regards as "the crucial, collective enigma of the West Indian literary scene" (4), Salkey's 1960 novel can usefully be read as an act of literary defiance, that is both complicated and radical in its shaping of erotic subjectivities.[5] The sexual narrative of London life for a West Indian man that unfolds in *Escape* does not take the shape of an avowal of an increasingly knowable homosexuality. Rather, it highlights the uncategorizable, queer nature of erotic desires and behaviors in ways captured by neither the terminology of the Wolfenden Report nor the vernacular of Selvon's fictionalized world.

The Erotic Compromise of the Respectable Homosexual

Reading *Escape to an Autumn Pavement* alongside Wolfenden's enquiry and report, as well as the circumstances that led to its commission, enables a differently inflected interpretation of its protagonist's, Johnnie's, refusal to occupy binary sexual identities. Alongside mass migration from the Caribbean and South Asia, sexual slackness, and in particular homosexuality, were increasingly regarded as a rupture, a disturbance, and even danger to the social fabric and cultural stability of post-WWII British life. In his instructive and nuanced cultural history, *Queer London: Perils and Pleasures in the Sexual Metropolis 1918–1957*, Matt Houlbrook (2005) describes the overlapping of perceived social crises in this period that led to the negative attention on sexual dissidence, the eventual liberalization of the law, and the subsequent and related categorization of sexual citizenship: "As the Empire was fragmenting, youth and family life were becoming increasingly problematic, and comfortable assumptions of the ordered social body were eroding, these narratives of sexual danger acquired increasing resonance. The queer, a predatory and lustful danger to the nation and its manhood, embodied a wider postwar crisis of Britishness" (239). A key response to this crisis came in 1954 when Home Secretary David Maxwell Fyfe, who was championing an "anti-vice drive" focused on London, appointed the Departmental Committee on Homosexual Offences and Prostitution in Great Britain, chaired by Sir John Wolfenden, then vice-chancellor of the University of Reading.

Wolfenden's "Report on Homosexual Offences and Prostitution" (commonly known as the Wolfenden Report) was published in 1957. Its principal finding was that the existing criminalization of homosexuality was a curtailment of individual morality and civil liberty. Its controversial first recommendation read as follows: "That homosexual behavior between consenting adults in private be no longer a criminal offence" (Wolfenden 1957, 115).[6] The Archbishop of Canterbury, Geoffrey Fisher; the British Medical Association; the Howard League for Penal Reform; and the National Association of Probation Officers supported this change in the law. All the same, the Cabinet refused to implement the report's findings. Indeed, it was not until Lord Aran's motion in the House of Lords in 1965 that the recommendations were taken up and the Sexual Offences Act of 1967 was passed, decriminalizing sexual relations between consenting adults over the age of twenty-one in private (excluding members of the Merchant Navy or Armed Forces).

Despite the fact that government ministers did not show much responsiveness to the report, the 155-page document was something of a bestseller. The first print run of five thousand copies sold out within hours, and it stimulated significant media attention, bringing the question of homosexual identity, as well as sexual freedoms, into public debate. Yet the terms of that debate may not be as clear as the short teleological and emancipatory history of decriminalization indicates. While there evidently was a reformulation of sexual citizenship in relation to homosexuality in the postwar period when Salkey was writing his novel, there was also an important counternarrative or erotic normalization promoted by the Wolfenden Report's emphasis on the containment and respectability of the newly defined homosexual.

Houlbrook (2005) argues persuasively that the elite social position of the witnesses who gave evidence to Wolfenden—Patrick Trevor-Roper, a Harley Street consultant; Carl Winter, director of the Fitzwilliam Museum; and Peter Wildeblood, the diplomatic correspondent on the *Daily Mail*—enabled the careful contouring of a paralleled social world of heteronormative/homonormative encounters predicated on shared values of "discretion, fidelity, and intimacy" (260). He contends that the report's construction of the "respectable homosexual" through the legitimate privatization of intimate and erotic lives forged a homosexual identity that could transition from criminal to civil status. Structured to mirror heterosexual conformity, with a different but stable object choice, this discursive construct was congruent with a privileged lifestyle that facilitated attachments and meetings within sheltered domestic settings and protected cultural enclaves, such as the ballet: "This respectable "homosexuality" was assembled from interwoven legal, scientific, and medical discourses and a particular moral politics of space . . . In short, the "homosexual" was constituted through and within border matrices of sexual difference, defined through his distance from places, practices and people repudiated as abject, immoral and dangerous" (243). Houlbrook is keen to point out the consequences of the report's construction and legitimation of "respectable homosexuality," as both the "ever-greater stigmatization of the disreputable queer" and the historical ambivalence of "a moment of political 'liberation,' which excluded and stigmatized vibrant forms of queer urban culture" (261, 270).

While it is precisely this sense of a constraining liberalization that Johnnie shuns in Salkey's novel, there is certainly a strong sense of the typography of regulation in relation to queer bodies that Frank Mort (1998) describes in his article "Cityscapes: Consumption, Masculinities and the Mapping of London since 1950." Here Mort details exactly the "waiting mob of diagnosticians, analysts, observers, recorders" that Johnnie dreads: "statistics, medicine, and the law, as well as newer practices of psychiatry and psychoanalysis, were all drawn on in the interests of productive surveillance" (890). Indeed, Johnnie's acute consciousness of being subject to scrutiny, commentary, and judgment even breaches the narrative surface: "What would an audience think? . . . What would the vast reading public of Sunday papers say? Queer lot." (Salkey 2009, 143). This sense of an exterior gaze dividing society into "them" and "us" through a biopolitical knowledge bank that directly invokes Wolfenden is called out again by Johnnie: "And *they* say there's something queer about a relationship like ours. *They*, the mockers; *they*, the intelligent critics; *they*, the wolf-hound boys; *they*, the . . ." (145; italics in the original). The debate around sexual citizenship framed by the Wolfenden Report's recommendations that society and the law should respect "individual freedom of actions in matters of private morality" (Wolfenden 1957, 24) orchestrated an expansion of sexual tolerance without meaningfully opening up questions around sexual desire or identification. In this way, the report, much like the constitutional reform in Jamaica, raised the promise of freedoms, but only as imagined within the purview of the bourgeois respectability to which Salkey is both fictionally alert and critical in *Escape*.

"My Kind of Freedom": Johnnie Sobert's Queer Belonging

My attention to Salkey's expression of erotic attachments as plastic, multiple, and positively open in *Escape* continues my exploration of creolized Caribbean sexualities. My interest here lies with how Johnnie's refusal to be interpellated by the identity of the homosexual, as much as by that of the heterosexual, is informed by his creolized Caribbean sensibility, which is strongly resistant to all such acts of identitarian assimilation. Indeed, Johnnie's unwavering focus on extreme self-determination is suggestively connected to the place from which he has escaped. Jamaica's process of incremental constitutional reform during the 1950s, in which the promise of independence and the compromise of its realities were both in sharp focus, led to a surplus of liberatory expectation such as Johnnie expresses.[7]

Throughout, the novel describes dissent and intraracial prejudices expressed among and toward different Black communities—West Indians, Indians, Africans, and African American GIs—all of which are represented as diverse groups that cannot be reduced or racialized by simplified versions of Black solidarity that risk homogenizing ideas of Blackness. The foregrounding of this resistance to reductive identity categories is formally announced by a somewhat curious and yet telling author's note that prefaces the work:

> Although all the characters and situations depicted in this novel are fictitious, I'm obliged to point out that the character called SHAKUNTALA GOOLAM, might, indeed, cause some offence in that, quite unwittingly, she has been given an improbable Indian name. Apparently, SHAKUNTALA and GOOLAM belong to different worlds.
>
> After naming her, I learned that SHAKUNTALA (Sanskrit) is Hindu, and GOOLAM which is properly GHULAM (Persian) is Muslim. . . .
>
> In the first instance I plead ignorance, and in the second innocence. If I'm allowed a third I plead invention. As it is, SHAKUNTALA GOOLAM barely exists in name, therefore, she has no other life and exerts no influence whatever beyond her appearance as a minor character in this novel. (Salkey 2009, n.p.; emphasis in the original)

Ostensibly relating to the inflammatory possibilities of hybridizing faith identities, Salkey's disclaimer on his choice of names, the wider politics of identity attached to naming, and the immunity of "real" life claims in fictional world-buildings can all be seen to resonate more generally in the novel to come.[8]

Salkey's tone here is demonstrably irreverent and sardonic. Moreover, in the fictional world of his novel, it is precisely the struggle to be free from the captive labor of identity tags and singular acts of belonging that almost obsessively preoccupies the protagonist, Johnnie. In this context, drawing attention to the seemingly clashing composite of his fictional female character, Shakuntala Goolam, can be read as a fitting prelude to the novel. This disruptive collision of allegedly mutually exclusionary identities (most provocatively suggested in the narrative by the unspoken "Jamaican queer") arguably primes the reader for the wider disputes with identity categorization that the novel stages throughout, although most intensely in relation to sexual rather than ethnic or religious identity.

The narrative itself opens with a consciously brazen and declarative first-person voice: "The name's Sobert. Johnnie Sobert. Jamaican. R. C. Middle class. Or so I've been made to think" (Salkey 2009, 15). Indeed, it is this ill-fitting conjunction between the bagginess of being and the narrow thinking of identity categories that provides a guiding interest for this novel in relation to faith, ethnicity, class, and—most strikingly—sexuality. As we soon discover, middle-class Johnnie has come to London from Jamaica, settling in "a small Hampstead bedsitter," which he calls a "private tenement kind of hell" (15). The anticipated "escape" of the title is Johnnie's evasion of an excruciatingly constrained and conventional life as part of the aspiring Jamaican middle-class, which has been plotted for him by his father and affirmed by his mother. In relocating to London, Johnnie seeks determinedly to unthink the regulated spaces and identities into which his future life has been mapped. Resistance to the normalized organization of social realities, and to the pressures that these realities exert on the conditions necessary for individual and collective freedoms, remains a central theme throughout the book.

The entire first chapter of Salkey's novel focuses on Johnnie's encounters with the individuals and couples with whom he shares a bedsitter and makes visible (and risible) the investments they have in the identity-based politics of racial, class, and sexual cohesion. In the opening meeting with his landlady, Mrs. Blount, Johnnie brusquely rejects her attempts to accommodate him by interpellating him as an exception to his ethnic group on the basis of his class position in comments like "you're different from the others I've seen working on the Underground" and "you're so intelligent, Mr. Sobert" (Salkey 2009, 15, 17). Johnnie's internalized retort, "House-owning bitch" (19) reveals his unforgiving attitude toward a politics of class identity that seeks to model inclusion and sameness based on mutual exclusion and difference. Johnnie's verbal exchange with Miss Goolam, a visiting student from India, is similarly punctuated by internalized interruptions that underline his willful repudiation of any grounds for similarity or solidarity based on identificatory categories—in this case, colonial consciousness. When she asks where he comes from, his first response—"A place damn' far away from India, Miss Goolam" (17)—is a clear refusal of common ground. His reference to her as a "thick piece of curry" (17) and his antagonism toward her idea that she will be improved by an English education further exemplify Johnnie's desire to dismiss narratives of colonial solidarity and of Western development in order to resist his own identity being regulated according to the dominant historical trajectory of his era. His parting allusion to her body, however, clearly insinuates sexual anticipation: "Not a bad effort under that great swaddling expanse of sari. Must see her for a little chat. Perhaps when we cross paths at the toilet, again" (18).

The third encounter, with Dick the English "fish-faced chauffeur" (Salkey 2009, 15), more directly brings a critique of gender and sexual identity into play. When Dick comments flirtatiously, "We're always meeting at this point, aren't we?" (18), Johnnie's reflections on Dick's body and dress are alert to his stylization as an act of both class and gender crossing dressing: "Tender chuckles from Fish-face. Long fingers with manicured nails. Third-class citizen with first-class citizen's grammar and accent. Harrods dressing gown. May be Aquascutum. Or even Burberry. Could be a Christmas present from the tramp for services rendered on the road. I wonder what his driving is like under pressure?" (18–9). As with Shakuntula, verbal quips do not conceal the horizon of sexual curiosity and availability encoded in this encounter. As their exchange develops, Johnnie gently rebuffs Dick's efforts to position him alongside other West Indians, "your chaps," even though Dick speaks empathetically of a narrative of colonial suffering: "Not their war. Not their climate" (19). There is a clear sense of intimacy in their ensuing exchange. Agreeing to share the bathroom for the prosaic domestic ritual of washing socks and towels, Johnnie's curiosity about Dick's sexuality is nevertheless divulged to the reader. In an uncharacteristically oblique reference, Johnnie draws on the Jamaican linguistic gesture toward same-sex desire, "I wonder if he's *that way*, really?" (20). Erotic interest is reciprocated when Dick begins to quiz Johnnie about his own preferences, using the landlady's disapproval of nighttime guests as a reason to inquire whether he had been sexually involved with the couple who had visited his room the night before:

> "So, you didn't . . ."
> "Of course not."
> Most peculiar moment, this. The look on Dick's face wants to tell me something. Very badly, most urgently. Can't make out whether he's glad or sorry. (Salkey 2009, 20)

Their thinly disguised erotic exchange continues when Johnnie asks Dick why he has not "snapped . . . up" Miss Goolam since they have lodged together for seven years, a question he follows up with the deliberately imprecise inquiry, "You're fixed all right, aren't you?" (21).

In Johnny's final encounter, with the "married unmarried couple," Mr. and Mrs. Trado, who act as rent agents for the landlady, his own identity story, as well as his resistance to it, begins to surface. When provoked by the racist slurs of Mr. Trado and his insinuation of racial surveillance, "Sobert, we're watching you closely. No funny tricks, now," Johnnie remains silent while his interior voice becomes increasingly vivid and pacey: "No use behaving the way my mother would want me to, responsibly and politely . . . the way a *little gentleman* is brought up to behave" (Salkey 2009, 24; italics in the original). Raging at the futility of the middle-class colonial aspirant who believes that they can evade racism through an exaggerated civility, "a whitewashed nig with lots of *coolth*," Johnnie nevertheless replays the sentence that hangs over his freedoms and conditions his identity performance through restraint: *"There aren't many houses in Hampstead that would have your kind"* (26; italics in the original).

Collectively, these opening encounters draw attention to the strangely creolized private/public space of the bedsitter as a jostling zone of identity competitions and factions that call upon typecast postwar identities both to stage discriminations and to invite alliances. In all these encounters, Johnnie is at pains to make himself wholly unavailable to racial, class, and sexual categorization and therefore to escape the normalizing organization of social identities and imaginings. Importantly though, while Johnnie closes down the offers of class and migrant solidarity made in his encounters with Miss Goolam and Dick, he does not dismiss the multiple erotic prospects and energetics that they present; even their names—Shakuntula (with its embedded variation of *cunt*) and Dick—suggest a crude parody of their sexual offers. In the fabricated community of the boarding house, human difference is presented as routinely classified in order to be understood and managed. Only sexual desire seems able to flow against the currents of engrained social segregation and racialized assumptions. Importantly, such desire, like Johnnie's own counternarratives railing against these currents, remains mainly unuttered and yet noisy within the narrative. It is as if spoken language is itself an act of "going public" that risks absorption into the normalizing discourses of a national imaginary that speaks and thereby instantiates its standards in the face of a postwar social turmoil from which it already knows it will never recover. Such a significant portion of the novel unfolds as an interior voice at odds with its social contexts that the novel's privileged interest in reflection over action is clear. From just these initial encounters, the reader comes to recognize that it is in the interstitial and internalized spaces of his voicings that Johnnie finds the freedom to escape—an escape from names and assumed identities that limit his agency and his freedom to broker new modes of sociality.

Johnnie's own intimate history begins to take form when he returns at night to find Mrs. Fiona Trado waiting in the darkness of his bedsit. Purportedly there to explain Mr. Trado's earlier racist outburst, Fiona divulges to Johnnie how she had found herself pregnant and abandoned by her former lover, Joseph, an African student, and how Mr. Gerald Trado had taken her as his partner not knowing that the baby had a Black father. When the baby was born both Gerald and her parents rejected the boy and he was taken to live with an aunt in Newcastle. Further exploding the veneer of marital normativity that the Trados perform, Fiona also reveals that Gerald is already married and that their own relationship is abusive and exploitative: "And when he's drunk enough he either beats me or uses me as a sort of public convenience, or both" (Salkey 2009, 44). Fiona's evident attraction to Johnnie resonates with colonial desire as the novel and Johnnie insinuate her particular attraction to Black men. While the blatantly race-based prejudices of this period are later drafted into the narrative by the discussion of pamphlets calling for the repatriation of "colored immigrants," the words of a street drunk and the indignant rage of Mr. Trado disclose the undertow of a racialized discourse around sexual potency and threat.[9]

Salkey's novel narrates a metropolitan world in which hustling to make a living inevitably means becoming embroiled in an economy of sexual transactions. Money and sex are as closely allied as sex and race. For both Johnnie and Dick, the relationships to bosses, colleagues, clients, and strangers are all fraught with claims on sexual availability. To remain afloat in the world this novel depicts entails constant and careful negotiations crafted to sustain desire without delivering satisfaction. At the nightclub, Johnnie dodges the sexual advances of both Biddy, his coworker, and Sandra, his boss. And he is aware when he attends to a male client that this encounter also carries the prospect of sexual demand: "That's the fix. On time. Saved in the nick. Might need to be saved from him, too. Anyway, later for that" (Salkey 2009, 86). Evading the consequences of the almost constant agitation toward erotic play that he experiences in public places, Johnnie finds himself sexually involved with both Fiona and Dick in the compressed space of the boarding house, yet he still eschews the conventional description of these attachments by object choice.

Johnnie knows that his sexual encounters with Fiona confirm a predetermined social contract in her mind: "Kiss and something's solved for Fiona. Something's pigeon-holed. Something's properly identified, and then documented, and then filed, and then forgotten" (Salkey 2009, 107). For Johnnie this prospect of attachment and containment occasions an unraveling. He constantly dissects language and comes no closer to experience. Fiona's world making around their liaison is a means by which to interpellate him into her heteronormative arrangement, a tactic that becomes unambiguous later when their relationship cools and she claims to be pregnant: "Don't you feel peaceful and very self-contained, Johnnie? I do. I could remain here like this for years on end. I could give you all the solace you've ever wanted, and still have enough for myself. I could escape like this for ever" (109).

For Johnnie, such containment is the situation to escape from. His escape is to think of Dick, and the difference that he experiences with Dick—not in terms of sexual orientation—but in terms of social orientation and freedom. "She doesn't understand her defeat. She doesn't understand Dick's victory. Dick's supremacy. Dick's gift of freedom to me. And her gift of aching, nervous tension; her gift of boring, irresponsible, conventional conduct; her cross, my cross. She understands none of it. . . . She doesn't understand that I'm outside her; not in with her in anyway. *I'm away.* I'm with Dick" (Salkey 2009, 110). Johnnie's identification with Dick here is as a dissenting figure and not a declaration of a chosen orientation within a binary structure. Indeed, when Johnnie moves toward articulating his relationship to Dick the self-questioning returns: "What am I heading for? Do I want to make a declaration? A credo? A better way of loving" (111). At this point in the novel, it is hard to determine whether Johnnie's resistance is focused on individuals, on orientations, or on sexual acts. What remains consistent is his resistance and refusal of identity scripts.

As the narrative unfolds, it becomes clear that Johnnie views Fiona and Dick as different erotic possibilities but not on account of their gendered identities. Sex with Fiona is dictated by her greed, by her needs. Johnnie exclaims, "Fiona wants me, wants her own way" (Salkey 2009, 132). Her desires seek to shape his identity, despite and against his own disorganizing yearnings. In contrast, his relationship with Dick is defined by its distance from the frenzied and sordid transactional relationships that dominate the world of the novel in which sex, money, and class-based power cannot be extricated from each other: "Dick owes me nothing; I owe Dick nothing" (141). Yet if what Johnnie values about his relationship to Dick at this point is the absence of the need to be defined, possessed, or obligated by him, then Dick's question, on which book two of the novel ends, suggests the gay Englishman's limited possibilities to think outside the relentless sociosexual imperatives that populate the novel's public and private spaces: "'What are you going to do, Johnnie? I think a change would do you a world of good. What d'you think?'" (146).

For Johnnie, the problem of object choice is a demand imposed by a social world organized according to a fabricated hetero/homo binarism. It is a problem he knows he must face and yet persistently declines to confront: "So there it is; Fiona groans on; Dick waits; I wait. There (and the world and his wife know it) must be a decision" (Salkey 2009, 132). By acknowledging the need to resolve this crisis over sexual identification, Salkey's novel brings it into sharper focus and refuses the social reassurance of a decision based on a stable sexual preference. Despite narrating how the question of sexual identification finally becomes unavoidable, evading definition remains Johnnie's, and arguably the novel's, defining queer achievement.

While Johnnie believes that what he shares with Dick is a yearning to live and love beyond and outside social definition—"We genuinely wanted a kind of freedom" (Salkey 2009, 177)—a shock awaits when, on Christmas morning, Dick tells him that he'll need to make a decision soon about his homosexuality. As Ellis (2015b) notes, "Dick's relationship with Johnnie is in the lineage of homosexuality as identity, which is why Dick forces Johnny [sic] to make a choice between him and Fiona" (108). Johnnie, who refuses both this lineage and this identity, seems genuinely perplexed, and yet he is also aware that his response to the identity word—"You're on the wrong track about my being homosexual"—is not adequate to his feelings: "That sounded feeble and positively stupid; yet it was a try" (Salkey 2009, 185). When Dick tells Johnnie that he has "carried out my own private tests," Johnnie asks, "Suppose you tell me how different it is to be truly homosexual and how difficult it is for one to become aware and certain of another, especially another who doesn't know he is" (185). Johnnie's response, "Look I'm no *queer*! I ought to know and that's proof enough, isn't it?" (186) shows hesitation in its final interrogative and the possibility of giving a bounded account of himself begins to shape the exaggerated question mark that the novel asserts around all such demands for sexual identification. Somewhere between Dick's empiricism and affirmation of a homosexual identity, and Johnnie's public denial of and private reflection on his attachment to Dick, sexual identity is put into question, if not into crisis.

As a homosexual man in London in the 1950s, Dick can only read Johnnie's recalcitrance as shame and casts him as "a dismal failure to me" (Salkey 2009, 187). For Dick, the proper terms of their relationship can only be established by Johnnie's consent to the identity of homosexual: ""I want you to return my love for you, Johnnie. And before you can do that, you've got to come to terms with what I spoke about earlier on. There is no mystery attached to it; no depravity either. I had to. Quite a lot of people have had to. Now it's your turn. If you don't you'll make a lot of people unhappy, including yourself, perhaps most of all" (188). Johnnie is almost persuaded by the force of this coming out narrative, "Somehow, I wanted to give in and have done with it. I wanted to tell him he was right. . . . I wanted to stop talking about it; thinking about it; being so near to it, and yet so far from it. I was terribly confused and resentful and fed up" (188). However, the confusion cannot be stilled because there remains no correspondence between his erotic feelings for Dick and the identity-fixing category of the homosexual. Importantly, Johnnie's wretched combustion of emotions is provoked not by his social fears of exposure or self-doubt but by the ongoing dissonance between singular naming and being, reminiscent of Glissant's (1995) Caribbeanness, which "does not tend toward the One, but opens onto diversity" (268).

Within the narrative, the determination of Johnnie's homosexuality becomes a matter of shared interest and an oddly democratic process that overturns the idea of sexuality as an individually elected identity, as Johnnie lays out his situation after the Christmas dinner to which Dick had invited Fiona: "Am I to be homosexual or not? Am I to be bisexual or not? Am I to be a whole man or not? You're the one being asked to use the casting vote . . . because Dick's voted that I am and I naturally have voted that I am not. Got it?" (Salkey 2009, 192). When Fiona votes for Johnnie being a homosexual, but then goes on to say, "And this doesn't mean I don't want you as my lover. I couldn't care less" (192), the very idea of sexuality being decided "naturally" or neatly, again comes to crisis, as does the idea of heterosexuality as a relationship based on inherently normative other-sex desires. What Johnnie had cherished in Dick, the absence of obligation, has now vanished. Both Fiona and Dick make attempts to bring Johnnie into normalizing, stabilizing sexual relations—to which they give meaning, and which give meaning to them. When Fiona earlier tells Johnnie that she is pregnant, she wills him to slot into the category of heteronormativity, paternity, and social recognition. Even when he rejects this, she remains convinced of her power to bring him to what she calls "our kind of love. Not Dick's" (194). Dick, on the other hand, sees Johnnie as suffering from socially inflicted misery, a "bondage" to heteronormative performance that only a coming out can cure. For Johnnie, both "solutions" are "identical truths," and his loathing for both is equal: *"Johnnie wasn't at home, wasn't admitting a thing, one way or the other!"* (194, 195; italics in the original). In Houlden's (2013) reading, which focuses on the "unsettled and unsettling presence" of the queer Black migrant in the English domestic space, this behavior of "simultaneous emotional co-starring," identifies Johnnie as a "sexually confused, middle-class young Jamaican who is caught in a love triangle between two white Britons, preda- tory Fiona and gentle, homosexual Dick" (115, 96). My own reading is con- cerned with Johnnie's creolized queerness and the political energetics of decolonization that shape his challenge to sexuality as identity defining. In this frame, Johnnie's indecision is a conscious evasion of sexual orientations such as hetero/homo, as well as of sexual-social arrangements such as trian- gles and couples. His refusals undo the reader's socially conditioned reflexes to read sexual desires and acts as expressions of a fixed erotic identity based on object choice and point to a creolized sensibility of plurality and fluidity.

When, early in the narrative, Johnnie tells Fiona that he wanted to escape Jamaica, his answer to her inquiry—"What are you going to do here that you couldn't do over there?"—is both mundane and monumental: "Live, I suppose" (Salkey 2009, 49). He describes the suffocation of his life as part of a self- proclaimed Jamaican middle-class whose imagined superiority is only sus- tained by "a tight bunch of people [who] move and hope and act as if they're being guided by it" and "which damn well strangles everybody" (50). When Fiona astutely remarks, "But, isn't that the West Indian problem? Not being totally anything identifiable? I mean, you're not Continental African and you're not anywhere near the other thing" Johnnie replies "No real identity, eh?" (52). As Johnnie confirms his unmooring to origins in this way, he begins to articu- late a particular version of Caribbeanness as a queer state of unbelonging. In part this is an expression of loss and alienation, and in part one of a freedom from containment that has a significant purchase for the novel's later interven- tion on the question of sexual identification: "Africa doesn't belong to me! There's no feeling there. No bond. We've been fed on the Mother Country myth. Its language. Its history. Its literature. Its Civics. . . . Can't you see that I don't belong anywhere? What happened to me between African bondage and British hypocrisy?" (52). Johnnie's expected life-narrative, in which race, class, and sexuality are mutually imbricated to assure self-improvement and familial uplift, was his father's vision of personal success posted back to the home in Jamaica from Panama where hard paternal labor was purposed to secure the prosperity, social ambition, and racialized transition of the next generation:

"The right life saved up for me. The life of endless respectable pursuits and conventional patterns of behavior . . . a girl three or four shades lighter than myself. Respectable people are married people. Shade's the thing" (81).

Johnnie's insistent and committed questioning of what self-determination means critiques the possibilities for freedom in a way that reflects both his connection to 1950s Jamaica, where the process of constitutional reform stirred the discourses of freedom and also showed them to be compromised, and to 1950s England, where the Wolfenden inquiry provoked questions around erotic liberation that ultimately sedimented homonormalization.[10] England's historical moment of homonormalization can be read most transparently through Dick, whose move with Johnnie from the lodging house, where he is both vulnerable to surveillance and to blackmailing, to residential housing where he hopes for a "queer domestic unit that mirrored marital life" seems to exemplify the Wolfenden "solution" (Houlbrook 2005, 129). Johnnie seeks no such accommodation in his persistent refusal to accept sexuality as identity defining. He leaves the domestic comfort of his flat with Dick to remain outside of definition—articulating his sense of a queer subjectivity willfully at odds with the demands of social coherence. "I've often wondered, and I still wonder, if there are many people who have my burning, nihilistic desire to be outside the law, outside the emotions of other people, outside the respectable and respected critics, the police, the magistrates' court, the newspapers, the public conscience of the masses, the nasty fangs of the purgative lawmakers and assessors" (Salkey 2009, 132). As Houlden (2013) argues "Salkey destabilizes both the hypermasculinity and the unhomeliness of many narratives of migrant life as well as the queer discourse of respectability with which the novel is engaged" (107). However, rather than emphasizing the novel's disruption on account of Johnnie's orientation within the English home, I wish to emphasize how Johnnie's Caribbeanness primes his creolized queer refusal of sexual categorization, as well as his more general dismissal of identity-based politics.

Within the world of the novel, Johnnie's refusal and inability to choose between Fiona and Dick becomes a way of resisting those technologies of the self that seek to manage and govern his production as a socially recognizable and legitimate subject. His framing of, and resistance to, the options laid out by a taxonomic system of identificatory categories strikes against Wolfenden's version of sexual accommodation, as well as the centuries-long investment of imperialist thinking in classificatory and comparative "expert" knowledge. Johnnie's assertion of his freedom and his kind of freedom suggests a privileged insight and resilience in the face of these tactics of social control: "They had made a farce of freedom, my kind, anyway. My kind of freedom didn't function for them. It wasn't even a selfish thing. It was just nonexistent. They made me know, in no uncertain manner, that truly 'whole people,' whatever that means, were tagged, always have been, pigeonholed, easily classified, easily lumped in a bundled mass, conveniently distributed to a waiting mob of diagnosticians, analysts, observers, recorders" (Salkey 2009, 195). It is this sense of a fundamental difference in how to be and how to know himself that shapes Johnnie's escape from middle-class respectability, first in Jamaica and now in England.

Salkey allows Johnnie the freedom to be inconsistent, restless, opportunist, and noncommittal. He is vigilant to the losses that accompany the stabilization of sexual identities—even at the cost of accommodation—yet his determination on freedom remains paramount. Johnnie's restless indecision emerges finally, not as the penalty of a colonial Caribbean consciousness as much as its strange reward. Ellis (2015b) is right that "Johnnie chafes at romantic enclosure" (113), but the suspension of the narrative at the point of Johnnie's retraction allows for more than an expression of his dissatisfaction with the domesticating habits expected of both hetero- and homonormalization. The novel ends without Johnnie having made a decision. Ellis notes "Johnnie's doubling-back, flitting between choices he does not want to make, and ultimately embracing a kind of suspension that similarly leaves the reader up in the air" (99–100). His own open preferences—disorganized and disorganizing as they are to both the hetero- and homosexual schema available to him— are arguably not written into the narrative precisely because Johnnie refuses to become legible in these terms: "I had a choice of lives before me. A choice of loves. . . . I knew I had to wait. For the truth about Dick, about Fiona, about myself. About my next move. That and only that was worth waiting for: the truth about myself, and the courage and ability to recognize it when it came" (Salkey 2009, 212).

Within a context of 1950s Britain, Johnnie's denial of a homosexual identity may ostensibly appear to dilute the transgressive or dissenting force of the narrative, but only if we take such a disavowal as a denial of his erotic attraction to Dick. If, instead, we acknowledge Johnnie's rejection of the only options available to him as a refusal to be disciplined by the social norms that dictate the terms on which he can experience himself as an erotic subject, his insistent openness models a creolized queerness. As Ellis (2015b) argues, this deliberate deferral is also critical in allowing the novel to render the anticipatory character of the queer diasporic subject on his own terms: "[Johnnie] suspends a decision about himself and his loves and the novel imposes an ending in which he, and the reader, 'must learn to wait and wait and wait'" (99).[11] I want to link this waiting to the novel's anticipatory politics of thinking otherwise that refuses available options in order to expand the range of imaginable possibilities. While sexual and erotic self-determination is seemingly not realizable outside the paradigm of the identity-defining binarism (hetero/homo) of 1950s Britain, it is still glimpsed as possible in Johnnie's imagination of the alternative, "my kind" of freedom. As Ronald Cummings (2018) argues in "Johnnie's

Letters: Epistolary Practice in Andrew Salkey's *Escape to an Autumn Pavement*," "the closing of the narrative frustrates the immediate demand for the consummation of this desire but at the same time does not foreclose its possibilities" (n.p.).

Conclusion

As the introduction to this book makes evident, one of the main questions that motivates my inquiry is to what extent the queerness of the creolized Caribbean primes a more supple, pluralizing experience and expression of erotic desires and attachments—even in the face of a dominant heteropatriarchal and homophobic culture. In one significant way, Salkey's novel answers this call. It does not allow us to conclude that Johnnie's escape is deficient or unfinished because he does not subscribe to either the heteronormative option of marriage and paternity inscribed in Fiona's discourse of completeness, or the homonormative coming-out story that Dick narrates. Rather, the novel allows us to see that Johnnie's escape lies precisely in his attachment to living beyond these normalizing narratives that would mistakenly define him as a product of his erotic preference, an understanding of identity that he resists, just as he resists the equally flawed and contradictory claims of both a middle-class Jamaican and a working-class Londoner.

Salkey's novel is not so much a direct response to the question of how queer the creolized Caribbean sensibility is, but rather a redrafting of the relationship between the two in such a way that the fluid, creolized identity resources of being Caribbean and the unyielding, inexorable appetite for self-determination (which arguably peaked in the Anglophone region during the decolonizing decade of the 1950s) offer an important and timely response to the socially conservative discourse-making project of twentieth-century metropolitan homonormativity. Caribbeanness, held onto by Johnnie in its promise more than in its reality (he, after all, seeks to escape the constraints and fraudulence of the invented middle-class and their attempts to differentiate themselves from fellow Caribbean citizens), becomes an ideal that is never fully realized on either side of the Atlantic. It remains, however, one that the novel renders in anticipation through its protagonist's relentlessly resistant interior narrative.

Though the novel itself "escaped" much attention as a narrative of a Caribbean man's accommodation in its own day, its inconclusive ending is congruent with other canonical works of migration, such as Lamming's (1971) *Water with Berries* or Selvon's ([1956] 1979) *Lonely Londoners*. Restoring *Escape* to this context brings questions of erotic agency into established critical discussions of how the West Indian male came to experience and know himself as a subject and citizen in the diaspora. While, as I. Smith (1999) points out, these are questions that bubble under the surface and between the lines of Selvon's *Lonely Londoners*, and are insinuated in the fragile and vulnerable masculinity portrayed in the majority of the canonical works by West Indian male writers in this period, the question of a Caribbean queer erotics that eludes and exposes the constrained binarism of object choice uniquely finds an extended and explicit meditation in Salkey's novel.

Discussing London in the first half of the twentieth century, Houlbrook (2005) argues: "The most remarkable thing about queer urban culture is that it was, to a large extent, composed of and created by men who never thought themselves queer" (7).[12] Possibly unsurprisingly, most reviewers of Salkey's novel in 1960 failed to appreciate the challenge that it presented. Their responses register frustration and bewilderment at the novel's presentation of sexual identity as productively incoherent and ambiguous. The reviewers' impatient questions jolt us back to the entrenched belief that heteronormativity and the sexual binarism represented an authentic reality, which the novel must somehow approximate. J. D. Scott of *The Sunday Times* asked, "In short, is Johnnie homosexual?" and Peter Green of *The Daily Telegraph and Morning Post* made the more revealing interrogation: "Is he abnormal or not?"[13] Only the Jamaican writer and critic, John Figueroa (1960) tried to understand the novel on its own terms as an inquiry into the Caribbean person's distinctive detachment from the customary moorings on which identity politics cohere: "It might be that the question of not knowing one's sex is merely an extreme form of not knowing oneself: that the position of not knowing one's relation to a given man and woman is the extreme form of not knowing one's relation to one's society, past and present" (n.p.).[14] While there is something of an apologetic explanation for the novel's emphasis on sexuality in this review, a strongly appreciative approach is articulated in a private letter to Salkey from the Jamaican novelist John Hearne who had travelled widely and recently settled again the UK, signed simply "John." Hearne writes: "You don't need me to tell you what a powerful and profoundly upsetting piece of writing it is. . . . I suppose you realise that it's the first time [—you've—] anyone from the Antilliary regions has done a man so big and individual. He comes bounding down the slopes of one's understanding like a runaway boulder and each time he strikes he shakes you a little more. He is [—I'm—] in for a hard time, or maybe he's got through to a floating part of himself. It doesn't matter, does it? . . . It is the first time reading a book by a West Indian that I've felt an area of experience brand new to me. Have felt compelled to live through a course of life not my own or not intellectually comprehended or sociologically foreshadowed."[15]

Perhaps then, it is not only today's readers—reading in what Ellis (2015b) calls "a critical moment when Caribbean cultural studies has begun more seriously to consider sexuality as a central part of the familiar analytical matrix nation-race-gender" (104)—who find the novel's queer questioning of what is it to be a Caribbean man striking. By narrating erotic orientations into the project of creole self-definition, *Escape* reconnects erotics to the project of Caribbean world building from which it is often expelled along with Caribbean queer subjects. Moreover, he privileges erotic freedom as the prism for addressing the ongoing issue of self-determination. There are many opportunities for Johnnie to find a place: racists willing to accept him as favorably middle class, women sexually attracted to his enticing promise of difference, West Indians who treat him as one of the boys, fellow colonials who embrace him as one of the oppressed. Johnnie refuses them all, just as he finally declines Dick's accommodation for him as a fellow homosexual. In this way, Johnnie does escape. His freedom is realized in terms of resistance and refusal and his decolonizing impulse to remain strongly intact and open to his creolized multiplicity of being despite others' narrow definitions of him.[16]

This refusal of Caribbean subjects' homonormalization is discussed in a contemporary context by Rinaldo Walcott (2009) in his analysis of the limitations of "rights talk" (after Miriam Smith's [1999] *Lesbian and Gay Rights in Canada*). R. Walcott questions what might be lost or denied by a rights-based sexual contract in terms of creole erotic subjectivities: "Rights talk comes with benefits, but those benefits in no way threaten the hegemony of state organization nor force the state to change its fundamental disciplinary apparatus of citizenship. Instead rights talk most often asks that queer citizenship mirror heterosexual citizenship. Heteronormativity and homonormativity collude in policing sexually desiring bodies, practices and communities in a tacit "sexual contract" with the state. A homopoetics of selfhood is not possible under those terms. The complexities of creole selves must be forcibly submerged, discredited and even deemed deviant" (R. Walcott 2009, 12). By returning Salkey's novel to its historical context—as part of the emergent canon of Caribbean literature focused on narrating the particularities of Caribbean lives—its provocative status in narrating Caribbeanness and queerness as mutually constitutive becomes highly visible yet remains importantly fluid in its focus on R. Walcott's (2009) "complexities of creole selves" (12). Tellingly, the novel's open weave means that Houlden (2013) can plausibly read the way in which "Johnnie and Dick's ménage conforms to heterosexual patterns of intimate life" (107) in order to argue for the queer being absorbed back into normative structures according to the novel's depiction of the Wolfenden effect, and Ellis (2015b) can equally plausibly read the novel as subtly queering socially normative structures, even in their expanded forms, sanctioned post-Wolfenden: "Dick and Johnnie show that it is entirely possible to be homosexual without necessarily having sex. The corollary is true of Johnnie and Fiona, who prove that it is possible to have heterosexual sexual intercourse without being straight" (108). Salkey's *Escape* narrates a creolized queer life in which flight becomes a repeated necessity to maintain freedom from social containment. It calls into visibility the choices that shape identities and the identities that shape lives, as Johnnie narrates his continued evasion of both. The note of suspense on which the novel ends suggests the effort and possible exclusion involved in eluding social compromise, but it also allows for a moment's pause within the relentless imperatives of normalization in which the pursuit of creole erotic self-determination and nonconformity can claim its imaginative hold.

4

Queering Caribbean Homophobia

● ● ● ● ● ● ● ● ● ● ● ● ● ● ● ● ● ● ● ●

Non-heteronormative
Hypermasculinity in Marlon
James's *A Brief History of
Seven Killings* and Junot Díaz's
*The Brief Wondrous Life of
Oscar Wao*

> You cyan be a shotta if
> You know you a fish
> —Ricky General, "A Wha Dis," 1999

> I sing a smaller song for the ways we exist
> flamboyantly and invisibly at the same
> time. The ways we exist incredibly.
> —Kei Miller, "A Smaller Song"

In this chapter, I explore another distinctive tension and overlap between exaggerated expressions of explicitly heteropatriarchal identities in Caribbean societies and their undoing. While the turbulent and uneven homonormative and heterosexual identities discussed in chapters 2 and 3 are often shown to cohabit with heterocolonial social structures, queer hypermasculinity arguably provides the extreme case of a paradoxical and fluid subjectivity. My focus is on representations of queer hypermasculinity in two novels that have won major international prizes for literature: Marlon James's (2014) *A Brief History of Seven Killings*, which was awarded the 2015 Man Booker Prize for "the best novel of the year," and Junot Díaz's (2007) *The Brief Wondrous Life of Oscar Wao*, which won the 2008 Pulitzer prize for "distinguished fiction by an American."[1] Both works undoubtedly share narrative ambition and daring, and both are consciously, dazzlingly excessive and extreme in their literary form and subject matter. Both also explicitly bestride Caribbean identities as they move between the region and the diaspora, rendering the impact of networks of political power, narcotics, and noxious masculinity in which the Caribbean and the U.S. are mutually implicated in everyday lived realities and human attachments. In *Oscar Wao*, the linguistic markers of this transnational interchange are clearly exhibited in the novel's English language medium, which is multiply creolized through code-switching collisions with Spanish, African American vernacular, and "nerdish." These deliberately speak of and to the Dominican American experience as polyvocal and multidirectional in its belongings, in what Lorgia García Peña identifies as "the clear rupture with the dominant thematic of nation-building and the trauma of the Trujillo dictatorship that dominated the works of the various decades of generations" that characterized Dominican literature from the 1960s onward as it broke "away from the patriarchal, Hispanophile, heteronormative structures that shaped the production of Dominican literature" (2018, 10).[2]

In James's fictional world, the trigger event (the assassination attempt on Bob Marley in his home in Kingston, Jamaica, on 3 December 1976) amplifies its reach outward toward the U.S. as it traces transnational networks of organized political and criminal interference and their unholy human repercussions over five intensely narrated days across the cities of Kingston, Montego Bay, Miami, and New York. In the fictional world of *Brief History*, to be a man is to carry the promise of sexual conquest and the threat of physical violence. The hypermasculinity perpetrated by its gang leaders, drug dons, and "bad man" youth is premised on the display and the mutual (over)validation of physical coercion and sexual supremacy. The diasporic Dominican world of Díaz's *Oscar Wao* unfolds mainly in New Jersey from the mid-1970s to the mid-1990s, but is constantly journeying back to, and across, the Dominican Republic from the mid-1940s to the mid-1990s, with a particular awareness of the shadow of violence cast by Rafael Trujillo's dictatorship, which persisted until 1961. Even though Yunior,[3] the novel's main narrator, footnotes this murderous history, Trujillo and his regime remain fully present and deeply define the lives and deaths that Yunior narrates. His is the

fukú story at the spine of the novel's proliferating tales and traumatized subjects. As Lola, Oscar's sister and the only other narrator, laments, for those
who are born there, "Santo Domingo will always be there. It was in the
beginning and it will be there at the end" (Díaz 2007, 210). In the context of
the novel, hypermasculinity in Santo Domingo translates as a relentless
expression of *el machismo*, with its underpinning performances of male sexual dominance, prowess, and reputation. Yet as Maja Horn has argued
"against the tendency to equate Trujillo's discourse of masculinity simply
with that of a stereotypical Latin American " strongman," or "caudillo,"
dominant Dominican masculinity is already complicatedly transnational, as
"Trujillo's own pervasively hyper virile discourse was, at least in part, a strategic response to the imperial and racialized notions of masculinity that
accompanied the U.S. presence in the country, especially during the U.S.
military occupation (1916–1924)" (Horn 2014, 1). In another context of further creolization, the machismo of American migrant Dominicanness in the
novel also intersects with U.S. hypermasculinity as embedded in the American fraternity culture—both based around the exploitation of women.

In his essay, "Caribbean Masculinity: Unpacking the Narrative," Linden
Lewis (2003a) notes how the common depiction of Caribbean masculinity,
emerging from both social studies and literary fiction, coheres around a narrow
characterization of man as "powerful, exceedingly promiscuous, derelict in his
parental duties, often absent from the household" (107). Lewis's own argument
is for a complication of this homogenizing categorization that can "distinguish
between hegemonic masculinity and other subordinated forms of masculinity"
and "hegemonic masculinity [that] refers to practices of cultural domination of
a particular representation of men and manliness[, which] refers to an orientation that is heterosexual and decidedly homophobic" (108). He proposes attention to "race, ethnicity, age, class, sexual orientation, and religion" (108) as
valuable ways to problematize Caribbean masculinity, but does not question the
organizing binarism of a hetero-/homosexual divide. While I acknowledge that
models of Caribbean masculinity do commonly place hypermasculinity and
homosexuality as oppositional identities, my argument here attends to how
these literary works by James and Díaz capture the queerness of extreme Caribbean realities where hardcore and non-heteronormative masculinities creolize
to become mutually expressive. My interest in reading these two novels as explorations of queer hypermasculinity lies precisely in locating how their frantic, disproportionate, exaggerated, and unmannerly fictions surface non-normalizing
masculinities that complicate the very hyperheterosexualized masculinity that is
seemingly normalized within their narrative arcs.[4] I attend to these overlapping
possibilities as an assemblage of Caribbean masculinity that can barely be read
without feeling sideways, and yet is not to be disregarded.

Related scholarship that draws attention to this oxymoronic entanglement of hypermasculine and non-heteronormative has emerged at the interface of queer and popular cultural studies and is critically invested in the ways dancehall and visual art draw attention to the performative and surface qualities of gendered identities to expose the idea of masculinity as a complex, often contradictory act of self-fashioning rather than as an essential characteristic. As Veerle Poupeye (2014) argues in relation to "gangstas and bush cockerels" in the work of Jamaican visual artist Ebony G. Patterson, the consistently creative engagement Patterson shows with these seemingly stereotypical figures of manhood recrafts them to reveal "the complexities and contradictions of black masculinity" (9). In a whole range of Patterson's visual works, the overlapping of bleached, adorned male bodies and the hard-core identities of violent hypermasculinity creolize the sexuality of the Jamaican male body in such a way as to aestheticize its contradictions and make this paradoxically creative genderscape compellingly legible. This overlapping of hardcore masculine and queer embodiment is also evoked in Kei Miller's (2013) essay "Maybe Bellywoman was on 'Di Tape (2011).'" Initially discussing the pragmatics rather than the aesthetics of crossed-dressed criminals, Miller notes how the drug lord Dudas and Jamaica's most wanted fugitive Nattie Morgan can both be understood within "the long line of bandits from our stridently heteronormative island who were not above wearing a bit of drag" (106). Yet Miller also reimagines these queer, violent hypermales through the lens of folklore and carnival, which embody the Caribbean normal queer contradiction: "And I imagine them—author that I am—this tribe of bellywomen, with comically large asses and pregnant bellies, holding on to the hems of their frocks with one hand, and their uzi guns with the other, and with almost balletic grace running and shooting and dodging bullets, at least for a little while" (106).[5]

The prized literariness of both *Brief History* and *Oscar Wao* are significantly and substantially invigorated by the sensibilities and vocabularies of popular cultural forms. In *Brief History*, these are the scenario-modeling narratives of crime fiction and Hollywood movies, as well as the belligerent acoustics of dancehall and reggae's revolutionary tempo for the dispossessed. In *Oscar Wao*, Oscar lives in and through the immersive, alternative realities of speculative, sci-fi genre-fiction and cult television shows. In their creative mediations of highbrow and popular cultural forms, both novels might be read as issuing a fictional response to Linden Lewis's (2003b) observation that "it is perhaps only at the level of popular discourse that sexuality is given its full airing" (7). In both novels too, the necessity of complicating received narratives (including that of masculinity) is communicated by their creolized literary character as well as their message. Their multiplying genres and layering of formal, compositional structures draw attention to the varying and heterogeneous ways in which lives can be framed and read. Moreover, the intricacies and intimacies of the individual lives and relations these novels represent also give a strong feel of how local and global modalities of violence conspire to make certain lives simply too much to bear without the intercession of fictional, lyrical counterimaginaries. In this way, both novels hint at the queering of hypermasculinity as an inward fold caused by, yet concealed within, its own unremitting violence, especially sexual violence.

As well as invoking and connecting global popular cultural forms with constructions of Caribbean masculinity, the lives in these two virtuoso narratives are also depicted as being snagged in the cultural and political traffic that buttressed the hegemony of a U.S.-centric, transnational, neoliberal world in the late twentieth century. In Sheri-Marie Harrison's (2015) essay, "Excess in A *Brief History of Seven Killings*," a spirited defense of James's novel against Nadia Ellis's (2015a) complaints of its excessive and indulgent character, Harrison (2015) foregrounds the break these authors make with Caribbean literary traditions in their shared attention to "displacing the centrality of discrete nationalism in Caribbean narratives and creating wild and risky new possibilities for thinking about the region's place in our contemporary reality" (n.p.). Arguing for Díaz and James as part of a new generation of writers, Harrison points out that "contemporary fiction written by immigrant and immigrant descended authors who live (or split time) in the United States and teach in writing programs in American universities, such as James, Chimamanda Adichie, Junot Díaz, and Teju Cole, constitutes a major site in which a recognition of the commonalities within global (rather than national) economic inequity is becoming visible" (n.p.). My interest is in how the move that Díaz and James make toward a narrative reworlding in the light of transnational neoliberal geopolitics is not only crucial to the more localized political literacies developed in these literary works, but also critical to their negotiation of localized erotic identities.

Given that violent masculinity is "the" identity that figures most prominently in representations of Caribbean societies held in the grip of global injustices and hypercriminalities, especially when read from the outside, these novelistic recalibrations of hypermasculinity are valuable to thinking through the prismatic possibilities offered within creolized queer realities. In a Jamaican context, Kei Miller (2013) highlights the limitations and negative impact of a neocolonial framework that reads sexuality from outside the local context. While Miller does not deny that an imported rights-bearing agenda may bring a particular vision to light, he nevertheless points out that it obscures other possibilities of locally negotiated and lived modes of erotic being and belonging:

> Such performances and the processes by which [sexually transgressive figures] have been accommodated do not map easily onto neo-colonial notions or cultures of "queer" or "LGBT." They do not necessarily live under the banner of "homosexuality" etc. However, in Jamaica, we live in a neo-colonial world

where words and concepts are being imported all the time—and far fewer of our own words and concepts are being exported. So the postcolonial subject begins to understand himself in the imported terms, through someone else's pitying gaze, and understands himself as oppressed. He wouldn't be wrong either. I just think it is all very complex. (Miller 2013, 102)

My reading of *Brief History* and *Oscar Wao* can attend to only a fraction of this complexity, and my focus is on how these novels describe lives that desire in multiple and contradictory ways and thereby contribute to an acknowledgment of the creolized queer texture of Caribbean societies. Such a reading emerges from blurring the lines that may appear so firmly drawn between a declarative, threatening Caribbean homophobia on the one side, and the demands of neocolonial global justice agendas on the other. Both James's and Díaz's novel have been read as confirming, or at least indulging, a hypermasculine culture. Nadia Ellis pinpoints a lack of empathy as the particular failing in James's literary engagement with the sexual ecology of 1970s Jamaica:

What this means is that, for all the potential of explicit sexual representations to challenge a reader and to inspire thought, James here mostly replicates the effect of sexual violence as *suffusion*. This effect is accurate in its way— misogyny, homophobia, and abuse, and the use of sex and language to convey them are, indeed, widespread in Jamaica. This novel, though, wed to a poetics of excess, sacrifices the potential for *empathy* (so much of the sex is presented as if narrators were hovering somewhere above the action); for *complication* (a rigid verisimilitude marks the sexism of the characters); or indeed, for *reflection* (since there is virtually no pause in the presentation). (Ellis 2015a, n.p.; italics in the original)

For Ellis (2015a), the sex in *Brief History* with its "highly confrontational and distinctly voyeuristic presentation throughout the novel, is both thoroughgoing (which is to say, constant) and somehow shallow" (n.p.). I will return to a detailed discussion of James's novel that takes up this question of erotic representation more closely. Interestingly, similar accusations of excess as a substitute, or poor excuse, for empathy have also been made against *Oscar Wao*. In his article for the Huffington Post, Anis Shivani voted *Oscar Wao* one of the fifteen most overrated books,[6] arguing:

[Junot Díaz] doesn't realize the fine line between presenting the dark underside of reality and glorifying it. The Dominicans in his books are obsessed with screwing—that's how this uber-nerd desperately tries to establish his street/ ghetto cred. . . . Oscar, the science fiction nerd, tries to lose his virginity—that's basically the whole story. His sister Lola thinks of nothing but fucking, his mother just wants to fuck, and when Oscar tries to fuck an older woman back in Santo Domingo, he gets killed—because the agony of the novel has to end somehow. (Shivani 2011, n.p.)

In her more searching and subtle academic article "Dictating Desire, Dictating Diaspora: Junot Díaz's *The Brief Wondrous Life of Oscar Wao* as Foundational Romance," Elena Machado Sáez (2011) makes a similar objection to Díaz's perceived endorsement of a negative heterocolonial order by arguing that "employing the appealing guise of polyvocality, *Oscar Wao* charms and entices the reader, especially the academic reader, into becoming complicit with the heteronormative rationale used to police male diasporic identity" (523).

While I recognize that both *Oscar Wao* and *Brief History* give voice to an almost suffocating normalization of heterocolonial and heteropatriarchal structures, albeit importantly shaped by different histories of colonialism and nationalism, my reading is directed at the ways in which both novels also undo this normalization to render queer, non-normalizing erotic lives that coexist with, and within, these structures. This critical intervention aims to feel sideways toward the vectors of non-heteronormative erotic desires and customs that coexist with and may even be interdependent on an apparent conformity to heterocolonial gender and sexual scripts. I also interrogate the possibility of a Caribbean queer hypermasculinity in which the performative pressures of masculinity are revealed and undone by discordant but deep entanglements of exploitation and care, tenderness and violence, homophobia and queer desire.

"Nobody Is Ever One Thing": Marlon James's *Brief History*

Marlon James's comment, "Nobody is ever one thing," made in relation to *Brief History* during an interview with Jeff Vasishta, may seem obvious, almost bland, until we reflect on just how constrained and compromised the ready-made rubrics commonly are for representing Caribbean masculinity.[7] And when the two things that a man might be are hypermasculine and queer, then the calibration tools of most sociological models are already spinning, particularly with regard to the typecast, hardcore men of Kingston's flourishing criminal world. As Donna P. Hope (2012) observes, "In Jamaica, as in many other territories, one's sexuality is often imputed from one's gendered performance. Thus, a man's sexual identity is ranked and identified based on how closely his masculine performance matches with or moves away from the hegemonic ideals of heterosexual masculinity" (106). Hope's own work is focused on shifts and instabilities within these dominant framings. In *Man Vibes: Masculinities in the Jamaican Dancehall*, Hope (2010) draws attention to a recent shift in dancehall's repertoire of masculinities toward "Fashion Ova Style" with its "feminized aesthetic" (125). Hope is clear that this "'softened' variant of dancehall masculinity" (125) is not a rejection or even a diminution of the homophobia of the dancehall where masculinity still parades itself as violence and promiscuity, shored up by conspicuous consumption and masking class anxiety. Nevertheless, she does argue that "this radically transgressive variant to dancehall masculinity . . . raises questions about the current constitution of hegemonic masculinity from which dancehall culture ultimately draws its strength" (142). Although Hope doesn't use the term, what she describes might also be characterized as a queer hypermasculinity in which both queerness and hypermasculinity coexist yet do not disqualify or diminish each other, despite their oppositional character in hegemonic social structures. This paradoxical performance of masculinity is also relevant in the ghetto worlds of *Brief History*, where reputation, show, and style are the critical means of expressing and asserting masculine power and where they similarly intersect with queer relations.

In his commentary "On That Island of Broken Penises," published in *Caribbean Quarterly*'s special issues on Caribbean masculinities, Kei Miller (2014) discusses the performance of Jamaican hypermasculine violent sexuality as it was shaped in "the [recent] time of 'daggering'" to "exaggerate sexual copulation to ridiculous proportions" (101).[8] Miller ends his piece with an observation on how the violence of hyper-heteronormativity that so visibly harms others (in this case women's bodies) should be recognized as self-harm too: "Instead, we must hold on to our brutal, national, heteronormative penises, and we must use them to inflict damage on others and then damage on ourselves" (105). As a non-heteronormative Jamaican man, Miller's closing identification here, with "ourselves," interestingly positions him as a Jamaican living within a culture of phallic masculinity that so systematically interpellates the male body that its own queer preferences and even practices are indiscernible, perhaps even irrelevant, in the overall cultural performance. As Michael A. Bucknor and Conrad James (2014) comment in their introduction to the issue, Miller's piece is a reflection on how popular cultural practices "ritualize queer sexual expressions under the most brutal heteronormative and patriarchal force" (5). This work may also be read as a provocation to unsettle the way in which hyper and queer Jamaican masculinities have persistently been calibrated on the "continuum that positioned, at the highest point, hardcore heterosexual masculinity as the ideal and, at the lowest point, male homosexuality as the most rejected category" (Hope 2012, 107). In the light of the dancehall scene as Miller (2014) narrates it, might there also be an argument for seeing the hypermasculine and queer as strangely aligned and curiously overlapping, as occupying an indistinguishable style and cultural space, even as mutually embodied? Indeed, as Bucknor and James (2014) also point out about Caribbean masculinity, "The more public the display, the more magnified the exposure is. And the very excess in public display seems to be a strategy to camouflage heteronormative and patriarchal complicity with transgressive intimacies" (1–2).

In the violent novelistic world of U.S.-sponsored neoliberalism, with its electoral interferences, its financialization, and its narco-imperialism, the hypermasculinity in *Brief History* is revealed to be but an accessory to the incessant crime of hemispheric exploitation. Yet the novel powerfully captures the translation of this structural violence into countless ruthless, intimate, and often shudderingly vicious personal onslaughts. At this level, the identity of those who perpetrate such crimes becomes a compelling focus for the reader. As Michael K. Walonen (2018) comments in "Violence, Diasporic Transnationalism, and Neo-imperialism in *A Brief History of Seven Killings*," "the constituent narratives of *Brief History of Seven Killings* explore how the efforts to attain and maintain this patriarchal social role of the don, which serves as the "glue" of the fraught Kingston ghetto social order, are predicated on public displays of violence and socializing young men into an order of masculinist aggression" (5). All the same, this is a crime novel where the reader gradually realizes that there is no detective and no criminal investigation that can identify accountability, let alone justice, in the organized chaotic world of global capital. In such a world, victims and perpetrators are almost bound to occupy the same bodies. Yet, if James's novel is focused on those men who cause harm and also suffer harm, Nadia Ellis (2015a) is right in arguing that it does not make these representations in order to cultivate empathy for those trapped in its everyday grasp. Indeed, as Harrison (2015) argues in relation to Demus, a youth within the gang planning to assassinate "The Singer" (Bob Marley), the novel actively repudiates a liberal, sociologically oriented downward gaze that can explain away the violence of those whose lives it determines and finally destroys.

> Demus pre-empts the hard luck story of poverty, victimization, violence and limited choices that is usually written about impoverished young black men like him. And these elements do indeed appear in Demus's story. But what he most wants us to know about—in his words, "where me coming from"—and to tell us before it can be co-opted by a writer, is that "people who say they don't have a choice is too coward to choose" (58). His explanation is not one of regret or repentance for his role in an attempt against the life of the "reggae superstar of the world," designed to explain and generate a demeaning sympathy for him and those like him. It is instead a choice he owns and one that to his mind is made consciously and courageously. (Harrison 2015, n.p.)

I want to argue that *Brief History* calls for a more complicated idea of feeling sideways. It does not render hypermasculine, hyperviolent, hyperheterosexual gangsters, who have themselves been demonstrably damaged by the heterocolonial neoliberal violence they execute, as subject to the "pitying gaze" (Miller 2013, 102). Neither does it dismiss the often heady mixture of their own oppression and the way they oppress others. Paying attention to non-heteronormative hypermasculinity in *Brief History* locates the capacity to feel sideways in the novel's most provocative iteration of being more than one thing. It shifts the focus toward the complicated queered male lives that the novel also brings to the surface in its hard-core voicings of life and death in Kingston and its diasporic ganglands. Indeed, within its extravaganza of drug-related crime, U.S. government–sponsored crime, as well as innumerable acts of violence and murder by shooting, stabbing, and burying alive, the idea that a criminal is a man who has sex with men brings one of Jamaica's most strenuous constructions of masculinity into crisis.

Sharae Deckard's (2018) conclusion to her brilliantly informed reading of *Brief History* foregrounds "the bleakness of its critique of the systemic condition of violence under neoliberal capitalism [which] is exacerbated by its lack of explicit representation of modes of collective resistance that could issue in an afterworld beyond capitalism" (189). Yet focusing on the novel's representations of queer hypermasculinity offers a way of attending to the one future-facing element that Deckard identifies in James's almost-stiflingly retrospective narrative. My reading of the queer gunman Weeper, and the relationships he has with Josey Wales (his superior who presents as a monogamous heterosexual) and with John-John K. (a gay American hit man) is motivated by Deckard's sense of "hearing [in] the stories of the dead, resuscitated here through the capacity of fiction to imagine the voiceless" the potential "to conceive of new futures" (190). While Walonen (2018) only raises the issue of queer masculinities in a footnote to his essay on the novel's violence, it is telling that he reads Weeper and John-John K. through a hegemonic model of Jamaican masculinity. Arguing that the same-sex-desiring gangsters "carry out killings in part to perform the identity of gunman as a means of showing that their masculinity has not been compromised by their homosexuality" (5–6), Walonen implies that their violent hypermasculinity is the performative identity designed to conceal their "true" or essential identities as homosexuals. To my mind the novel renders a world of complicatedly creolized sexualities in which hypermasculinity and queer desires can and do coexist and where having sex with a man is not necessarily to identify or to be identified as a homosexual, nor is it a guarantee of being any less violent or homophobic. Presenting such queer hypermasculinities that are simply unintelligible in terms of the hegemonic model of a defining object-choice binarism (as described by Lewis [2003a] and Hope [2012] earlier) is entirely in keeping with James's exploration of the internal folds and wrinkles of blanket narratives of Jamaica and Jamaican men.

The homophobia prevalent in Jamaica is a sustained form of violence that has its roots in colonial power and has been inflamed in recent decades by the discourses of evangelical religion and the lyrics of the dancehall that coincide historically with the timeline of *Brief History*. The casually colloquial homophobia that underpins the vernacular of masculine bravado pervades the novel, and homophobic slurs are not only the substance of intentional invectives but also the commonplace lexicon of frustration, disappointment, and anger, with no explicit link to sex. The normalization of hypermasculinity seems to depend on this systemic, low-grade denigration of same-sex desires and desiring subjects. James's narrators incessantly ventriloquize a homophobic vernacular, including both those who are friends and allies of those having sex with men and those men having sex with men. But there are also moments within this stylized oral history when an open discussion of male-male erotics can be heard that queers, but does not erase, the prevalent homophobia.

In terms of thinking through Jamaican queer hypermasculinity in *Brief History*, my emphasis is on Weeper, a notoriously violent gangster whose desires for men exist alongside his casual and frequent sexual relationships with women. The reader first encounters Weeper, the gang enforcer in Copenhagen City, West Kingston, through the voice of his superior, Josey Wales, a duplicitous rising star in the city's criminal network who takes the (intentionally) failed shot at "The Singer." Right from his narrative introduction, Weeper's sexual prowess is foregrounded by a "gun rubbing against his nuts" (James 2014, 41), which threatens a fate worse than death for a Jamaican man. This embodied sexuality is further bookmarked between the stories of two women "Weeper like to fuck" (40). As Wales's history of Weeper unfolds, his homophobic rhetoric peppers his narration, though the curses of "pussyhole," "sodomite," and "batty fuckers" are simply insults and not accusations (40, 41, 43). Furthermore, when Wales does come to narrate Weeper's same-sex relations, it is in no way as if they contradict or undermine his fucking women or his fathering children, and Wales's language is strangely restrained. Indeed, in letting Weeper speak directly to his experience, Wales prevents his story from being silenced: "*Brethern, coke was the only way me could fuck in prison*, he say to me, knowing that no man in the ghetto would dare come up to him and call him battyman because of it. That man still send him letters from prison" (43, italics in the original). Unlike Weeper's atheism, which he also decided on in prison and with which Wales admits he has "one or two problems" (42), there is no value-based judgment on his sexual practices. Weeper's non-heteronormative hypermasculinity is marked here by his insatiable need for sex, which both corresponds with hypermasculinity's emphasis on sexual prowess and virility and, at the same time, queers it. The fact that his object choice is dramatically out of line with a homophobic hegemonic construction of masculinity appears perversely irrelevant here.

Much later, when Weeper is failing to keep control of the Jamaican drugs operation in the U.S., Wales reconsiders his tolerance of Weeper's perceived sexual transgressions. Now that Weeper is no longer shielded by the halo of hypermasculinity defined by effective violence, Wales reflects: "Is years now I know the man not only fucking man but is really the one getting fuck, and no matter what he say, he still sorry to leave prison. Is years now I supposed to kill him for that, but why?" (James 2014, 466). While Weeper's active sex with men could be explained away as a necessity of incarceration, as the passive queer who is fucked (rather than doing the "shooting") and who still yearns for the emotional attachment to a man he knew in prison, Wales knows that Weeper can no longer be recuperated within Jamaican hardcore masculinity. Yet, it is Wales's own absence of homophobic or violent intention toward Weeper that is also a non-normalizing reality here.

Given Weeper's paradoxical identity as a hypermasculine queer, it is perhaps consistent that his experience of prison was also contradictory—a place where he was free to develop attachments and interests queer to his ghetto world of Jamaica. As a young man with a love of reading, Weeper discovers Bertrand Russell's monumental 800-page study, *The History of Western Philosophy* (1946) in prison. While it is well known that Russell was an active supporter of legal reform and the decriminalization of homosexuality, and a signatory of A. E. Dyson's 1958 letter to *The Times* calling for a change in English law, there is only one mention of homosexuality in the 1946 study that Weeper so cherishes.[9] It is, however, a telling one. Russell (1946) refers to how "homosexual love, both male and female, was a recognized custom in Sparta, and had an acknowledged part in the education of adolescent boys. A boy's lover suffered credit or discredit by the boy's actions; Plutarch states that once, when a boy cried out because he was hurt in fighting, his lover was fined for the boy's cowardice" (103). Here, in Russell, as in Weeper's life, is the mixed material of non-heteronormative hypermasculinity, with its regard for reputation, hardness, and courage, set right beside the prize of intimate attachment, loyalty, and dependency. Similarly, in James's narrative there is no sign that Weeper's sensitivity, learning, or queer attachments have compromised his hypermasculine capacity for violence. The two exist right beside each other, as Wales takes his time to explain:

> Now every Weeper story have only one hero, and that is Weeper, except for the man who send him letters still, the man who he love to talk about all the time, this man who did this, this man who did that, this man that teach him this, and with a little coke or even less H, he let the man do that and both of them feel good. Weeper will talk about the man like he couldn't care less what anybody else think, because everybody know Weeper is the fucker that will kill a boy right in front of his father and have the father count his last five breath. (James 2014, 65).

It is as if Weeper's unflinching capacity for violence so swells his hypermasculine persona that it eclipses his queer longings in the explicitly homophobic culture he inhabits. Wales claims that "Weeper earn the right to do what he want to do, even if it is some sodomite business. He'll talk about it all the time but *sideways* like an Aesop fable, or a riddle and rhyme. He can shape it and mold it and make it Greek, his word, not mine, I don't know what the fuck he's talking about with that Greek shit" (James 2014, 69; italics added). Wales may not have read Russell, but he can still understand what it means to live by insinuation and paradox, and he is willing to grant Weeper his right to opacity. The novel's own sideways move here is to arouse a sense of what this way of being may mean for Wales too.

Much as in Díaz's novel, where we come to know the non-normalizing Oscar Wao through the eyes of Yunior, whose insistent proclamations of his own heteronormativity are set in tension with his deep, unending fascination with Oscar, in *Brief History* we come to know Weeper through Josey Wales, or at least at first. In this way it is obvious that Josey Wales is important to Weeper's story. It is Wales, after all, who makes the decision to send Weeper to the U.S. where he can live without being a sexual outlaw. But what Weeper means to Wales is less clear. In the world of hardcore Jamaican masculinity, Wales is already incongruous in his monogamy. A curious "one burner," Wales claims to have "a rule" with women: "If your titty prettier and your body hotter than [his] woman, I'll deal with you. Otherwise fuck off" (James 2014, 41). But a decade of monogamy in a culture of male uninhibited hypersexual promiscuity seems unlikely according to this rule, unless it is also a cover. In the first two sections of the novel that Wales narrates, Weeper is the very first thing on his mind: "Weeper taking his own good time as per usual" and "Weeper is a man with a whole heap of stories" (40, 65). There is also the hint of rivalry in Wales's reflection on Weeper's obsession with his prison lover and opaque references throughout to Weeper's call on Wales: "Waiting on Weeper. Now there's a title for a song, a hit record too" (42); "Make sense that I would be in a bar seeing women dancing, and man watching, and music playing and what I doing? Thinking about Weeper" (65); "I want to pick up his glasses and put them on, maybe see the world how he sees it" (169), or even more obliquely "Is years now I supposed to kill him for that [being fucked by men], but why? . . . I can't set a man on his tail because that man would find out. And there are some things that only Weeper can do" (466). Whether the novel edges us toward Wales's queer desire for Weeper or for the queer possibilities open to Weeper, in the stories Wales tells to protect his own identity and Weeper's, and in his insistence on the exceptionalism of this queer gunman, the novel does at least allow for such possibilities to be imagined.[10]

Weeper's own four, first-person narrations arrive once the novel shifts to the United States and tell a brief history of erotic freedom in his diasporic home, "This is America and me can do what me want so fuck what any of you want to say" (James 2014, 500). The first opens with his story of contesting homophobic violence in an encounter with the victim that ends in them having sex. As Weeper thinks back to his meeting with this White man, who has been his lover for the past three weeks, he looks out of his apartment window in New York to witness the same imprint of violence that framed his Kingston life: "Streetlight throwing darkness in alleyway where man get kill, woman get rape and pitiful fool get mug with two butch-slaps, the tax for being a sucker" (445). What is not a crime here and what Weeper can and does voice with impunity in the U.S. is his erotic life with men in all its snarled desires for intimacy and distance, control and abandonment. It is not, however, that Weeper is not still aware of his subordinate status in this national imagining. Translating what Walonen (2018) calls "the Hollywood mediascapes that made increasing inroads into Jamaican society in the years following the country's independence" (6) into his own life, Weeper indulges in a non-heteronormative account of the classic movie bedroom scene. Although he supposes that such a scene could never make it into Hollywood, this literate gunman still enjoys a moment of countercultural imagination: "Think like a movie. This part you put on your clothes, boy wake up (but boy would be girl) and one of you say babe, I gotta go. Or stay in bed and do the whatever, the sheet at the man waist but right at the woman breast. Never going to be a movie with a scene like this bedroom ever" (James 2014, 446–7). In other ways too Weeper's brutal sexual candor directly challenges a simplified grammar of erotic identities, from his refusal of the active/passive categorizations of men who have sex with men, "Don't think the man getting fucked must be the bitch," to his conflicted minglings of sex and emotional attachment, "I shut him mouth and show him what my hole was for. I love you—I don't mean that, I said" (446).

In Weeper's second named section, a dialogue about men having sex with men—addressing the taboo of Black men taking the passive role, of crying out with pleasure, of giving oral sex, and of tongue kissing—unfolds at the same time as Weeper and his White lover are having sex. In Weeper's frantic internal dialogue the desire to abandon the restrictions of his Jamaican hypermasculinity collides with his irrational anxiety of being seen by Josey Wales, who is on a plane from Kingston to New York. Finally allowing himself full expression as an erotic subject, Weeper realizes that being open to the sexual possibilities between men is to affirm rather than to deny his masculinity: "But it just feel like man grabbing a man to be a man. In bed and so soft we feel like two faggots. We sound like two faggots. So what? Then we must be faggots" (James 2014, 501). In this way, Weeper queers his Caribbean hypermasculinity in terms of the hegemonic model that Wesley Crichlow outlines as a result of his sociological studies:

> For most young men in the Caribbean, the success and strength of their
> manhood to a large degree depends on how well they can perform "normative,

straightjacket or dominant masculinity" to obfuscate any form of tenderness or effeminacy. Their hypermasculinity is an apparatus or sum total of collective surveillance and regulation of what is supposed to be male. . . . To that end, most men police and deny expressions of tenderness in order to perform, instead, a certain cheerful obsequiousness, hypermasculinity and, by extension, heterosexualization. (Crichlow 2014, 31)

In one sense then, the novel is surprisingly simply in its representation of gangsters who also have queer desires. Weeper's ability to embrace his erotic subjectivity comes close to the end of his life, when he is addicted to cocaine and outwitted by the Jamaican-born Eubie (who dropped out of law school to fulfill his potential in organized crime). In Weeper's last two narrated episodes, his increasingly untenable existence is exposed. In the first, his spontaneous execution of a man who calls him the very term, "faggot," that he has just named himself, is a random act of violence, but one that shows his growing vulnerability. In his final episode, Weeper accompanies Josey Wales and Eubie on a killing spree in a crack house. The loss of confidence in Weeper's power is demonstrated when, on two occasions, Wales turns the gun on Weeper only to walk away.

Given that Wales had consciously pardoned Weeper for his same-sex crimes in Jamaica and arranged for him to be in the U.S., it is ironic that it is in New York that Weeper is killed on Eubie's orders. The irony of his murder is further compounded by the fact that it is John-John K., the gay White American hit man, who is sent to bring Weeper to his end. In K.'s narration of their first and final meeting, the exchange is hallmarked by their vigorous and entertaining dialogue on sex and violence. Their personal rapport is evident, even in the face of the imminently fatal encounter they both recognize their meeting to constitute. Their shared queer hypermasculinity in turn queers the character of this assassination story, as homicide blurs with suicide and affection with murderous intent. When Weeper persuades K. to let him have a last "hit" to soften his death, "If you going to take me out, at least make me go out 'pon the sky, no man?" (James 2014, 596), he instructs K. to inject him with cocaine. Not knowing that it was a syringe of pure cocaine, K. watches as Weeper goes into a seizure and thrashes to his death. As K. describes it, he too is seized in the moment and finds himself called to embrace Weeper: "And me I don't know why, I don't fucking know but I grab him around the chest and clutch him even though he was on top of me. I don't know why but I was hugging and holding him and squeezing him and he was just shaking, man, shaking, and shaking some more" (597–8). It seems strangely fitting to the oblique creolized queerness of James's novel that Weeper and his story end in a perverse consummation in which intimate violence and male-male desire become indistinguishable from each other.

"What More Sci-Fi Than the Antilles?": Mythic Hypermasculinity and Queer Forms of Queerness in *Oscar Wao*

In *Brief History*'s world of relentless, but diffuse violence, moments of queer hypermasculinity are as arresting as they are fleeting. In *Oscar Wao*, Junot Díaz manages his creative exploration of historical violence rooted in the Dominican Republic, and its legacy of impossible, fantasized hypermasculinity, according to a very different narrative scale; one that is structured around the relationships that have developed between Yunior, who reveals himself as our main narrator toward the middle of the book, and the de León family, his diasporic Dominican peers. The world of almost everyone in Díaz's novel is overshadowed and distorted in some way by the monumental history of violence shaped by "Trujillo, one of the twentieth century's most infamous dictators, [who] ruled the Dominican Republic between 1930 and 1961 with an implacable ruthless brutality" (Díaz 2007, 2, footnote 1). Trujillo's rule is narrated in the novel's footnotes as the historical background that still foregrounds the present reality of the novel's characters, including those now living in the U.S. The ways in which sexual and gendered violence were an intrinsic part of Trujillo's dictatorship is made clear from the start when Yunior streams his mention of the dictator's mustering of one of the largest militaries in the world with the fact that he was known for "fucking every hot girl in sight, even the wives of his subordinates, thousands upon thousands upon thousands of women" (Díaz 2007, 2–3, footnote 1).

In its straddling of the Dominican Republic and the Dominican diasporic community in New Jersey, the novel calls into view the extreme claims that the dictatorship made on Dominican bodies to perform according to a fantastical version of the nation and their ongoing legacy for those who left. For Oscar and Yunior, who grow up as "dominicano/as living abroad, Dominican ethnicity is a marker of difference within larger pan-ethnic groups such as black or Latinxs, a way to culturally identify with the Caribbean and to assert (trans) national belonging to the Dominican nation" (Lorgia García Peña 2018, 1). Yet successful belonging as a male dominicano is only guaranteed when supported by a successful, or at least persuasive, performance of *tigueraje*, a brand of hypermasculinity defined by Lipe Collado in *El Tiguere dominicano* (1981) as "the mythic paragon of barrio masculinity who gains power—riches, women, control over others—apparently from nothing" (Collado 8–9, translated by Ramírez 2018, 133). In *Colonial Phantoms: Belonging and Refusal in the Dominican Americas, from the 19th Century to the Present* (2018), Dixa Ramírez discusses how this identity acts as a historical echo in *Oscar Wao*, drawing attention to "the oppressive pressure of performative masculinity" (135) for both those who can comply with its demands and those who fail or refuse. In the novel, the legitimating demand for an impossible and disfiguring obedience to gendered, sexed, and raced identities is narrated as it transmits across time and place in the form of a trans-generation curse, or fukú. Although the main body of the novel narrates the intimate and intense world of families, friendships, fraternities, and neighborhoods, the legacy of a ferociously declarative Dominican hypermasculinity against which all men are to be measured and according to which most choose to announce themselves remains relentlessly defining.

Several critics have drawn attention to how this heteropatriarchal imperative propels the novel or, as Maja Horn (2014) argues, the way in which "the novel's entire plot could be summarized as Oscar's quest to have sex with a woman for the first time" (130). Certainly, the repeated, relentless demand on Oscar is foregrounded and tracks the novel's narrative arc, but plot is not story and, arguably, the novel is more interested in the fact that "many men, especially those like Oscar, cannot measure up" (Ramírez 2018: 135). If Yunior's own womanizing and his stated purpose to "fix Oscar's life" (Díaz 2007, 175) drives the plot as it affirms his hypermasculine centrality, then I would argue that Oscar's alternative, nerdy, failed masculinity and the queer attachment that develops between him and Yunior constitutes the story. While Oscar's queerness is alleged within the narrative on account of his lack of heterosexual prowess and his inability to perform Dominican hypermasculinity, I want to read Oscar as queering the life story presented to him and that of La Patria through his rearrangement, rather than absence, of heterosex. Moreover, if the plot of Yunior's "Project Oscar" (176) is directed at fashioning Oscar to be more like the hypersexualized *tiguere* that Yunior projects, it is telling that the story reveals a pull in the opposite direction, as Yunior's oblique and enduring desire for Oscar is glimpsed through the cracks of his performance of Dominican hypermasculinity.

It hardly needs pointing out that the narrative of *Oscar Wao* flaunts, even oozes, extreme heteronormativity and that its cocktail of hypermasculinity and Dominicanness reaches its saturation point alarmingly early in the novel and in Oscar's life. Introduced in terms of his negative capacity, Oscar enters the novel marked by failure: "Our hero was *not* one of those Dominican cats everybody's always going on about—he *wasn't no* home-run hitter or a fly bachatero, *not* a playboy with a million hots on his jock. And except for one period early in his life, dude never had much luck with females (how very un-Dominican of him)" (Díaz 2007, 11, italics added). Setting aside the absurdity of attributing terms like *playboy* or *little macho* to a prepubescent, Oscar's one success in hypermasculine terms is, tellingly, a relationship with two girls when he was seven. Equally attracted to the beautiful Maritza and to Olga who was not beautiful, but willing to wrestle and play with his Star Wars dolls, Oscar finally loses both in trying to conform. Interestingly though, the legacy of this triangular circulation of erotic energy comes to typify Oscar's encounters—from his attachment with Yunior, the narrator, who is in an on-off sexual relation-ship with Oscar's sister Lola, through his intense friendship with Ana Obregon that connects him to her violent boyfriend, Manny, and finally, fatally, to his obsession with Ybón Pimentel, an older prostitute in the Dominican Republic who is claimed by her boyfriend, the police capitán. Throughout, Oscar is positioned beside hypermasculine males and, while he is unable to win in the sexual contests he finds himself in, his tenderness and companionship provide opportunities for a feeling sideways around the bru-tality of heteropatriachal sexual relationships. For Anna and Ybón, being with Oscar offers an intimacy and rapport that are evidently absent from their sexual partnerships.

In addition to his queer proximity to the erotic via the lives of others—and according to a rule of three, rather than the heteronormative two, Oscar's disproportionate acts of being also queer him. His physical obesity and his oversized afro are identified by Yunior as "anti-pussy devices" (Díaz 2007, 20) that estrange his birth claim to Dominican masculinity. Moreover, his exag-gerated appetites for reading, film, television, and later for writing, are all directed at speculative genres and the idea of imagining other worlds. Identi-fied most frequently as a nerd, at points in the novel Oscar is called a *parai-guayo*, defined by Collado as a man "who assumes he will lose and constantly pities himself" and a freak (Collado 8–9 translated by Ramírez 2018: 136). Certainly the narrative seems to congregate abundant evidence against Oscar's hypermasculinity and therefore against his Dominicanness. Oscar can never refute these doubts—"Who the hell, I ask you, had ever met a Domo like him?"—not even with his repeated assertions: "But I am. Soy Dominicano. Dominicano soy" (Díaz 2007, 180, 49). All the same, when Yunior says that Oscar "Couldn't have passed for Normal if he'd wanted to" (21) it is perhaps not the plot's drive toward normal that presents the compel-ling path. Indeed, in this throwaway phrase of detraction, Yunior surfaces the way in which "normal" itself is only ever a performance, an act of passing. Arguably, it is the excessively heavy veneering of heteronormativity, which Yunior marks here as "normal," that eventually collapses in this narrative, undermining its own credibility and drawing attention to itself as a fragile, surface construction that is constantly under threat. Moreover, while Yunior's insult works in the service of the plot and Yunior's own perfor-mance of hypermasculinity, the implied question of what Oscar actually desires opens up the possibility of an interesting counterstory. Indeed, what is most destabilizing about Oscar is not the idea that he is unable to pass for normal but the idea that he may not desire that norm.

There is no mention of Oscar having same-sex desires in the narrative; in fact, Yunior tenaciously affirms Oscar's heterosexual longings and fantasies to the point of suspicion. There is, however, a strong sense in which the heterocolonial, Dominican American culture (based on a binary object choice) in which Oscar lives can only understand him as gay if he is not having sex with women. He is called a faggot at school, and when he leaves for Rutgers his *tio* (uncle) gives him a box of condoms: "Use them all, he said, and then added: On girls" (Díaz 2007, 49). Later, at a college Halloween party, Oscar is assigned his queer name because, in his Dr. Who costume, Yunior "couldn't believe how much he looked like that fat homo Oscar Wilde, and [he] told him so" (180). The way in which queer sexuality is simply read off the surface of nonconforming gendered bodies within the Dominican diasporic community is also evident when Oscar's sister Lola shaves off her long hair and, having transgressed the appearance of Dominican femininity, is labeled and scorned as *lesbiana* (37). In this context, Oscar's queerness is both highly visible and utterly unrecognizable. He becomes an unreadable figure in the world into which he was born and socialized, and finds himself compelled to invent other worlds and to speculate on other realities. Throughout the narrative, there is a mismatch, an unsettling asymmetry, between Oscar's erotomania and his virginity, the intensity of his erotic feeling and his failure of sexual encounter.

In the final section of the novel, Yunior relates Oscar's obsession with Ybón, a Dominican prostitute whom he pursues against the advice of his family. As Yunior aligns Oscar with his hypermasculine "project" and plot line, he narrates this "last-ditch attempt to put him back on the proper path of Dominican male-itude" (Díaz 2007, 283). Casting doubt over the "truth" of their sexual encounter, Yunior calls the reader into his "Oscar Redemption Program" (179), asking, "Can't we believe that an Ybón can exist and that a brother like Oscar might be due a little luck after twenty-three years?" (285). For some critics, Yunior's direct narratorial intervention here is an act of erotic censorship. On this point, Elena Machado Sáez (2011) argues: "The novel's conclusion supposedly resolves the ambiguity of Oscar's sexual identity as a virgin since he engages in a hetero-sexual act, having sex with Ybón. But in light of the fact that this act (like the novel as a whole) is a fiction constructed by Yunior as narrator, the motivation for 'resolving' Oscar's queerness is tied to the threat which that identity represents to Yunior's own sexuality" (548). In my reading of Oscar's queer queerness, it is not the object of his sexual desire that is ambiguous, but rather his mode of erotic connection. When, at the end of the story, there is a consummation, this too is deliberately queer to the masculine, national identity it is read as affirming: "Guess what else? Ybón actually fucked him. Praise be to Jesus" (Díaz 2007, 334). What seems to be made most visible at the point of his assent to heterosex is Oscar's sexual dissent (he is the passive object and not the hypermasculine sexual conqueror). Whether it is Oscar's own story or Yunior's account of his story that is being told here, the plot falters as it succeeds. Having experienced the so-called climax of penetrative heterosex, which is described at the very end of the novel, Dominican hypermasculinity is finally the negative against which Oscar is defined. What Elena Machado Sáez (2011) describes as Oscar's "transformation into full-fledged heterosexuality" (524) strikes me as a queer transformation, unless we conform to Yunior's plot, through which normative Dominican male sexuality can be read entirely according to object choice.

Redefining his erotic subjectivity, Oscar's story (or Yunior's account of his story) focuses on the cherished intimacies of everyday proximities:

> He wrote that Ybón had little hairs coming up to almost her bellybutton and that she crossed her eyes when he entered her but what really got him was not the bam-bam-bam of sex—it was the little intimacies that he'd never in his whole life anticipated, like combing her hair or getting her underwear off a line or watching her walk naked to the bathroom or the way she would sit on his lap and put her face into his neck. The intimacies like listening to her tell him about being a little girl and him telling her that he'd been a virgin all his life. He wrote that he couldn't believe he'd had to wait for this so goddam long. (Díaz 2007, 334–335)

Oscar's non-normalizing consummation comes in finding an affective rapport, rather than in sexual conquest. His preference is not for the "bam, bam, bam of sex" which clearly carries an echo of the violence with which heterosexual relations are presented in the rest of the book (Díaz 2007, 334). In his insistence on the value of intimacy and the surplus of desire that denies a utilitarian politics and the sexual imperatives of the state, Oscar is arguably at his most non-heteronormative, when he does finally have sex with a woman. His lived repudiation of the aggressive hyper-heteromasculinity associated with being dominicano, which involves suppressing emotions and objectifying women, may be freakish in terms of the machismo culture that is validated at the surface of the narrative and drives the stated quest of the plot. However, by refusing this distorted and damaging hypermasculinity, which depends on "acquiring, maintaining and reproducing power" (Lewis 2003, 97), Oscar continues to seek an alternative world in which the possibility of consenting human contact and nonviolent pleasure has not been erased by the nation's or the diaspora's historical backstory. In this way Oscar might be seen to have achieved what Díaz has declared he wants for his characters, the "kind of love that could liberate them from that horrible legacy of colonial violence. I am speaking about decolonial love" (Díaz 2016, 396–397).

Oscar's non-normalizing sexuality ultimately resides in his expression of surplus desire, uncategorizable longings, and historical yearnings that are grounded in the fantasy of an unharming, democratic touch that positions him beyond and outside Dominican masculinity. Indeed, as Maja Horn points out, while "Oscar's death was neither wondrous nor mysterious [. . .] he is killed as a result of his overstepping the scripts of hegemonic masculinity in the Dominican Republic," his elected vulnerability to the violent consequences on non-normalization provokes an inversion in the nation's gendered script of victims of sexual transgression, as "in the Dominican Republic more often this results in the murder of the woman involved; such femicides by jealous partners in fact constitute a widely recognized and ongoing crisis in the country" (Horn 2014, 128).

Given the strenuous focus within this novel on the suspected queerness of Oscar and the way in which critical attention has often focused on Yunior's power as the narrator/dictator,[11] it is easy not to pay attention to just how alike Yunior and Oscar are, and how Yunior longs for and depends on Oscar, dreaming of him even years after he has died. If Yunior does finally make Oscar conform to the exclusive life plot of Dominican heteromasculinity, then he also allows him the narrative space to be weirdly sentimental. Moreover, if the narrative is seeped in the ways in which Yunior, Lola, his mother, and others try to normalize Oscar (helping him to lose weight, stop writing, get outside, cut his hair, etc.), it also more obliquely reveals how his queer life and nonconformity have their own charm too. Yunior not only dreams of Oscar years after he has died, but he has preserved his archive, "books, his games, his manuscript, his comic books, his papers" in "four refrigerators" and he now writes obsessively, "Learned that from Oscar" (Díaz 2007, 330, 325). Right from the beginning of the novel Yunior confesses their likeness: "These days I'm nerdy like that" (4). Indeed, despite Yunior's shrill voice-over of Oscar's life, it would seem that Oscar has, in fact, presented the center of gravity toward which Yunior has found himself moved. As Oscar's story surfaces to disrupt the heteronormalizing dynamics of Yunior's plot, Yunior is no longer so invested in the vigorous and arduous recital that being an old-style dominicano man demands. As Horn argues, "Dominican male scripts, this story strongly suggests, are largely responsible for Yunior's long, drawn-out personal misery" (2014, 137). As Yunior imagines himself through Oscar, he learns how to be "a new man . . . a new man, a new man" (Díaz 2007, 326). This is not the newness of a "suppressed homosocial romance that cannot be rendered as part of a Dominican diasporic history" that Machado Sáez (2011, 524) reads as the novel's censored story. For, while Yunior's oblique desire for Oscar may strangely be the only straight form of queerness in this novel, Oscar's queer desires are not object based, but calibrated by their nonviolence, reciprocity, and care—and it is this that Yunior may finally recognize as his "newness" too.

The novel implicitly asserts through its coexisting, as well as competing, generic claims to biography, autobiography (or *testimonio*), comic book, sci-fi, pornography, history, and ventriloquism, that the same life, the same story, is terrifyingly susceptible to how it is told. The idea that it is narrative alone that can bestow stability on the ontological commotion of what Díaz refers to in a 2007 interview as "the masculine derangements" of a dominicano national identity (Díaz quoted in M. O'Rourke 2007, n.p.) means that social identities are powerfully inscribed before social bodies enter them, but also that they are available for redescription. Yunior claims ethnographic methods in telling the de León family history (referencing family photographs, the oral history of Belicia, letters, and, of course, Oscar's journals). He then later admits that he has also "thrown a lot of fantasy and sci-fi in the mix" (Díaz 2007, 285). Ultimately the lives rendered by *Oscar Wao* are not to be distinguished as truth or fiction, as hypermasculine or queer. Deliberately disruptive of such authorizing identities, this novel "destabilizes the very distinctions between the natural and the artificial, depth and surface, inner and outer through which discourse about genders almost always operates" (Butler 1990, preface xxxi). In a space of such extreme, wild imaginings as the Dominican Republic under Trujillo, a lived self is knowingly projected, both real and unreal at once—as Oscar himself states, "what more fantasy than the Antilles" (Díaz 2007, 6).[12] Finally then, the only differences that the novel registers as valuable to know are those between gestures that are motivated by taking power and those that are not. In this way, the novel also responds to Aaron Kamugisha's (2012) question of "how in the teeth of a sexist culture so oppressive of women in its historical and contemporary manifestations, one can illustrate the diminution of men's lives by this same culture" (42).

Conclusion

To read *Brief History* and *Oscar Wao* for whether Weeper or Wales, Yunior or Oscar are "really" hypermasculine or same-sex-desiring is to miss the queer poetics and politics of these frenetic, disorienting literary worlds. In their different ways, both of these novels are invested in representing opportunities, choices, thoughts, feelings, and fantasies that cannot be resolved into a coherent identity or even a coherent self. As Yunior confesses near the end of his narrative, "Which is to say if you're looking for the full story, I don't have it. Oscar searched for it too, in his last days, and it's not certain whether he found it either" (Díaz 2007, 243). To acknowledge the possibilities of more open-ended stories of masculinity that are both contested and contradictory is, in these novels, to imagine multiply discrepant masculinities in which unbelonging is only as excruciating as belonging. In this way, both novels confirm Rafael Ramirez's (2003) observation: "To live like a [Caribbean] man, the constant reproduction of male discourses, the fierce competition for acceptance as a macho, the persistent threat of devaluation to the sphere of the nonmacho, is very painful" (247). Momentary encounters aside from such pain form the quiet, queer epicenters of both narratives. Within cultures where non-heteropatriarchal Caribbean men are denied visibility as legitimate masculine subjects (and often also as legitimate Black and national subjects), there is a queer logic to hypermasculinity's assertions of invulnerability and effortlessness becoming the shelter to, as well as the repudiation of, its queer avatars. By allowing for ways of being and of knowing that cannot be described and can hardly be discerned from within the heterocolonial order, these works make space for the queered presence and value of virtually illegible Caribbean masculinities.

5

Imagining Impossible Possibilities

● ●

Shani Mootoo's *Moving Forward Sideways Like a Crab* and Selected Writings by Thomas Glave

> What is the Caribbean in fact? A multiple series of relationships.
> —Édouard Glissant,
>   *Caribbean Discourse*

> Queerness is essentially about . . . an insistence on potentiality or concrete possibility for another world.
> —José Esteban Muñoz, *Cruising Utopia: The Then and There of Queer Futurity*

This book comprises readings of literary works that have been consciously directed at expanding the critical terrain for thinking about literature as a supple and often subtle imaginative platform for undoing the rigid categorizations of sexual identities based on singular object choices and cis-gendered constructions. The creative works discussed so far represent multiple and overlapping erotic desires and sexual attachments beyond, alongside, and even within these orthodox models, which already exist with meaning in a creolized Caribbean. By reading across this wide range of Caribbean writings in English, the aim has been to argue that literary representations of fluid, intersecting, and queer lives are intrinsic to representations of creolized Caribbean communities and their lived realities, and that the seemingly spectacular contradiction of *Caribbean queer*, is also a commonplace reality—an everyday impossible possibility.

In this final chapter, I turn to works that insist on a more consciously defamiliarizing and deconstructive reading of eroticism, embodiment, and sexual identities. In different ways, the works of Mootoo and Glave under discussion here ask us to notice and to challenge the thresholds of erotic intelligibility. I read these works as paying serious attention to the question of seemingly impossible possibilities by representing transitioning and radically embodied lives and by telling stories that dare the reader to be equal to the openness of their imagination in thinking around social transformation. Although markedly different from each other in their literary form and register, both Mootoo's and Glave's works expose and unfasten the normalizing effect of the familiar. They offer an imagined transformation of being, and a reach toward questions about the power and use of the erotic that are unimpeded by citizen-shaped identities. The difficulty of accessing the erotic as a humanizing resource uncontaminated by social drivers that look to profit from sexual transactions or to manage and contain sociosexual relations is the subject of Audre Lorde's (1984b) essay "Uses of the Erotic: The Erotic as Power."[1] I read Mootoo's and Glave's fictions as engaging with the obstacle to transformation that Lorde (1984b) identifies as "the fear that we cannot grow beyond whatever distortions we may find keeps us docile and loyal and obedient, externally defined" (58). Through their distinctive styles of address—Mootoo's digressive, hesitant, and retrospective style that decelerates the move toward fixed meanings and Glave's speculative and dazzling shift into postspecies ecologies of desiring subjects to dislodge all preconceptions of embodiment—these writings move the discussions about erotic and sexual being in directions that demand fresh conversations. They affirm Lorde's (1984b) argument that "recognizing the power of the erotic within our lives can give us the energy to pursue genuine change within our world, rather than merely settling for a shift of characters in the same weary drama" (59).

Indeed, although this book is a work of literary criticism, it takes its bearings from a lived world where contestations over erotic entitlements and sexual citizenship carry high stakes. Thinking about the work that literature might perform in this context, I argue here for the value of speculation, and of the literary imagination more generally, as a means by which to stretch and expand horizons of the possible. In their address to queer forms of embodiment that move beyond and yet still toward a reconceptualization of the human, these writings point to the ways in which rights need to remain in step with a dynamic politics of citizenship shaped by, as well as shaping, changing conceptualizations and discourses of the human within human rights.

"The Grey Area of Freedom": Shani Mootoo's *Moving Forward Sideways Like a Crab*

Despite a widespread recognition of the Caribbean as a place of transverse and multiple relations, there has been little work to date focused on transgender and transsexual figures in literary works. Between 2014 and 2016 three publications redressed this gap in different ways. In *Island Bodies*, Rosamond King's (2014) comprehensive study of *Transgressive Sexualities in the Caribbean Imagination*, King offers a reading of three Caribbean novels that engage with transgendered characters in a sustained way: Shani Mootoo's *Cereus Blooms at Night* (1996), Michelle Cliff's *No Telephone to Heaven* (1987), and Mayra Santos-Febres's *Sirena Selena vestida de pena* (2000). King concludes that in these works the trans characters perform a symbolic function and that the narratives stop short of exploring the trans experience in and of its own right: "Trans individuals also deliver other individuals—and sometimes themselves or each other—in the sense of *rebirth* to a truer incarnation or a better understanding of themselves. This linking of deliverance to trans people incorporates unconventional genders into Caribbean social orders by having them literally *serve* the dominant, conventional genders in the social hierarchy. The literature thus accepts trans characters as part of Caribbean culture but does so in a backhanded maneuver that keeps them in subservient, marginal roles" (King 2014, 25; italics in the original). King points here to the deficiency of these literary works to release trans individuals from the dominant schema of gender convention and their missed opportunity to create a rich and humanizing rendering of their lives. For her "in the Cariglobal imagination the portrayal of trans people is a backhanded one that acknowledges their existence while refusing them the possibility of full lives or citizenship" (20).

Keja Valens's (2016) essay, "Excruciating Improbability and the Transgender Jamaican," which appeared in *Trans Studies: The Challenge to Hetero/Homo Normativities*, edited by Yolanda Martínez-San Miguel and Sarah Tobias, mines the "productive intersection and collaboration between knowledge production, social justice, and activism" (2) through a reading of Patricia Powell's 1998 novel *The Pagoda*. Valens (2016) argues that Powell's imagining of her central trans character, a Chinese forced migrant named Lowe in nineteenth-century Jamaica, brings awareness of the complicated relations between nonbinary identities and the historical forces of colonialism: "Caribbean cultural critic Édouard Glissant's *Poetics of Relation* guides my understanding of Powell's novel as forging and revealing connections between the pain of colonial experience and resistance to it, between resistance to the colonial order and the colonial order itself, among bodies and stories and histories that are not neatly separable into any binary, be it colonizer/colonized, black/white, or male/female" (Valens 2016, 66). Valens is interested in "the trans relations in *The Pagoda* as offering ways around, through, and under heterocolonial patriarchy that do not destroy it or point to any move out of or beyond it" (80). In her reading, value is placed on Lowe's deferral of a fully realized identity story and on the ways in which "the novel never settles . . . on one 'right' way to articulate Lowe's status" and offers "no single true gender or sexuality for Lowe to 'be'" (79).

Both of these critical interventions emphasize the pressure that trans identities exert on the conventions of cis-gender norms. For King, "the first step in understanding how trans individuals reveal and reinforce ambiguities in Caribbean binary gender is recognizing how they deconstruct that system" (King 2014, 40).[2] For Valens (2016), the trans characters in *The Pagoda* bring to light an "excruciatingly improbable poetics of relation [to] transgress and transfigure the gender binary that occasions them" (79). In my reading of Shani Mootoo's novel *Moving Forward Sideways Like a Crab*, another 2014 publication to bring a Caribbean trans person to the fore, I want to explore King's (2014) idea of the literary refusal of full citizenship alongside Valens's (2016) interest in the movement across multiplying possibilities of being rather than toward a final identity destination.

Recognizing the demands for rethinking gender difference and sexual relations that Caribbean trans experiences and lives necessitate corresponds to the critical move of "feeling sideways" that I outlined as a localizing methodology in the introduction to this book. Indeed, critical attention to this novel works most productively when it follows Mootoo's own literary course, and that of her trans character Sid/Sydney, in terms of "moving forward sideways."[3] Importantly, while the novel's focus is on the life of a trans person, it insists on feeling sideways toward others, both in its story and in its narrative form, allowing space for a deliberately unhurried and necessarily incomplete understanding of how creolized Caribbean subjects might practice gender and sexuality in different ways. Moving sideways here involves a change in pace, as well as in direction, as the reader (including the reader/narrator internal to the narrative) is slowed down through repetition, reflection, and digression. It also involves paying attention to insistently lateral narratives that detail parallel but nonidentical human complexity. In this way, Mootoo's writing queers the temporality of linear progress and moves us sideways to craft representational space and conceptual ground from which to explore lives that are continually navigating how gender and sexual identities are experienced and what meaning they might carry and fail to carry.[4] As Sydney, the central trans character, comments, "But there is hardly ever a single answer to anything. And isn't it that the stories one most needs to know are the ones that are usually the least simple or straightforward?" (Mootoo 2014, 32–33).[5]

The telling of life stories is a guiding motif in this novel as it explores the relationship between Jonathan Lewis-Adey, a Canadian writer in his forties whose career is faltering, and Sid Mahale, whom he first knew as Siddhani, the Indian Trinidadian female partner of his White English biological mother, India, who left their home and Jonathan when he was ten. When Jonathan is finally reunited with Sid in Trinidad—decades later—she has transitioned to Sydney. The novel opens with seven pages from Sydney's notebook, written toward the end of his life and in his full awareness of Jonathan's desire for resolution, even closure, on that defining episode in his own life story when Siddhani left. Indicatively, the narrative opens by calibrating the impossibility of representing the fullness of being: "Surely it is a failure of our human design that it takes not an hour, not a day, but much, much longer to relay what flashes through the mind with the speed of a hummingbird's wing" (Mootoo 2014, 2). It is not just Sydney's imminent death that queers his sense of time, making it both exceptionally rich and impoverished at once, but also the relationship between life and story, which is always a complicated and complicating one. Reflecting on how to explain his departure and his transition to Jonathan truthfully and responsibly, Sydney contemplates that he "could explain to him that I came to realize that the imagining and dreaming, the wishing and the knowing that led bit by bit to the being I am today had actually started long before I left Trinidad and went to live in Canada" (6). While unlikely to meet Jonathan's demands, the emphasis here on the primacy of the imagination, on being over identity, and of the rootedness of a reimagined self in Trinidad are all significant to the novel's representation of a Caribbean trans life.

Although the main body of the novel comprises "A Memoir by Jonathan Lewis-Adley," the narrative rocks between the story that Sydney needs to release and that which Jonathan wants to receive. Its meaning arguably rests in the ellipses between the two, where a space opens up and expands into a shared awareness of how precarious and how powerful it is to try to understand and to tell another's life, and another life. Although Sydney recognizes that it is an unwelcome interference to Jonathan's demands, he also needs to release the story of a third life—that of his adolescent friend and love Zain, who supported him in his transition and whose public conformity to a heterocolonial script also belied the fullness of her being. Unable to separate the story of his own life from Zain's untimely death, Sydney continually relives their time together and their correspondence. Yet this intense reflection only makes the inadequacy of his story to carry the density of their deeply enmeshed connection more palpable:

I could say, I arrived one cold and snowy morning at a building in Toronto, entered a room at an appointed time with a bag full of cash and changed my life forever. And I could leave it at that. Perhaps these are the stories that would satisfy Jonathan. But they are only a fraction of the truth, and I need to tell him the rest. I need to tell him how I have battled with the belief that had I only been a different person, Zain would be alive today. *Had I been a different person.* This, more than anything, is what needs to be said. Still, that would only be a fraction of the story. (Mootoo 2014, 8; italics in the original)

Sid's painful sense of being different and her migration to Canada are traced back to the "gulf that existed between Sid and her parents—on account of her inability and refusal to conform to their idea of what a good daughter was" (Mootoo 2014, 41). In their professional, middle-class, Indian Trinidadian world, respectability and their good name are secured by gender conformity and the expectation of looking, living, and loving within the heterocolonial order. Sid fails to meet any of these expectations and consequently remains a mystery and an outsider to her family. As even her caring mother tells her, "I don't understand all of this instability, this kind of life you people live" (99). In Trinidad, which is her home and the place she feels she belongs, Sid was painfully aware of "the incongruity between what [she] was and what [she] wanted" (77). This incongruity is articulated at various points in the novel, as Sid's impossible desire for a Trinidadian female partner, for living at home and for a relationship of shared understanding and care spills out. Even on his death-bed, Sydney feels sideways toward an impossible past for Sid, "What if in Trinidad she had seen that the mould in which women were cast could be broken, and yet women not themselves be broken?" (293). It is characteristic of the narrative style that while telling the story of one life, the novel moves sideways at the same time to represent lives unlived, but not unimagined. In this way, the novel delicately proliferates and magnifies the possibilities for multiple different configurations of gendered and erotic being that seemed impossible to Sid, but that Jonathan glimpses in others' queerly possible lives after Sydney's death.

It is in Canada, after her break-up with India, that Sid learns about the option of surgical and hormonal interventions for gender reassignment. Although resigned not to take this path while her parents are alive, Sid has been given the money necessary to make that choice by Zain and, soon after her funeral, joins a clinic group for those undergoing gender reassignment. In the company of transitioning peers, Sid's emotions are heightened and restless.

Whenever . . . I saw the ones who were no longer women but were not yet men either, my chest would heave, and from deep inside would well a confusion of emotions. I would be breathless with the excitement of recognition. I would want to collapse with relief at the prospect of my own change. I would feel envy and impatience that I was not further along on my own path. But I felt fear, too, that in becoming like them I would find too late that I had given up more than I had intended to, fear that there were steps on that journey that, once taken, were irreversible. (Mootoo 2014, 107)

The pull of no longer being a woman, as her home society defines it, is strong here, but so too is the hesitation around loss and around ever matching an unconventionally gendered being to a male body. The seeming gender clarity of transitioning from woman to man, or man to woman, is not correspondent with the complex, nonbinary sense of unbelonging to any such conventional gender category that Sid expresses: "The crime that there isn't a word, beyond *male* or *female*, to describe someone like me" (Mootoo 2014, 288). On many occasions throughout the novel, Sydney returns to the memorable walk to the clinic as if it is the idea of the journey across, between, and through genders that is more significant than the arrival or destination.

Inquiring deeply into his motivation for undergoing this change, Sydney surfaces the need to escape a category that does not fit alongside an almost contradictory need to be accommodated within the existing social ground.

What I felt in my very bones was that I could no longer live my life as a woman; I no longer wanted to be identified by others as a woman, and treated, as a result, in predictable and predetermined ways. It was easier to change myself than wrestle with society. Above all, I desperately needed a kind of annihilation, and a rebirth. I did not want to stand next to a woman and feel, ever again, that I had to guard my love for her, or that I dared not touch her in public in the ways I wanted. . . . I did not want a body that attracted hatred and brought harm to those women I cared about. (Mootoo 2014, 108)

Later, on reflection, Sydney recognizes that there was no opportunity to discuss the regendered destination on offer, or the more searching and increasingly pressing question of what correspondence can ever be possible between a socially constructed binary identity and a multifaceted interior sense of being: "Looking back now, I realize that no one had ever asked me directly if I wanted to be a man, for I would have had to answer 'no.' I remember saying, however, I could not bear the body in which I—this 'I' quite separate from any body—existed" (Mootoo 2014, 108).[6] Here, and arguably throughout this novel, the concern is more profoundly about how being and body are forced to reconcile within such a limited range of options: "Our options then were black and white, between this and that. The grey area of freedom we longed for existed only in dreams" (108).

As well as marking the damaging limits of social intelligibility, the novel also edges toward a sense of those seemingly impossible possibilities within the already imagined "grey area of freedom." It is intent throughout on feeling sideways by representing erotic agitations as necessarily in excess of both assigned and elected gender categories. After Zain's murder—which Sid suspects was a crime of passion with homophobic intent, provoked when Zain's male lover discovered them in each other's arms—she ponders: "If I were asked if we had ever kissed, or been sexual with each other, I would truthfully say we hadn't, but my answer would elide the intensity of our bond and the intimacy that at times had blinded me, and that she had felt too" (Mootoo 2014, 94–5). Refusing the defining line between sexual acts and sexual desire, between the conformity of a fixed gender/sexual identity and the ambiguity of the erotic, Sid/Sydney recognizes a texture and density in Zain's connection that exceeds the categories through which sexual subjectivity is permitted to articulate itself.[7] Indeed, Sydney had tellingly confided in Jonathan that his relationship with Zain was "better than a romance" (36). As the novel unfolds, his connection to Zain, rendered "painstakingly" (130) and in "bewildering detail" (146), feels sideways across their friendship to reveal these fuller dimensions.

The localized charge between Sid and Zain is one of the first items narrated in "Sydney's Story (as he told it to me)" when Sydney admits, "In all my years away, no one ever touched me or treated me like Zain did. Was this peculiar to Zain, I often wondered, or was it the way of women from our culture? And was it only they who could ever satisfy me?" (Mootoo 2014, 53). Reflecting on an earlier moment of the same visit home, when they had been taking a sea bath together, Sid focuses on that within Zain which cannot be known or reached through her social identities: "You are a mother of two adult children, the wife of a businessman, you are a Trinidadian woman, you are an Indian woman, a Muslim woman, you live here in this country, but who are you, really?" (61). In keeping with its insistent sideways glance at how who we are is always in excess of how we can be named, the novel reveals how Zain's conformity to the conventional gender script is only a fragment of who she is. While Sid is disciplined and "sexiled" by her inability to meet the expectations of the dominant society and "do what was right" as an Indian Trinidadian woman (211), Zain's seeming correspondence with this gendered script also marks its controlling limits.[8] In relinquishing her dreams of a career in medicine in favor of marriage, maternity, and supporting her husband's business, Sid recognizes that Zain is "spinning her top in the mud of all that was steady, familiar, and expected of her" (42). Yet the limits of expectation do not hold for Zain either, and it is her unexpected love for Sid that likely costs her her life—a suspicion that Sydney endlessly replays as guilt and inadequacy.

Interestingly, this significant day out—replete with intimacies, revelations, and fears—is relived in Jonathan's memoir at the end of the novel. Infused with the stories he has been told by Sid and the letters between Sid and Zain that he has read, he rewrites their story in his own words "but faithfully" (Mootoo 2014, 233). In Jonathan's version, Zain kisses Sid in the darkness of their journey home, perhaps faithful to his sense of what constitutes an erotic attachment and the declaration of love he reads in one of Zain's letters to Sid (154). In Tuli Chatterji's (2016) reading of this episode, she emphasizes that, "though Mootoo does not indulge in describing the events 'happening in the car' when their breath, skins and bodies met, we are made aware of how Zain and Sid in their own ways were participating in decentering 'national or public values'" (123). Chatterji's (2016) reading is focused on "Sydney's attempt to initiate an Indo-Trinidadian liberatory space" (123) and on the ways in which the relationship between Sid and Zain challenges the constructions of sexuality that are legitimated on a national level. She argues that Mootoo "calls for feminist interventions to recognize Indo-Trinidadian identities that don't fit so easily within a homosexual terrain and also have not been politicized in the regional, diasporic, and global study of feminist epistemology" (Chatterji 2016, 129). While I would agree with Chatterji's reading in relation to the novel's general disturbance or creolization of conventional erotic and gendered identities, I see Jonathan's rewriting as an exception to this, rather than its culmination. In my reading, focusing on acts of "moving forward sideways," Jonathan's fictional inclusion of a kiss between Sid and Zain is arguably a diminution of their relationship, given Sydney's unrelenting attempts to step aside from the necessity of such direct correspondences between desire, identity, and act in order to explore more opaque erotic intensities.

After Sydney's death, Jonathan observes that he and Zain were "the warp and weft" of Sydney's life (Mootoo 2014, 151). In one sense, this is a simple acknowledgment of how interwoven the two were with Sydney's sense of being, but it also helpfully invokes threads moving in different directions, creating a fabric on account of their tension. After Zain's death, Sid realizes that nobody else knows the quality of their intimacy and connection, or how in letters and unspoken moments they had crafted a delicate fabric of relation that gave a structure for Sid/Sydney's sense of being. Inhabiting that paradox of invisibility and uniqueness, Sid relates a defamiliarized sense of being "a little piece of thread . . . hardened into a filament of wire so fine I was practically invisible" (163). The weave of connections that her relationship with Zain crafted cannot be perceived by others, who remain blind to the impossible possibilities of their attachment. Indeed, Zain's lover's partial (mis)perception of their relationship is deadly.

For his part, Jonathan is absorbed and impatient in his desire to pull on the now seemingly invisible thread leading back from Sydney to his childhood life with Sid. Moving forward sideways, he finally comes to appreciate that it takes "time, desire, and patience on both our parts" (Mootoo 2014, 21–22). During Sydney's life Jonathan remains reluctant to hear his stories of transition and is resistant to thinking otherwise about the possibilities of gender: "I did not really believe that there was an acceptable story" (44). Gradually through acts of translation, Jonathan begins to reconcile his understanding of the world with Sydney's, acknowledging, "How Zain must have loved Sid. She might not have called it 'love,' but she must have felt it" (115). Through both Sydney's and Jonathan's repeated re-envisioning of their significant relationships and moments in their lives, the novel stretches out the terrain of the possible and feels sideways toward queer thinking about lives—both inner and outer—and the categories into which they are admonished to fit. For Jonathan, it is only in the queer temporal distortion of the deathbed and the wake that he is able to open himself to this fuller range of possible lives. As "time and habits and ways shifted forwards and backwards and sideways, without reason" (29), the distinctions between life and the end of life, public and private, the permissible and the taboo are suspended. Symbolically, in Sydney's parting letter to Jonathan the signature is simply an *S*, as if leaving the space for the sense of an expanded, not yet representable being, not fully accounted for by either Sid or Sydney— both themselves ambiguously gendered in English.

After Sydney's death, it falls to Jonathan to manage the household and lead the funeral arrangements. Jonathan's increasingly bicultural identifications culminate in his cultural transvestitism as the Hindu son who lights Sid's funeral pyre. As a sideways narrative of transition, this uncontroversial, expected creolizing of Jonathan highlights the everyday fluidity and multiplicity of the Trinidad he comes to know.[9] Indeed, within this milieu, the anomalous refusal of gender and erotic fluidity is a clear paradox. As Maria Cristina Fumagalli, Bénédicte Ledent, and Roberto del Valle Alcalá (2013) argue in the introduction to their collection *The Cross-Dressed Caribbean*, "cross-dressers, hermaphrodites, transgendered people, and transsexuals haunt Caribbean literature, where sexual 'eccentricities' often become a key to understanding the Caribbean and its 'mongrelized' identity" (14). Only during the wake does Jonathan meet the other trans people who "were his friends. They were his family," alongside those who sought to make Sydney's life both possible and affirmed. These include the tailor who made suits for Sydney and whose sister was "like Sydney" (Mootoo 2014, 268, 228).

During these gatherings, Sydney's house becomes an evidently queer space, where many possible ways of knowing gender, family, and intimacy are brought together without needing to reconcile. In the company of the trans women he meets, Jonathan reflects on how their identities shift, on what changes and what remains. His conclusion is a move toward feeling sideways around gender categories and toward an ethical sense of being in the world:

"I had come face to face with women and men who presented themselves in ways that did not match their voices and their bodies—and yet, at the end of the night I was left with no sense that lies had been told. No secrets had been imposed on anyone. Everything was out in the open" (264). It is also in this space, where Jonathan's preference for openness develops, that he finds himself attracted to Anta, the adult child of the pundit who leads Sydney's funeral. Anta shines out as an exception to the narrow binarism that had overshadowed Sid/Sydney's life. As "the daughter *and* the son her mother had wanted, and . . . the daughter and the son her father had wanted too" (272, italics in the original), Anta was not socialized to conform to the gender binary, but rather to cross it. Through his desire for Anta, Jonathan also finds a way to queer himself. As Chatterji (2016) notes, "His conscious rejection of a colonial heterosexual ideology to be with androgynous Anta . . . inaugurates a paradigmatic shift in the political and linguistic representation of desires that need not necessarily be mapped in terms of heterosexuality, homosexuality, transgender, or cross-dresser" (116).

Yet, even in this state of openness, consonant with his now creolized sensibility, after he has allowed Sydney to release the completeness of his story and listened carefully to what it means, Jonathan feels a sense of inadequacy: "I wanted the impossible: to correct the misconceptions that had swirled around him when he lived, and to organize how he was remembered" (Mootoo 2014, 290). Importantly though, in naming this task as impossible Jonathan has also recognized that, in a paraphrase of Valens's (2016) reading of trans identity in *The Pagoda*, there is "no single true gender or sexuality" for Sid/Sydney to be (79). While being left with a seemingly impossible task may not appear to be an encouraging end point for Jonathan, in fact, it is. The most important misconception that Sid/Sydney, and the novel, seek to address is that of finding a meaningful correspondence between the multiplicity, complication, and potentiality of being and the narrowness and conformity required by social identity. As Jonathan reflects on Sydney's investment in the value of imagining impossible possibilities and on his "foresight, openness and generosity" (Mootoo 2014, 162), he recalls his most meaningful inheritance: "I was reminded of how he used to encourage me to wish for and to dream of the impossible. The implication was that the act of wishing and imagining was of equal value to—and sometimes of greater value than—the realization of dreams" (182–3). Finally then, Sydney has proven the value of slowing down life stories such that the plasticity and multiplicity of being can be noticed, appreciated, and understood. In this way, *Moving Forward Sideways Like a Crab* models the potential of feeling sideways and enables Jonathan to achieve his impossible desire of reorganizing the understanding of Sid/Sydney within the context of Trinidadian creolized sexualities beyond the inadequate possibilities of the heterocolonial order.

In this reading, *Moving Forward Sideways* shifts the trope of deliverance that King argues has emerged as a literary device to represent and yet ultimately marginalize the Caribbean trans character. While Jonathan's account may be seen as his way to deliver Sid, his ability to tell this queer story is only made possible by Sid's deliverance of the creolized Jonathan and their combined narratives center a trans life. Most importantly perhaps, what *Moving Forward Sideways* consciously refuses to "deliver" is the equivalence between a full life and citizenship, which King also finds wanting. Rather, the narrative decelerates and intensifies thinking around the relations between being and social identity to allow for possibilities that are not beyond imagination, even though they are not yet realizable for Sid/Sydney. Narrating the potential freedoms of a creolized queer Caribbean on the one hand and the social absorption of imposed historical categories through which Caribbean heterocoloniality has been organized and governed on the other, *Moving Forward Sideways* plots the distance between the terms of a full life and those of a livable life.

In this sideways move away from a focus on category-based identities and toward the complexity and crowding of desire, experience, and reflection, which are consistent only in their instability, the horizon of sexual citizenship may appear to recede, but it also expands. Unsettling the binarism of cis-female and male, the novel recognizes how lived negotiations of gender and sexuality already fall within Trinidad's creolized queerness, even though they are publicly invoked to mark its limits. By exposing how narrowly defined gender and sexual identities represent just a fraction of being, and therefore just a fraction of the knowable, the novel feels sideways toward an alternative politics of inclusion. In its imaginable world co-citizenship rests not on collective norms (even if more extensively conceived), but rather on a shared recognition of the potential of giving ourselves and embracing others differently, multiply—an evolving citizenship that is conferred through a deferral of identities rather than a confirmation.

Ecstatic Fluidity and Radical Embodiments: Thomas Glave's "Whose Caribbean? An Allegory, in Part," "He Who Would Have Become 'Joshua,' 1791," and "Jamaican, Octopus"

In the works by Glave that I discuss here the emphasis also lies with developing a literacy around the Caribbean subject as a slippery body that is knowingly contingent, pluralized, and unfinished. In common with Mootoo's *Moving Forward Sideways*, their acts of decolonizing representation are those of expansion, openness, and speculation. In Glave's writings, though, the submerged possibilities for queer connections become a compelling and recurring trope of ecstatic fluidity. First emerging in his short fiction "Whose Caribbean? An Allegory, in Part" ([2004] 2008b) and again in "He Who Would Have Become 'Joshua,' 1791" (2007), the aquatic as a queer ecology becomes a defining trope in "Jamaican, Octopus" (2012). When set alongside the intransigent and hardened nature of gender and sex norms as characterized within Jamaican national discourses (both official and popular), the imaginative value of these speculative works becomes evident.[10] The persistent assertion of a safe distance between Jamaicanness and non-heteronormativity delineates the social grammar from which Glave's creative interventions depart radically and purposefully. The extreme undoing of gendered and sexed bodies in these works calls for a dialogue between the real and the speculative, showing their rich interconnection in illuminating each other and the terms of queer im/possibility. As both a writer and an activist, Glave has repeatedly articulated in his works the acute sense of an inner, as well as a social, alienation that is produced by the custom and habit of constructing same-sex-desiring subjects as shameful mistakes in the Jamaican natural order. In his essay "Again, a Book of Dreams," Glave (2013a) demands that the reader recognize the psychological impact that being treated as beyond human recognition has on the queer subject: "What can be more psychically injurious than to make inescapably clear that everything about those whom the world at large considers *perverse* is simply wrong: wrong human being, wrong way of being a human (and thus not quite human), wrong way of seeing and looking, wrong way of thinking, wrong way of living, and then of course very wrong way of loving: formidably wrong" (Glave 2013, 78–79, italics in the original). The totalizing wrong of same-sex desire that Glave invokes here has a long history in Jamaica, where postemancipation concerns around dissenting bodies were mapped onto the emerging penal codes of British colonialism in the 1860s. At that transitional moment, certain acts and bodies were represented as both "wrong" and outside nature. These representations and their value-laden vocabularies were intimately tied to the colonial project's self-interest and entrenched racism of that period. However, they have continued to have juridical legitimacy and theological standing until the present day and point toward how the postindependence imagined community has also reiterated a heterocolonial model of family, nation, and citizenship.

Taking this longer view of the criminalization of same-sex acts in Jamaica brings into focus how this notion of the "wrong way of being a human" (Glave 2013, 79) is intrinsic to the historical legacy of colonialism, which relied on the control of Black bodies both through direct power and through racialized discourses of embodied inequality—a move analogous to the later tactics of homophobia. Historian Jonathan R. Dalby's (2014) research on sexual laws and outlaws in Jamaica during the nineteenth century argues that their designation was most strenuously concerned with preserving colonial power relations and with asserting the entitlements that certain bodies had to rule over others in the interests of plantation capitalism.[11] Two aspects of Dalby's historical research are relevant to my reading of Glave's literary works, which radically reassemble the representational and anatomical grammars of desiring Jamaican bodies. The first is Dalby's argument about the focus on sexual crimes committed by Black Jamaicans and the disciplining of their bodies as a means to characterize and castigate the island's majority Black population, whose reconfigured labor practices since their postemancipation flight from the plantations had threatened the social hierarchies of the White elite, as well as their economic dominance and sense of identity.

Dalby notes how the reporting of these crimes expedited public anxiety, which was primed to respond to threats of "deviant" sexuality and the associations between Blackness and sexual immorality already embedded in the discourses of colonial racism: "Newspaper reports of judges' comments on assize court calendars increasingly concerned 'unnatural' and 'nameless' offences, and a degree of moral momentum built up in 1848 and 1849. Indeed . . . the high point of the panic appears to coincide with a surge in prosecutions of sodomy and bestiality and a fall in prosecutions of rape and carnal abuse. . . . The climax came in the early summer of 1849, when the news broke about the discovery of serial sodomy in the General Penitentiary" (Dalby 2014, 148). Importantly, Dalby reads this linguistic fashioning of a sexually deviant minority as part of a wider struggle over claims to economic and social power at a key moment of historical transition. In his interpretation, this foregrounding of sexual crime "was less about sex, or crime, or law-breaking, and much more about elite anxieties over where emancipation was leading. It was linked to one of the last battles in the continuing '*war of representation*,' and marked a near-decisive victory for the planters" (Dalby 2014, 154; italics added).[12]

The second aspect of Dalby's research that can be read productively alongside Glave's imaginative evocation of a decolonized Caribbean erotic is his attention to the definition of sodomy as unnatural and beyond social inclusion. Noting the correspondence between the application of the legal codes and the amplification of certain acts as archetypes of Black criminality and barbarity, Dalby (2014) points out that "the high point for sodomy prosecutions came significantly in the late 1840s and early 1850s, when sex offence prosecutions as a whole were at their maximum, and it was homosexual deviance which became the particular focus of the scare in these years" (142). The particular wording of the standard bill of indictment for sodomy at that time enunciated the neat coalescence of legal and theological discourses that produced the heterocolonial order through which Nature was exclusively defined: "referred only to 'that most horrid, detestable and sodomitical crime (not among Christians to be named) called Buggery,' the perpetrator 'not having the fear of God before his eyes, but being moved and seduced by the instigation of the Devil, and *not regarding the order of Nature*'" (141; italics added).

This characterization of sodomy as an especially abhorrent crime continued in Jamaica's now notorious 1864 Offences Against the Person Act.[13] That no other crime in the Jamaican 1864 Act is categorized as "unnatural" is also true of the British Offences Against the Person Act (1861), but—as Joseph Gaskins (2013) identifies in his comparative account of law making around the crime identified as buggery in Jamaica, Trinidad and Tobago, and the Bahamas—this emphasis on the unnatural is a specifically Jamaican framing that maps non-heterosexuality onto sexual otherness. Gaskins (2013) argues that "utilising a discourse of morality and the 'natural,' this law has served to foster a popular culture rife with homophobia and abuses by state agents. The 'unnaturalness' of homosexuality has become an especially prolific ideological anchor for homophobic rhetoric among religious leaders, popular artists and politicians" (434). Codified as criminal within that code and designated as "detestable," "abominable," and "unnatural," buggery was linguistically marked and called out in Jamaica as the act that did most violence to the so-called natural orders instantiated by the heterocolonial worldview.

Although the way that sexual governance coordinates concerns of capital alongside those of morality may have shifted in the twentieth and twenty-first centuries to focus on sex workers and sex tourism across the Anglo-Caribbean region, Jamaica's 2010 version of the Offences Against the Person Act shows little change since 1864. The penalties for "buggery" are still "to be imprisoned and kept to hard labor for a term not exceeding ten years" (Offences Against the Person Act 2010, 26)."[14] The consistent enunciation, across more than two centuries, of a decree against male-male anal penetration has seemingly shaped a deeply embedded concept of Jamaica as a nation in which the incommensurability between sexual queerness and Jamaicanness is so solidified as a religious and moral imperative as to make its undoing difficult to anticipate.

It is against this sedimented ground of national representation, in which the history of morality remains entangled with the history of colonial violence and through which certain acts and bodies have consistently been positioned as unnatural for centuries, that Glave's extreme alternative reimaginings of Jamaica take their ethical force. I want to argue that, although rendered in somewhat magical realist terms that willfully dis-identify the heteropatriarchal state as their point of reference, Glave's submerged Jamaica can be read most productively alongside the island's deep historical consciousness of the degradation of male same-sex relations.[15] His radically crafted, but steadily reimagined, Caribbean lives challenge the historically tenacious construction of a national assemblage from which Glave and other queer Jamaicans are excepted.

"He Who Would Have Become 'Joshua,' 1791" is narrated by an African woman, who is bound and repeatedly sexually assaulted by the White slaver "ghosts" in the hold of a slave ship during the Middle Passage, and whose memories, prophecies, and visions are shared among her companions without the breaking of silence. Releasing the remarkable history of enslaved men and women who "did not sprout wings yet arose out of their rigid forms among us all and flew: *flew up out of here and out over the water and then into it*" (Glave 2007, 420; italics in the original), the narrator focuses on "the beautiful one," who is also chained in the cave. Protected at birth from drowning by his riverbank delivery, and therefore by his belonging in part to river, "the beautiful one" would spend his days at the bottom of the river "breathing that green water" (Glave 2007, 425). In an animistic world where both air and water can be breathed—where both plants and humans speak silently, and where life and death are constantly in open transition—erotic arrangements are equally supple. In an alternative creation story, the beautiful one and his beautiful male lover, "their legs caressed by slinking weeds, remained hidden beneath those waters for seven uninterrupted secret days" (420). Although not commonplace in the community's life, neither their submersion nor their erotic attachment is seen as extraordinary: "None of us, not even their parents, were especially surprised. Since the sun had first scorched its way across the earth and birds had discovered the use of their wings, it was hardly the first time such things had been known, whether with men, women, or all those somewhere in between" (432). In this fluid, rapturous world, their sense of individuality and of corporality dissolves:

> And so down there—but this part, of course, soon became obvious—they became part of one another. The laughing one, as was his destiny, breathed in, in addition to water, the one who loved him and whom he loved, losing for that time nearly all memory of who he previously had been. Pressing his mouth so tightly to the beautiful one's down there as he pressed his face everywhere else, he looked in that other face and saw, more than once, his own eyes staring directly back at him. The same happened to the one who brought him down there: in those depths, opening his eyes to look down at his own hand holding the laughing one's hand, he felt his companion's form pushing against him, holding him as the weeds swirled between their legs, lingering over their thighs, and thought, "Is that my hand, or his? Is this my arm, or his?" And believe me now when I tell you that he could not summon an answer, nor did he ever summon one, to calm his pounding heart. (Glave 2007, 433–434)

Fulfilling the narrator's terrible and prophetic vision, the beautiful ones are captured and enslaved. Against the unexceptional ecosphere of their free lives, which are replete with queer reciprocated pleasure, it is the repeated assault of forced oral sex with the ghosts on the slave ship that constitutes "the unimaginable" (Glave 2007, 426) of this tale. Resisting that violence and determined to fly, the beautiful ones refuse the totality of a world that refuses them:

> Their mouths remained steadfastly clamped shut, their eyes firmly closed, as, touching fingers whenever they could in darkness and throughout the light that edged increasingly closer to them, they began to dream of the long journey that would soon take them out over all that spreading water out there and then into it, down, deeper, farther, until, their skins soaked unto even the blood beneath as the river had wrapped them in its belly for those seven days and nights, their breath stopped. "Not again," they each thought, "not ever again. Not ever again on the tongue," they each thought, "nor in the throat, leaving that bitter heat and taste behind. Not in the mouth, nor anywhere else," they thought. (Glave 2007, 436)

The story ends with the beautiful ones' flight, "their hands joined in that clasp that could not and would not ever again be parted" (Glave 2007, 437), in a literary imagination of Tinsley's "Black Atlantic, Queer Atlantic" where "intense shipmate relationships" marked the "feeling of, feeling for the kidnapped . . . [and] asserted the sentience of the bodies that slavers attempted to transform into brute matter" (2008: 199). At the close of the story the narrator awakens as she breathes in the seawater after her captors have thrown her dead body overboard. In common with Glave's other submerged worlds, here water is "the key to flight" (422) as the literary fluid births impossible possibilities. Yet, while "He Who Would Have Become 'Joshua,' 1791" pitches the unexceptional queer desires of young men in an animistic world against the detestable and unnatural violent acts of real-world enslavement and its sexual abuses, Glave's other two submerged narratives contend with the more contemporary world of Jamaica.[16] In this context Glave's speculative creative work also intertexts with Tinsley's lyrical and theoretical rearrangement of knowledge categories in *Ezili's Mirrors* (2018) that also privileges the Black queer Atlantic as a site of erotic creativity and agency.

In both "Whose Caribbean? An Allegory, in Part" (2008b) and "Jamaican, Octopus" (2012) the flawed and discriminatory world of the Caribbean, and more particularly of Jamaica, is represented alongside, and intertwined with, renderings of fantastical "natural" worlds in a tidalectic dynamic. In the oceanic underworlds of both texts, the fundamental conceptualizations of bodies, identities, and nations are exquisitely rearranged into an alternative natural order that is released from the constraints of normative gender, sexual, and species differentiation. By establishing a distance between socialized forms of normative embodiment and imagined freedoms, Glave goes beyond a call for accommodation to existing orders and provokes us to question on what grounds, and for whose benefit, the human has been constituted within epistemologies driven by heterocolonial structures and desires. In this way, his writings connect to Mootoo's novel in their shared desire to find new ways of thinking about being.

"Whose Caribbean? An Allegory, in Part" invokes an aquamarine child of indeterminate gender and species, whose yearning for freedom from repeated exploitation and for a quiet belonging both opens and closes his account of the formation of the Jamaica Forum for Lesbians, All-Sexuals, and Gays (J-FLAG) and its vision for "a nation welcoming to all, irrespective of sexuality and perceived gender transgressions" (Glave 2008b, 180).[17] The dreamer-child's gender-, sex-, and species-defiant anatomy suggests an entirely transformed and transforming version of Caribbean queer belonging:

> The child—let us know him/her as "s/he"—possessed a slender penis of startlingly delicate green, the truest color of the sea that s/he had always loved . . . as s/he also possessed a pair of luminous blue breasts the tone of the purest skies, which, on the gentlest days, nuzzled their broad, soft chins against the sea. Nipples did not grow at the end of the child's breasts, but rather berries the inflamed color of hibiscus in its most passionate surrender to the sunsets and dawns that for millennia had washed over that place. The child also possessed a vagina and uterus, which, as was common knowledge among all who knew him/her, produced at least two or three times per year, without assistance from anyone, a race of brazen dolphins. (Glave 2008b, 177)[18]

Yet, while this Caribbean child is at once fantastically liberated from the accepted divisions of gender and intimately connected to, and generative of, his/her surrounding natural world, his/her consciousness remains saturated with images of the violent and unfree history of the region, of enslaved and physically bound Black bodies: "their wrists bound with heavy chains and thick cords on so many mornings and late afternoons on a public square's auction block" (Glave 2008b, 178). Throughout this piece, the question "Whose Caribbean?" circulates not only as an interrogation that points to the exclusion and subjection of queer bodies. In ancestral space of the ocean, that question feels sideways toward an exploration of the extended timeline of the nakedly capitalist organization of Caribbean peoples and the colonial and neocolonial appetites for desirable, but disposable, bodies:

> S/he prays not to be perceived as "other," perhaps, by those among whom s/he has long dwelt, occasionally in the realm of history-tinged dreams, while received as an exotic morsel by many of those in pursuit of sun, sex, and the two-bit, so-called third world trade long ago made a reality by marauders, and held tightly in place by those of today: the International Monetary Fund, the

World Bank, the transnational corporate behemoths, and, first and foremost as nexus of all three, the United (severely capitalist, fiercely indifferent to human and most life) States." (Glave 2008b, 179)

While the Caribbean child's wildly embodied plurality serves as an imagined configuration of possible worlds to come, if the hospitality of the mind can reach to such an invitation, this piece is also deeply committed to thinking about the possibilities for self-determination within the increasingly globalized heteropatriarchal supremacy that governs "our increasingly *de*freedomized (if we are not constantly vigilant) twenty first century lives" (Glave 2008b, 185). In this way Glave offers what Kara Keeling names "freedom dreams," after Robin D. G. Kelley, dreams "that issue from Afrofuturist imaginations . . . [and seek] to explore where they open to another world (versus where they simply make compromises with what we currently know), yet not to define those dreams and render them knowable" (2018, xiv).

Clearly, the altered state of Caribbean sexuality symbolized by the marvelous autonomy and anatomical camouflage of Glave's all-sexual child represents a world seemingly beyond belief, but the writerly tides of this piece propel questions of erotic self-determination and self-description firmly back into the real world of contemporary political struggles to make clear that being able to think differently about bodily freedoms is not an imaginative indulgence, but a national and international necessity.[19] Rousing the historically charged Caribbean waters of what it means to be fully human, Glave (2008b) reprises the delusional and damaging practice of species demarcation that has historically functioned as an assault on Black humanity, turning it inward to show the exclusion of Black queer subjects as "those people who are not even really people" (184).[20] Between the fantasy of a nonbinary erotic ecology and the reality of homophobic dehumanization, Glave delivers the altered consciousness of a radical rehumanization founded on "a dream that will shortly transform to waking" (Glave 2008b, 188).

This same intermingling of radical imaginings and the call for social transformation underscores Glave's (2012) prose meditation "Jamaican, Octopus," in which bodily limits become porous and subject to profound reorganization in a submarine Jamaica that is saturated in bodily and erotic possibilities incomprehensible to the landed nation. This extended work of queer submersion becomes paradigmatic of the speculative realism that informs all of Glave's watery narratives as they variously call into question the fullness of the reality that passes through notions such as nation and citizen. As Glave (2013) describes in the opening to his essay "This Jamaican Family: The Word, and Dreams," from his collection *Among the Bloodpeople*, the conceptualization of a heteropatriarchal nation creates a powerful sense of consensus that depends on exclusion:

Whether or not you accept it, you finally understand that this is the message, delivered by them in shouting silences and stiffened backs whenever you summon the bravery to refer, even obliquely, to *that*: the simple message that *that*, as far as they're concerned, doesn't exist in this family; that, as true, proud Jamaicans still unmoved by North American and European "foreign" values, they will never reflect on the profundities or who you are in relation to *that*; and that by now, you should already have developed the good sense—good taste—to speak with them about other things, about anything other than *that*. (Glave 2013, 21; italics in the original)

"Jamaican, Octopus" puts extreme pressure on our imagining of the Caribbean world, specifically Jamaica, by shaping a radical departure in terms of a politics of the flesh. In a national context where to be queer is to be excluded from the category of human on account of the historical inscription of same-sex erotics as antithetical to human nature, the grounds for a transformed and appreciative conceptualization of fluid and multiple sexualities cannot easily be identified. The creative exertion of Glave's narrative is to imagine beyond the current reality. "Jamaican, Octopus"—still responding to the question "Whose Caribbean?"—crafts a world of aquatic belonging for queer subjects based on an alternative understanding of seemingly impossible possibilities. In his rendering of this submerged and speculative Jamaica, Glave establishes his narrator's inclusion and proximity to the nation through vernacular gestures of co-belonging, "back deh so inna Jamaica, right deh so" (Glave 2012, 371). These form part of his broader creative tactic of refusing, in the most fundamental terms, the separations of the natural and unnatural that have been mobilized to underpin Jamaican homophobia and maintain the thresholds between included and excluded bodies.

More explicitly interested in the potential of creative and imaginative writing to contest established, "naturalized," ideas of the human, this work asks readers to recognize that, while national identities may act to structure and to discipline unruly dimensions of erotic being and experience in ways that come to appear natural, there are other possible configurations of sexual subjectivity: "And so perhaps it can indeed be possible for a writer of fiction who has tried his very best to live *and survive* in octopus skin-survive if only for a few minutes, even-to write, and imagine, such unthinkable, unspeakable words. Unspeakable words and realities that I first witnessed under the sea, but also heard presented directly to me over the years, in Jamaica and elsewhere, out of the mouths of more-or-less men" (Glave 2012, 373; italics in the original). Rather than directly contesting the homophobia embedded in the idea of Jamaicanness and the commonly articulated refusal to believe in the integrity of same-sex desire and pleasure as a model for sexual citizenship, Glave (2012) offers a radical reimagining of the excluded experience of queer desire, which has been positioned as stranger to the Jamaican nation. In his underwater counterworld of "free" and "jubilant" (371) reciprocated desire, which is both creatively distant from and critically proximate to the real Jamaica, this work narrates the task of finding a language and a body in which the "intimate and tacit understanding" (368) of queer desires, feelings, encounters, and pleasures can be made knowable, if not fully available to epistemic stability.

In effect, this piece issues an ontological challenge to the heteropatriarchal claim on the real world of Jamaica by imaginatively undoing that world as it is "naturally" known: "Who, given so much of what we have heard about Jamaica's fury in recent decades," asks the narrator: "would ever have imagined that not only octopuses could dart and jet and jettison their arms among the corals, but that more-or-less men, sometimes drowned and sometimes not, could delight in the actuality of their pussies even as they exulted and somersaulted with a brethren's automatized penis in their celebrating hands?" (Glave 2012, 372). Claiming that, as a consequence of his "brief sojourn into the depths of octopuses and rays, cuttlefish and blueheads, [his] life had forever altered" (370), the narrator's life story as an octopus proceeds from an ecology that evokes both an almost precolonial planetary co-belonging and an ancestral re-belonging in the historically unforgettable "Sea of We"—the final resting place of so many African bodies drowned on the Middle Passage. Liberated from the historical burdens of colonial and national identity categories that exploited raced, gendered, and sexed bodies, Glave's submerged worlding represents both individual freedom and collective belonging in a state of open mutuality and compatibility: "I would tell everyone how at last, down there, as I drowned and drowned again, I could see that we were free, at last free, I mean really *free*. I could see as the young boy I was that, in the Sea of We, the 'we' was, in part, a group of men assembled at the place to which the elderly gentleman, under the sea, directly took me" (371). Despite the mention of the octopus as a creature that needs to be able to survive in a hostile environment, and the marvelous anatomical corollary of the male octopus's third arm from his right eye, which is reserved for sex, this piece—like "Whose Caribbean?"—is also only allegory in part. Indeed, as the opening statement declares, the memoir explores "the idea, or rather reality, of myself as an octopus" (368). Glave releases Jamaican queer subjectivity, and by implication human subjectivity, from the requirement to represent itself within what have come to be accepted as normative discourses and equivalences. Readers are asked to imagine encounters both as and with embodied beings outside the anthropocene; to imagine what bodies and identities might feel like within a sensual planetary ecology in which social ascriptions-from gender and sexual norms through to species thresholds-are brought into crisis. The piece is textured by eruptions of the erotic and the fantastic-of drowning and of living under the sea, of drinking whole tubs of bathwater, of "more-or-less men who, so freely, performed those acrobatics beneath the waves, and so gently, yet firmly, assuredly, detached each other's penis for the onward journey" (373). As Amia Srinivasan observes "the octopus threatens boundaries" (2017, n.p.), and one way of approaching this work is to understand it as a disturbance of the thresholds that determine the natural and the unnatural, the inside and outside, and the difference between embodied experiences and ideas of corporeality produced by historical discourses and disciplined by the social imperatives of heterocolonial history.

In its radical undoing of how the familiar and the strange are mapped onto bodies, the current of Glave's nonrealist writing tugs at a forceful reconsideration of the cultural and psychic impact caused by the normalization of hetero-reproductive Foucauldian technologies of the self. As an octopus, whose "very strangeness makes [them] hard to study (Srinivasan 2019, n.p.), the ability to detach and discard limbs is an unremarkable reality that flows here into that of "more-or-less men" (Glave 2012, 371) whose detachable and translatable sexual organs reimagine bodies that are freely in transition—bodies that cannot be explained by biological deterministic positivist knowledge. The emancipatory impact of such a reimagining for queer subjects is clear: "For if *they*, cavorting and somersaulting, leaping and balancing, could have a pussy, then I knew I could as well" (372; italics in the original). Importantly though, "Jamaican, Octopus" does not present itself as fantastical in the sense of being unrelated to the real. Rather, Glave asserts an ontological defiance to the epistemic violence and dominance of the global north that underpinned colonial constructions of reality: "I do not, and will not ever, write anything in a book that is not grounded in and proven by hard, incontrovertible fact: the sort of concrete 'truths' without which the West, for example, cannot long survive, or at least continue envisioning itself as 'the West'" (Glave 2012, 373). In this respect, Glave's fantastical writing is an act of translation from the unthinkable to the thinkable that transforms possibilities for recognizing legitimate historical subjects. Its speculative character chimes with the queer Caribbean futurism of Nalo Hopkinson's writing, which Hopkinson has stated "starts from the principle of making the impossible possible" (Nelson 2002, 98). Its presentation of Black queer survival as a submerged reality also compellingly echoes Tinsley's realization of queer being, in her encounter with Sharon Bridgforth's *Dat Black Mermaid Man Lady*: "Finally *this* is how you learn to breathe underwater when you're black and queer. (Sing). You let yourself fall under the sea, tonbe dan lanme; and there you look at the Black Mermaid man lady with fishes and fishes and pearls and flowing down behind and realize that you *are* himher, you are that safe coral castle at the bottom of the ocean floor where you can take in what you need" (2018, 166, italics in the original).

Collectively, these submerged speculative writings vividly shift the expected thresholds of ontological experience beyond what might be seen as normal human variation and toward seemingly unrecognizable and inassimilable difference so as properly to agitate understandings of gendered and sexed embodiment naturalized within the social imperatives of anthropocentric heteropatriarchy. Rather than making space for the accommodation of different sexual subjectivities, Glave's work renders a submerged paradigm of experience where bodies are released from all accepted reasoning around the configurations of sexual encounters and claims to sexual citizenship. In this way, his work draws on the imaginative potential of speculative fiction to reengage and reframe discourses of the normal and natural as they relate to sexual desires and behaviors, and to bring the classifications used to do the work of social normalization into clearer view precisely by propelling them into crisis.[21] Again, this insistence on an imagination beyond the familiar, translatable, and acceptable idea of erotic embodiment chimes not only with Mootoo's novel but also with Lorde's sense of the seemingly impossible already-possible of excluded subjects (for her women) connecting to each other outside and beyond the heteropatriachal frameworks that seek to define them. Lorde's promise of the transformation such a shift can deliver is relevant to both Mootoo's and Glave's reimagining of erotic relations: "Within the interdependence of mutual (nondominant) difference lies that security which enables us to descend into chaos of knowledge and return with true visions of our future, along with the concomitant power to effect those changes which can bring that future into being" (Lorde 1984a, 112).

In the oceanic underworlds of Glave's imaginative texts, the fundamental conceptualizations of bodies, identities, and nations are exquisitely rearranged within an alternative natural order released from the constraints of normative gender, sexual, and species differentiation. Yet, by establishing distance between socialized forms of normative embodiment and imagined freedoms, Glave goes beyond a call for accommodation to existing orders and provokes us to question on what grounds and for whose benefit the human has been constituted within epistemologies driven by colonial and neocolonial desires. By streaming realist and fantastical worlds alongside each other in incrementally explicit ways, to "ask how to make a workable present out of a painful past" (Tinsley 2018, 166), these submerged imaginings construct a powerful narrative crosscurrent that both challenges homophobia and questions heteropatriarchy. They craft a fluid world of seemingly impossible possibilities, which reveal an erotic ecology that, in Audre Lorde's (1984b) words, acts as a "well of replenishing and provocative force" (54).

In this composite queer ecology of submarine and sideways realities, it is no coincidence that Glave calls upon Kamau Brathwaite's invocation of Caribbeanness—"The unity is submarine" (Brathwaite 1974, 64)—as his epigraph to "Jamaican, Octopus." In this work, the oceanic is a regionally specific medium the promise of which undoes the historically entrenched "ideoscape" of Anglo-Caribbean/Jamaican heteronormative nationalism to imagine fluid relational possibilities, extreme anatomical plasticity, and an expansive and permeable network of co-creative human and nonhuman bodies. By asking us to imagine surprising bodies that break free from normative modes of sexual identity, these works also feel sideways toward the circumstances under which such expansive possibilities of being might arise. In the case of Jamaican same-sex desire and erotic practices, the distance between the thrilling effusion of bodily possibilities and the suffocating imposition of social impossibilities urgently needs to be reimagined and contested. Speculative writing here is restorative of real human possibility, and especially valuable when we consider that the 1864 laws—still defended in Jamaica as a means of preserving moral and spiritual good—were an explicitly colonial act of legislation, designed for capitalist gain from reproductive bodies, which could not be liberated to know themselves as meaningful outside of heteronationalism.

Conclusion

Both Glave's (2012) "Jamaican, Octopus" and Mootoo's (2014) *Moving Forward Sideways* create literary worlds constituted by acts of feeling sideways, where disorientations of the real provoke moments of rearrangement in which the terms of the imagination expand and the impossible and possible are no longer so clearly mapped. By challenging the reader to re-examine the construction of the "wrong human being, wrong way of being a human (and thus not quite human)" (Glave 2013, 78), both writers engage the pressing task of rethinking the value of erotic being outside of the current frame of citizenship. In line with the feminist political labor of Audre Lorde's (1984b) essay "Uses of Erotic: The Erotic as Power," these works call for a searching consideration of possibilities for erotic living that can be imagined beyond the invented, imposed terms of sexual identities:

> When we live outside ourselves, and by that I mean on external directives only rather than from our internal knowledge and needs, when we live away from those erotic guides from within ourselves, then our lives are limited by external and alien forms, and we conform to the needs of a structure that is not based on human need, let alone an individual's. But when we begin to live from within outward, in touch with the power of the erotic within ourselves, and allowing that power to inform and illuminate our actions upon the world around us, then we begin to be responsible to ourselves in the deepest sense. For as we begin to recognize our deepest feelings, we begin to give up, of

necessity, being satisfied with suffering and self-negation, and with the numbness which so often seems like their only alternative in our society. (Lorde 1984b, 58)

In this way, these works, like Lorde, "gesture towards a renewed expansiveness for eros as epistemology," as advocated by Lyndon Gill (2018a) in his inspiring work *Erotic Islands: Art & Activism in the Queer Caribbean* (198).

In a creative vision of postgender, postspecies Jamaican unity that rewrites the idea of home, Glave queers the lens of belonging. In his "blue place of dreams and imagining," the natural diversity of being can be awash without restraints, allowing an agency "to work, move, even swim, sentence by sentence, toward a language that might in some way capture, represent, even directly (or at least figuratively) illustrate, the ways and hows of becoming the varying and occasionally connected whos whom I wish (and sometimes, depending on the day and environment, do not wish) to be" (Glave 2012, 369, 368). In this way, Glave's radically speculative writings, like Mootoo's paralleled and digressive acts of narration, offer a creative and fresh imagining of Caribbean queer belonging that eschews the domestication and social accommodation of so-called sexual minorities in favor of a transformative ecology in which bodies are liberated from the historically entrenched reproductive and capitalist demands that have limited their possibilities.

Conclusion

●●●●●●●●●●●●●●●●●●●●●

> Queerness is not yet here. Queerness is
> an ideality. Put another way, we are not
> yet queer. We may never touch queer-
> ness, but we can feel it as the warm
> illumination of a horizon imbued with
> potentiality.
> —José Esteban Muñoz, *Cruising Utopia:*
> *The Then and There of Queer Futurity*

Highlighting the conceptual kinship between creolized Caribbeanness and queerness allows us to extend the established idea of Caribbeanness as newness, liquidity, and differently known differences to understandings of sexuality as expressed and lived in the region. The works that I have discussed throughout this book collectively build a literacy of creolized sexualities in their erotic mul-tiplicity and capture the constant creative undoing of normalizing categories and social restraints. By representing intricately queer and entangled lives these diverse literary works extend the portrayal of what it means to live and to love in the Caribbean, importantly including an expansion of heterosexuality and a challenge to both conforming and dissident masculinities. They bring into view creolized sexualities that may be no less transformative for being quiet rather than noisy, turbulent rather than resolved, anticipatory rather than com-plete, and marked by social density rather than surface outness. In this way, they make space in our thinking for a Caribbean erotics that can carry yearn-ings for the project of living together and living for the future deeply entan-gled with what it means to live in societies scarred by colonialism, its legacies, and its late-capitalistic avatars.

Drawing attention to inclusive and pluralizing representations of sexual possibilities within the Caribbean literary imagination in English not only allows for a reconsideration of the anomalous binarism that seeks to organize sexual identities in official discourses of the Anglophone region, but also engages with locally expressed erotic lives. Mootoo's (2008b) *Valmiki's Daughter* brings what is already known about the region's cultural plurality into orbit with what was, until very recently, denied within official governmental and religious statutes, by describing a wide spectrum of sexual tendencies in terms of the provisional prismatics of creolized being. Like Forbes's (2008) *A Permanent Freedom*, it reveals how heteronormativity functions as an invented social description whose specified and narrow norms consistently fail to correspond with more complicated and varied lived attachments and attractions. These works enact a gentle, but permanent, subversion of the ideas of heterosexuality, marriage, and the normative. The pressure on categorical identities is also the substance of Andrew Salkey's ([1960] 2009) novel *Escape to an Autumn Pavement*, with its uncompromising insistence on resisting the necessity of sexual essentialization and erotic normalization. In his rendering of a diasporic creolized queer sensibility, Salkey crafts an anticipatory belonging that highlights the inadequacy of discourses around sexual accommodation, such as those emerging in Britain in the late 1950s.

Although importantly diverse constructions of the Caribbean masculine identities of husband, father, and lover come to the fore in all the works discussed, the insubstantiality and performativity of what is avowed as "Caribbean masculinity" is most acutely observed in the overlaps between hypermasculinity and queerness in Marlon James's (2014) *A Brief History of Seven Killings* and Junot Díaz's (2007) *The Brief Wondrous Life of Oscar Wao*. In both of these epic novels, the scale of literary world building is proportional to the striking and extreme recital necessary to uphold the precarious fiction of hardcore masculinity. In their overlapping of queer longings and homophobia these novels bring to light a contradictory Caribbean masculinity in crisis whose outward expressions of domination and violence mask tender queer longings and lives.

The narratives by Mootoo and Glave, with which I conclude, share a frustration over how bodies are given meaning and look to reimagine possibilities for being that move beyond the paradigms of heterocolonial gender and sexual binarisms, which are so demonstrably constrained and compromised in the identities they promote, sanction, and imagine. By moving sideways, away from claiming a wholeness within the terms that would guarantee citizenship, these works emphasize the capacity, and even the obligation, of the imagination to entertain multiple possibilities—including seemingly impossible ones—in order to reconceptualize subjectivities that are humane in their fluid, dynamic, and incomplete nature.

The arousals and rearrangements of being that I have illustrated within the creolized Caribbean queer literary imagination throughout this book, work toward a more thorough and radical rethinking around the nature of erotic attachments, desires, and relations. Their evocation of impossible possibilities profoundly challenges the inculcated assumption that that which is familiar as the norm is the only likely version of how a life can unfold. By lyrically loosening the hinge between representations and rights—such that the realism of heteropatriarchy's claims and their injurious effects are backgrounded against acts of imagination that endorse other ways to be (to feel, to know, to live, to fuck, to be safe, to connect, to marry, to parent, to love)—these works also dismantle the impossibility of belonging for queer subjects. At the same time, they create new versions of queer belonging and of speculative rights that necessarily exceed, and undo, the limits of being queer under state-centric forms of citizenship.

While this book is keenly committed to reading the undoing of heteronormativity in Caribbean literary works and worlds that may not directly relate to the struggle for LGBTQI rights, my argument for the visibility of creolized sexualities consciously expands the possibilities for understanding and articulating sensitive and often embattled questions around erotic desires, possibilities, and entitlements in the social world beyond the novels.

When we accept that the Caribbean is a queer place, we clear ground from which to contest the assertions of heteronormativity underpinning the longstanding homophobia that appears in the region and, importantly, the limited conceptualizations of sexual attachments, behaviors, and identities that form part of the refusal to embrace, acknowledge, and celebrate erotic diversity. Both the long-time supple imaginings of Caribbean writers around issues of belonging and the ongoing displacements of sexually diverse subjects in the region suggest that such thinking remains significant. Indeed, although it has not been my focus here, the link between redescribing Caribbeanness in its innately inclusive expressions and rights-based activism beyond the page is an important and energizing one across the Anglophone region.

I want to conclude by mentioning the work of the Colin Robinson, which offers an inspiring example of how a committed responsibility to imagine fuller Caribbean lives can bridge the crafting of literary and wider cultural worlds. Robinson was the cofounder of CAISO (Coalition Advocating for Inclusion of Sexual Orientation), one of Trinidad's widely recognized umbrella LGBT/human rights advocacy groups. In his capacity as a community activist and organizer, Robinson had "long done policy-related writing and editing," yet he insisted "that what may be seen as business and professional writing is indeed creative work" (Robinson 2020, n.p.). Rooting the possibilities of social change in a transformed understanding and perception of the lived world of human relations, under Robinson's leadership, CAISO advocated for a deep, local engagement with the structures of social power and cohesion, insisting on (as its motto states) "making sexual and gender diversity part of T&T's national identity" (https://www.queensu.ca/snid/caiso-caiso-negotiating-sex-rights-and -nationalism-trinidad-and-tobago). Robinson's position was consistently to argue that genuine co-belonging is not a legal right but a cultural commitment based on an ethic of mutual care and respect that underpins, rather than sequesters, an agenda around sexual inclusion. Indeed, reflecting on CAISO's accomplishments, Robinson was clear that their "most important achievement is that our discursive work has been key to changing how sex and gender diversity in TT [Trinidad and Tobago] are *imagined*" (Robinson 2020, italics added).

Robinson's emphasis as an activist on the reimagining of lives that are dynamic, locally grounded, interconnected, and multiply resistant to the heterocolonial order connects to the creolized sensibilities of the literary imaginations that I have explored in this book and also emerges powerfully in his own imaginative writings. A collection of Robinson's poems, *You Have You Father Hard Head* published by Peepal Tree in 2016, gathers together poems that had been published or broadcast individually over twenty-five years. Although the poems travel across the region and into the diaspora in an arc that maps Robinson's own life journeys and also range significantly in tone, register, and form—from a celebration of erotic connection and pleasure, and acts of remembrance for the dying and dead, to a meditation on the lifelong shadow cast by his father leaving when he was just five—there is a strong common thread in their rendering of a distinctively Caribbean queer life. In common with many of the works already discussed in this volume, Robinson's works seek to apprehend rather than comprehend Caribbean queer desires and lives and to pay poetic attention to their intimations, their affective density, their possibilities. If this volume shows Robinson's investment in the power of the imagination and of poetry to render the miraculous texture of intimacy, of arousal, and of pleasure, then it also shows how matching the linguistic enchantment of the writer to the political imagination of an activist transpires only by eschewing the possible equivalence of any single word and conjuring the often inexplicable, invisible, intangible actuality of interior life. Following his own advice that "one must be open to a little / unravelling" (Robinson 2016, 16), Robinson's poems are often acts of undoing and of unknowing that invoke states of the possible as fertile and legitimate sites of queer becoming. Wary of the self-realization associated with coming out, in "Signifying in the Knees (for Joel)" the persona laments the penalty of a categorical identity and its negative capacity for meaningful self-determination, associated elsewhere throughout this volume with noticing, experiencing, and describing the world in its multifaceted, shifting, nuanced tones:

i had lost the magic of
signification the linear
language of being
out wrecked destruction on my
imagination" (19)

Here, the line break between *being* and *out* signals how "outness" is far from the guarantee of an acknowledged completeness, acting rather as a conforming identity that denies the fullness of a desiring self—both latent and realized in oblique, surreptitious desires: "the roar of secrets" (19).

In some senses the emphasis on being over identity, suggested in the above statement, is connected to the necessarily tentative gestures of desire for queer Caribbean subjects, as in "Riding Boundaries (for Larry)," with "the reflection of my own / desire imagining / we sniff each other secretly / i dropping innuendo carefully straining / to hear suggestion between your sentences" (66). In another way, it expresses how desire is most fully itself when it defies explanation in the positivist world, as in "Gardening for 18 Years (for Patrick)":

has anyone ever been in love with you this long
kept desire alive singlehandedly
beyond all reason   all yield   all futures (64)

Yet against his dread of a spoiled creativity, Robinson's poetry clearly embraces the exhilarating task of reimagining and rewriting the Caribbean through the lens of creolized queer desire. Mining an imagined possible that sits aside, if also askew, the declared real, appears deftly in "We did not Follow the Hummingbirds (for Tracy Robinson)," which recounts time spent in Jamaica. Upturning the now infamous naming of Jamaica as the most homophobic place on Earth, the poem voices the personal consequences of this island's declared intolerance: "i have always been unreciprocally in love with Jamaica" while also rendering an alternate queer Jamaica that defies its official description in "the unfolding magic of this passionate place / my human rights friend once called / the gayest place he'd ever been" (41). In "Connel, Morning," the poet persona channels the queer promise of Port of Spain "before it opens / to retrieve a lost belonging," (49) rereading the familiar, unremarkable, unyielding city as home. As this attachment and grounding are affirmed, the poem circles back to the early moment of this same day that made this homecoming possible: "I rose this morning to the stroke of / a trinidadian" and the imagined possibility of a queer creolized urban life that "strums hope and meaning into these streets" (50).

Both in his role as CAISO's "director of imagination" and in his poetry, Robinson emphasized the effectiveness and necessity of the imagination to the work of social transformation, mirroring the pathway so brilliantly illuminated by Audre Lorde: "poetry is not a luxury. It is a vital necessity of our existence. It forms the quality of the light within which we predicate our hopes and dreams toward survival and change, first made into language, then into idea, then into more tangible action" (Lorde 1984c, 37). Robinson's poetry and activism bridge the holistic project by both advocating for a better reality and imagining different terms on which that reality may be acknowledged and lived. As with all the literary works discussed in this book, in recognizing the creolized Caribbean as inherently queer we also recognize its advanced (rather than belated) status as a place in which the intersecting permeabilities and multidimensionalities—of ethnicity, gender, class, and sexuality—create an exemplary creolized ecology of fluid possibilities and illuminate the prospect of a non-heteronormalizing future.

Acknowledgments

I want to begin by acknowledging that my thinking on creolized sexualities has developed through the opportunities that I have had to work with other scholars and activists in the Caribbean and the diaspora over the last decade. Significant support for the research informing this book was also provided by the British Academy and the Arts and Humanities Research Council (AHRC). In 2010 the British Academy funded a small yet significant collaborative project, Breaking Sexual Silences, with Professor Evelyn O'Callaghan at the University of the West Indies in Barbados. For our final, packed out public event, we were able to listen and learn from Thomas Glave, Oonya Kempadoo, Pat Saunders, and Faith Smith. In 2013, I was in Trinidad as part of two amazing collaborations between the Institute for Gender and Development Studies (IGDS), the Caribbean International Resource Network, and the activist group Coalition Advocating for Inclusion of Sexual Orientation (CAISO). The first was a critical sexualities short course at IGDS chaired by Rosamond King and Angelique Nixon, with Colin Robinson of CAISO, John Campbell of St. Augustine, and myself as tutors. The second, funded and facilitated by my AHRC fellowship, was "Sexualities in the Tent," two days of gatherings among academics, students, activists, and the public, where we shared literature, music, debate, and strategy. I thank Angelique, Colin, Rosamond, Krystal Ghisyawan, Gabrielle Hosein, Sharon Mottley, Jason Jones, Beverly Bain, Rachael Espinet, and Vidya Kissoon for their intellectual and individual flair that made these events, culminating in a wall mural and disco at the then Bohemia, instructive, pleasurable, and memorable in equal parts. In November 2013, I held a workshop at the University of Reading where Bernadine Evaristo, Lawrence Scott, Denise deCaires Narain, Wendy Knepper, Kate Houlden, and Keon West shared their work and ideas addressing Caribbean sexualities. In December 2013, in collaboration with Annecka Marshall and IGDS at Mona,

Jamaica, I coordinated a workshop, "Embracing Jamaican Sexualities", that focused on bringing together different activist, creative, and intellectual perspectives, with contributions from J-FLAG, Pride in Action, Caribbean Dawn, and SO((U))L, and the first screening of "The Abominable Crime" alongside a striking performance of "Who am I? Man? Let's talk . . ." by Umoja. These connections with Caribbean colleagues and cultures have been a vital part of my work and also my world. The overlap of intellectual challenge and a shared commitment to new conversations means that many of these exchanges are happily imprinted, even today.

I have also been lucky enough to be invited to share parts of this project over many years at NYU, Miami, Brunel, Pittsburgh, Mona, Cave Hill, Cambridge, Durham, and Birkbeck, and at CSA in Grenada and ACLALS in St. Lucia. It is important to say how much the thinking behind this book has grown from being part of an expansive community of critical thought. In addition to those already mentioned, I am grateful to my exchanges with Ronald Cummings, Curdella Forbes, Thomas Glave, Jack Halberstam, Lyndon Gill, Taitu Heron, Ifeona Fulani, Antonia MacDonald, Patricia Mohammed, Kei Miller, Rachael Minott, Agostinho Pinnock, Sheila Rampersad, Kim Robinson, and Faith Smith, which have also helped to shape my thinking. Indeed, whatever is good about this book has been energized and inspired by working with a community of scholars and activists reimagining and redescribing Caribbean sexuality studies.

I moved from the University of Reading to the University of East Anglia (UEA) during the writing of this book and wish to acknowledge my colleagues at both institutions. Jonathan Bell, Julie Farwell, Sophie Heywood, Nicole King, Daniella La Penna, Ronan McDonald, Andrew Mangham, Mary Morrissey, Andrew Nash, David Sutton, Julia Waters, and Nicola Wilson—thank you for being my fabulous colleague companions at Reading. At UEA Katy Cubitt, Katie Cooper, Claire Hynes, Claire Jowitt, Tessa McWatt, Anshuman Mondal, Jeremy Noel-Todd, Rachel Potter, Jos Smith, Rebecca Stott, Henry Sutton, and Nonia Williams have made my work and life in Norwich richer and happier. I am immensely grateful to the brilliant Keja Valens, who gave me extraordinarily smart and generous transatlantic feedback on this book and whose challenge and confidence in this work has been a continual inspiration. I owe special gratitude to Marta Fernández Campa, who made the move from Reading to UEA with me and whose illuminating and interdisciplinary insights have been particularly enriching. Senica Maltese's attention to this manuscript was meticulous and crucial in keeping my sentences to a vaguely reasonable length—thank you! To the series editors and manuscript reviewers who took considerable time to offer engaged and incisive pointers, thank you for making this work much stronger and clearer. Special thanks are due to both

Kimberly Guinta, my editor at Rutgers UP, and Yolanda Martinez-San Miguel, for being exacting and encouraging in equal measure.

I want to give thanks for my PhD students during this time who have been among my finest teachers: Nicola Abram, Mags Chalcroft-Islam, Ashley Hickson-Lovence, Amorella Lamount, Ayanna Gillian Lloyd, Jen McDerra, Zakiya McKenzie, Lotti Mealing, Nalini Mohabir, Milena Rodella, Rebecca Romdhani, Ayan Salaad, Surya Simon, and Andrea Stuart. Traveling the dissertation journey with you has kept my thinking alive and my intellectual horizons wide. I so admire the wonderful work you have done.

I wrote this book and worried terribly about not writing this book through my most difficult times, including the monumental loss of my sister and my mother. The openness, warmth, and hospitality of fellow academics, whom I now count as precious friends, helped to sustain me. Loving gratitude is due to Bashir Abu-Manneh, Jon Bell, Susan Breau, Michael Bucknor, Thomas Glave, Denise deCaires Narain, Nicole King, Bénédicte Ledent, Andrew Nash, Susheila Nasta, Evelyn O'Callaghan, Emily Taylor, Keja Valens, Tessa McWatt, and Julia Waters. Having such respected and treasured interlocutors, comrades, and friends has enriched not just my work but my life.

For Jem, to whom I am almost afraid to count my debts, another heartfelt thank you for scanning and copying, feeding and fetching teenagers, late night tea and hot water bottles, early morning lifts to the airport, and, especially, for caring for my mother with such gentleness. None of this would have been possible without your indefatigable love and support for us all. This book is dedicated to the absolute blessings in my life: my sons, Max and Asher, and my nephews, Charlie and George.

Notes

Introduction

1   As Valens (2016) explains, "The heterocolonial order enforces an interlocking series of divisions and connections between civilized and savage, white and black, man and woman, chaste and perverse, normal and abnormal, among other things, which derive from the combination of the norms of heterosexuality and the principles and practices of colonialism and subject the Caribbean to their (often contradictory and destructive) orders even as they create the Caribbean and its subjects as we know them" (66–67).

2   The International Resource Network's web project Theorizing Homophobias in the Caribbean: Complexities of Place, Desire, and Belonging, which was launched in 2012 and edited by Rosamond King, Angelique V. Nixon, Colin Robinson, Natalie Bennett, and Vidyaratha Kissoon, is a highly nuanced multimedia collection of activist reports, interviews, film, creative writing, visual/performance art, and critical essays that establishes localized understandings around sexual possibilities and their limits. The project was driven by the need to foster more complex understandings of the Caribbean as a place, and to demonstrate the breadth of issues and concerns already in conversation throughout the region: "Our use of the term 'homophobias' insists upon local understandings and contexts while expanding awareness of the differences and similarities across the region and its diaspora" (King and Nixon 2012, n.p.).

3   Lugones (2007) brings the work of Anibal Quijano on the coloniality of power into dialogue with the work of feminists of color, substantially the work of Oyèrónkẹ́ Oyewùmí and Paula Gunn Allen on Yoruba and Native American cultures, respectively, in order to develop her theory of how heterosexualism operates as co-constitutive with colonialism to determine the nature of exploitative structures. She argues, "*Coloniality* does not just refer to racial classification. It is an encompassing phenomenon, since it is one of the axes of the system of power and as such it permeates all control of sexual access, collective authority, labor, subjectivity/intersubjectivity and the production of knowledge from within these intersubjective relations. Or, alternatively, all

control over sex, subjectivity, authority, and labor are articulated around it" (Lugones 2007, 191).

4 For details of the historical and changing contemporary situation, see the blogsite of the Caribbean International Resource Network: https://caribbeanirn.blogspot .com. "The *Caribbean IRN* is a network that connects activists, scholars, artists, and other individuals and organizations who do research and work on issues related to diverse genders and sexualities in the Caribbean" and their website archive (https://ufdc.ufl.edu/icirn, hosted by the Digital Library of the Caribbean) is a comprehensive collection of relevant documentation.

5 This study focuses on literary and critical works in English and describes how works from this region, often characterized as more homophobic and sexually conservative, can be read within the paradigms of fluid/trans/opaque sexualities that have also emerged from studies of the Hispanophone, Lusophone, and Francophone regions. It is therefore also in dialogue with works that foreground the shared queerness across the wider region, including Maja Horn (2014, 2018), Martinez-San Miguel (2014), Murray (2002), Tinsley (2010), and Wekker (1999, 2006, 2008).

6 A police raid occurred at the Stonewall Inn in Greenwich Village, New York City, in the early hours of 28 June 1969. The uprising by LGBTQI members of the community is considered to mark a turning point in the gay liberation movement in the U.S. and global north.

7 This same term is used in Ireland as in Brendan Behans's 1954 play *The Quare Fella.*

8 The *créolistes* are a group of Martinican writers who founded the *Créolité* literary movement in the 1980s in promote the distinctive creolized properties of (Francophone) Caribbean cultures and languages. Their manifesto text, *Eloge de la créolité (In Praise of Creoleness),* was published in 1993 by Patrick Chamoiseau, Jean Bernabé, and Raphaël Confiant.

9 For work that takes a pan-Caribbean perspective to explore sexual identities across linguistic boundaries see Rosamond King (2014) and Yolanda Martínez-San Miguel (2014).

Chapter 1   The Queer Creolized Caribbean

1 In the seventh chapter of her book, Puri (2004) reads works by the Indian Trinidadian writer Ramabai Espinet and singer Drupatee Ramgoonai to elaborate a dougla poetics that offers "a symbolic *resource* in the reconfiguration of racial and gendered identities" (221).

2 This essay forms part of a book discussion for Yarimar Bonilla's (2015) *Nonsovereign Futures: French Caribbean Politics in the Wake of Disenchantment.* See Beckett (2017).

3 As Wynter (1970) moves through nineteenth century sources to map the further European incorporations of the doctor-play, including excerpts from Shakespeare, she pauses to explain: "In the nineteenth century 'acculturation' between African cultural patterns and European civilization came to a peak" (39). Speaking of Jonkonnu dances in the postemancipation period, she explains that these "ceased to exist in the creolized form and became the preserve of the peasant. The dancers of Lacovia whom Beckwith saw, who leapt and danced, retained the dance in it [*sic*] original form even though they may have forgotten its true meaning" (Wynter 1970, 42).

4 Born in Montserrat in 1939, Markham lived mainly in Britain from 1956 but resided in Northern Ireland while poet-in-residence at the local university in the late 1980s.

5 Glissant (1989) similarly focuses on Trinidad as a locus of intrinsic and embedded "accepted difference" in *Caribbean Discourse*: "From now on true that if Trinidad and Quebec did not exist as accepted components of Diversity, something would be missing from the body of world culture—that today we would feel that loss" (98).

6 His reading of Oliver Cromwell's letters is followed by a confrontation with the English Historian Samuel Rawson Gardiner's denial of Cromwell's figures of Irish transportation. Moreover, J. Williams (1932) openly cites sources in which his core findings are put under suspicion: "Robert Dunlop, in his Preface to *Ireland under the Commonwealth*, tells us . . . At the time I was of the opinion that the view taken by Prendergast in his well-known book—The Cromwellian Settlement of Ireland—was not an entirely impartial one" (21).

7 Williams' disciplinary methods of historical inquiry are remodeled by the Caribbean space such that he partly responds to, and partly explains the impossibility of responding to, Brathwaite's (1975) call for histories of creolization: "Caribbean culture can be seen in terms of a dialectic of development taking place within a seamless guise or continuum of space and time; a model which allows for blood flow, fluctuations, the half-look, the look both/several ways; which allows for and contains the ambiguous, and rounds the sharp edges off the dichotomy. What we need now are specific histories of the process" (6).

8 For more information on the media's reaction to this statement, see Fallon (2011).

9 See Achebe (1997), Brennan (1989), Said (2001), and Said (1986).

10 The name *Side*, is a synonym for *athwart*, being a corruption of *Sayed* (like, of course, Edward Said's last name).

11 In his earlier autobiographically informed novel, *The Enigma of Arrival*, Naipaul (1987) dwells on his distant proximity to his English landlord, a queer figure whom he never actually meets but to whom he feels himself connected by the historical geography of Empire: "I was his opposite in every way, social, artistic, sexual. And considering that his family's fortune had grown . . . with the spread of the empire in the nineteenth century, it might be said that an empire lay between us. This empire at the same time linked us. This empire explained my birth in the New World, the language I used . . . [it] explained my presence there in the valley" (174). However, a more particular resonance between queer subjects robbed of a comfortable, unconscious sense of belonging to their space of living—even if they have never left home—and those dispossessed by Empire surfaces later when the narrator states, "I felt an immense sympathy for my landlord, who, starting at the other end of the world, now wished to hide, like me. I felt a kinship with him" (Naipaul 1987, 208).

12 Said is discussing Naipaul's 1981 *Among the Believers: An Islamic Journey*, but with a general resonance to his authorial position in relation to postcolonial subjects.

Chapter 2   Creolizing Heterosexuality

1 Following Calvin Thomas's (2000) provocative work *Straight with a Twist*, which explores "straight negotiations with queer theory" (30), two further publications helped to sketch out the motivations and effects of this turn within sexuality

studies: Michael O'Rourke's (2005) "On the Eve of a Queer-Straight Future: Notes toward an Antinormative Heteroerotic" and Richard Fantina's (2006) edited collection *Straight Writ Queer: Non-normative Expressions of Heterosexuality in Literature*. O'Rourke (2005) calls for a radical recognition of "non-normative heterosexualities, the queer practices of straights, and the lives and loves of those men and women who choose to situate themselves beyond the charmed circle at the heteronormative center" as core to the dehegemonization of hetero-erotics (121). O'Rourke (2005) also focuses explicitly on alternative readings of sex acts that deprioritize the heteronormative: "I want to focus here on the queering of the (heteroerotic) vagina and (homoerotic) anus, the penis/vagina and active/passive binary splits, and the potential for non-phallobsessed and non-hierarchical hetero-relationships" (113). In a similar gesture, Fantina's (2006) collection of literary criticism also draws attention to "queer heterosexual practices . . . transgressive acts and counter-hegemonic gender positions" (14) in nineteenth- and twentieth-century British and American narrative works as a means to map and discuss how queer heterosexuality can contest heteronormativity. The core critical impulse of these works is to draw out the incoherent character of hetero-sexuality in order to dismantle the established and embedded status of heteronor-mativity, as M. O'Rourke (2005) defines it: "the presumption that everyone is heterosexual, that only heterosexuality is normal or culturally intelligible, and it describes several intermeshing ideological state apparatuses which try to ensure that everyone is heterosexual in particular ways. Heteronormativity and heteropa-triarchy are imbricated since only specific types of heterosexuality are considered normal, licit, or proper, and the married, procreative, opposite-sex couple with children is valorized and reified as the normative sexual lifestyle. Opposite-sex partners are the only proper objects and procreative sex is a compulsory norm. The lines of demarcation are so strict that anything which crosses over the monoga-mous, familial line is deemed to be deviant, pathological, illicit, culturally unintelligible" (111).

2 The wider adoption of these terms occurred when Ulrichs sent the German Richard von Krafft-Ebing-one of the most prominent psychiatrists in Europe-his publications in 1866, the year in which the first edition of Krafft-Ebing's bestsell-ing *Psychopathia sexualis* was published. Although this work was written mainly for lawyers and doctors considering sexual crimes in court, the intense interest in sexology among prominent psychiatrists-such as Wilhelm Griesinger, Carl von Westphal, Krafft-Ebing, Paul Moreau de Tours, Jean-Martin Charcot, and Valentin Magnan-meant that a proliferation of sexual classifications emerged as so-called perversions to be identified and diagnosed. In this way, a vocabulary that was initially advanced by same-sex-desiring men to legitimate their own erotic preference was now sequestered by psychiatric discourses, with the ultimate effect of organizing the idea of healthy, sane sexual norms around a heteronormative imperative.

3 For more detailed engagements with the intersections between decolonizing and queer studies see Patrick E. Johnson, ed. *No Tea, No Shade: New Writings in Black Queer Studies* (Durham, NC: Duke University Press, 2016).

4 For a rich discussion of queer faith traditions, focused on Spiritual Baptists in Trinidad and Tobago see Gill's essay "I Am a Messenger" (2018b).

5 See Alison Donnell, "Living and Loving: Emancipating the Caribbean Queer Citizen in Shani Mootoo's *Cereus Blooms at Night*," in *Sex and the Citizen:*

Interrogating the Caribbean," ed. Faith Smith (Charlottesville: University of Virginia Press), 168–180; Curdella Forbes, "Yearning for Utopia: Earth, Body, Deviance and Festive-Carnival Failure, *Cereus Blooms at Night*," *Ariel: A Review of International English Literature* 41, no. 1 (2011): 111–142; and Heather Smyth, "*Sexual Citizenship and Caribbean-Canadian Fiction:* Dionne Brand's, 'In Another Place, Not Here' and Shani Mootoo's *Cereus Blooms at Night*," *Ariel: A Review of International English Literature* 30, no. 2 (1999): 143–160.

6   The same caution is not exercised by heterosexual men in the novel for whom infidelity is seemingly the accepted norm and seen to amplify their standing, as Nayan's friend Bally confirms: "And what you do outside of the house have nothing to do with what you doing inside. That is the beauty of the thing. Inside. Outside. Two different thing" (Mootoo 2008b, 249).

7   Later, Viveka reflects that it is her encounter with Caribbean Literature that has "provoked her to want to experience a Caribbean-ness, and a Trinidadian-ness more specifically, that was antithetical to her mother's tie to all things Indian and Hindu" (Mootoo 2008b, 99). Of course, it is this same investment in literature's ability to offer a redescription of the fullness of Trinidadian reality that the novel itself engages.

8   See Edelman (2004) and Bersani (1996) for canonical works of queer theory that critique the universal politics of "reproductive futurism."

9   John Howard's (1999) insightful study *Men Like That: A Southern Queer History* offers a helpful model in attending to the specificities of place and time that demand a locally responsive understanding of intimate lives—in his case in rural Mississippi.

Chapter 3   Caribbean Freedoms and Queering Homonormativity

1   Thomas Glave is cofounder of J-FLAG, which—as described in its website— stands for the Jamaica Forum for Lesbians, All-Sexuals and Gays and "was founded on Thursday December 10, 1998, as the first human rights organization in the history of Jamaica to serve the needs of Lesbians, Gays and Bisexuals and Transgendered (LGBT) peoples." "About," J-FLAG, accessed February 8, 2019, http://jflag.org/about/.

2   The Wolfenden Report presented the findings of an investigation committee led by Sir John Wolfenden in 1957. Their task was to "consider the legal ramifications of homosexual convictions and how the judicial system should treat those convicted" (Lutes 2000, 643). One of the recommendations put forward in the Wolfenden Report was the decriminalization of consenting homosexual relationships between adults provided these were mostly limited to the domestic sphere. The report itself can be accessed via the British Library portal at http://www.bl.uk/learning/timeline/item107413.html.

3   Lisa Duggan's definition of homonormativity has been widely acknowledged and referenced in gender and queer scholarship. Duggan argues that homonormativity reinforces rather than challenges power relations by privileging assimilation and the adoption of heteronormative structures, such as marriage or the military, thus contributing to the stigmatization of other lifestyles or modes of activism that oppose or revise those structures. She defines it as "a politics that does not contest normative heteronormative assumptions and institutions, but *upholds and sustains them*" (Duggan [2003] *The Twilight of Equality*, 172; italics added). However, there

are many other definitions that point to a more varied history of activism and critique of the term. Trans activist Susan Stryker identifies a genealogy of the term from the early 1990s as "an attempt to articulate the double sense of marginalization and displacement experienced within transgender political and cultural activism" (quoted in Martínez-San Miguel and Tobias [2016], 237).

4 *The Lonely Londoners'* status as an iconic publication and representation of West Indian postwar migration is widely acknowledged in criticism and scholarship of Caribbean and Black British literature (Dawson 2007; Forbes 2005; McLeod 2004; Nasta 1988, 2002; Procter 2003; and Zehnder 2003). Originally published by Longman in 1956, the novel was reprinted by Penguin in its Penguin Modern Classics series in 2006. The novel's portrayal of the city and its changing social history, narrated from the perspective of West Indian, African, and Indian migrants—as well as its use of creole—originally revised a tradition of British metropolitan literature and, in time, established a new tradition of diasporic writing. As Nasta (2006) notes of Selvon in her introduction to the Penguin edition of *The Lonely Londoners,* "Often heralded today as an ingenious alchemist of style or 'father of black writing' in Britain, Selvon . . . has influenced succeeding generations of writers" (vii). Nasta (2006) also highlights how Caryl Philips, "now a major contemporary writer himself, locates Selvon not only in terms of a tradition of black writing—a precursor of contemporary figures such as David Dabydeen, Zadie Smith or Andrea Levy—but more significantly as a key figure in the literary reimagining of Britain during the post-war years" (vii).

5 It is also interesting to consider Edgar Mittelholzer's 1950 novel *A Morning in the Office* within this context. In this work, obsessions with race and class within a colonial situation are often represented as having a sexual charge. The novel's insistence on rendering the unanticipated and uncensored interior life of its characters creates space for thoughts of infidelity, multiple attractions, and queer desire that commonly run against the racialized narratives that are ventriloquized at its surface. The voicing of strong sexual feelings on the part of its female characters is notable and within the heteronormative world of the novel; sexual yearning is usually gratified in this narrative, although often not with the fantasized subject. In the office of Essential Products Ltd., objects also tell tales, and for Mr. Reynolds, the same-sex-desiring figure, it is not insignificant that his green beret (his object story) is not even his as he struggles to claim an attachment to his erotic inner life, which is rendered as both reflective and regressive. For a more detailed reading of the erotics of this novel, see Faizal Forrester (1994).

6 For a summary of this parliamentary history and links to the relevant acts, see "Regulating Sex and Sexuality: The 20th Century," UK Parliament, accessed February 8, 2019, http://www.parliament.uk/about/living-heritage/transforming society/private-lives/relationships/overview/sexuality20thcentury/.

7 The 1950s in Jamaica was the decade of constitutional reform leading up to political independence in 1962. In 1953 Alexander Bustamante, a labor leader and head of the Jamaican Labor Party, became the island's first chief minister under the Crown Colony system. In 1957 Jamaica's Council of Ministers replaced the Executive Council of the Crown Colony, and a Ministry of Home Affairs took over some of the responsibilities of the colonial secretary and the British-appointed attorney general. In 1959 there was a new constitution in Jamaica with internal self-government agreed within the federation. Although these measures effected a significant transition in terms of local political determination, they were

a compromise, and Jamaica's colonial status remained. Perhaps more importantly, it was the brown middle classes (from which Johnnie flees in the novel) who were the beneficiaries of this transition, which failed to transform the future lives of the majority as only a small percentage of the population had wealth and income.

8   Faith identities and identifications had been shown to be genuinely incendiary and even fatal in the wake of Indian Partition. On 3 June 1947, the British colonial government announced through All India Radio the partition of "British India," into India and Pakistan, as two sovereign states. This geographical division had major implications in the religious and sociopolitical landscape of the new nation-states, and would determine a long history of strained relations among communities. Provinces with a predominant Muslim population were to form part of Pakistan. However, the Punjab and Bengal provinces—with a mixed population in terms of religious faith, Muslim, Hindu, and Sikh—were split to the west and east of the peninsula, respectively, as a result of the partition. The period following the partition of these two states and independence from British colonial rule was marked by episodes of extreme violence and mass migration. The conflict and the movement of migration started in 1946 in anticipation of the imminent partition, preceding thus its official announcement (June 1947) and its declaration in August that summer, ten months earlier than originally established. As Rini Bhattacharya Mehta and Debali Mookerjea-Leonard (2015) write in the introduction to *The Indian Partition in Literature and Films: History, Politics, and Aesthetics*, "A massive cross-border migration of population had commenced in the weeks leading to the event, as numerous Muslim families left India for Pakistan, and Hindus and Sikhs left Pakistan for India" (1). From the 1946 communal riots in Bengal, to the Great Calcutta Killings (16–19 August 1946), violence erupted across the Punjab and Bengal.

9   In Ellis's (2015b) reading it is the fraught and passionate friction between the White working-class Trado and Johnnie that focalizes the novel's queer energy, "where desire and identification are not sexual per se but intense, hostile, and evocative of sexual intimacy" (129).

10 The Wolfenden Report makes the limits of its freedoms clear: "This limited modification of the law should not be interpreted as indicating that the law can be indifferent to other forms of homosexual behavior, or as a general license to homosexuals to behave as they please" (Wolfenden 1957, 44).

11 Ellis's quotation comes from the original 1960 Hutchinson edition of Salkey's *Escape to an Autumn Pavement* (38).

12 *Escape*'s metropolitan literary geography also offers an interesting inter- and subtext to the novel's engagement with erotic freedoms. Johnnie settles in Hampstead, at once a sign of the middle-class identity he wishes to disavow and of his proximity to London's queer subculture. Although the book makes no direct allusion to Hampstead as a historic cruising ground, its notoriety as one of very few public spaces in which gay men could encounter each other becomes another language of erotic possibility that is referenced, but unspoken, within the novel. Given the many regions of the metropolis that Johnnie could have settled in, other than Notting Hill or Brixton, where there was a concentration of West Indian bachelor migrants in the 1950s, the significance of Hampstead as a place of sexual opportunity cannot be ignored. While Johnnie's several street encounters with men are framed by his seeming naivety, the novel elsewhere insinuates that his knowledge of public space is not entirely innocent. When Fiona asks him where he

is walking to one morning, Johnnie's response, "Up to the Heath inevitably" (Salkey 2009, 101), insinuates a knowledge of cruising not recorded elsewhere in the novel. In daytime, the Heath becomes a place for Fiona and Johnnie to share sexual intimacies—an open, public place where heterosexual encounters are freed from the regulating eyes of the bedsit: "For luck's sake, who's seducing whom?" (Salkey 2009, 103). When Dick and Johnnie move into a house in Piccadilly, they are not far from Soho in the heart of the West End—a district known for its sex clubs and gay bars. Significantly Dick is referred to as "the man with a thousand routes to the West End" (Salkey 2009, 104), in a double meaning that plays both on his job as a chauffeur and the idea of his polymorphous perversity.

13 Peter Green, *The Daily Telegraph and Morning Post*, 15 July 1960, p.17. Salkey kept a scrapbook of reviews where this review was pasted. There are no further details.

14 From John Figueroa's review, "A Choice of Lives," published in the *Tribune*, 5 August 1960. As with the Peter Green review, it was found in Salkey's review scrapbook; no further details are available.

15 Private letter from John Hearne to Andrew Salkey, 7 July 1959, held in the Salkey Collection now archived at the British Library. Quoted with permission of Shivaun Hearne.

16 One reading of Johnnie's defiant individualism might be to read him as taking the promise of decolonization to deliver freedom very seriously and applying it to the individual level in the spirit described by Fanon (1988) in *Toward the African Revolution*: "The liberation of the individual does not follow national liberation. An authentic national liberation exists only to the precise degree to which the individual has irreversibly begun his own liberation" (103).

Chapter 4 Queering Caribbean Homophobia

In Jamaican DJ Ricky General's (1999) "A Wha Dis," he addresses the cultural prohibition against cunnilingus as part of a staunchly heteropatriarchal identity in which a man bowing is seen as giving women agency. In the lines quoted here, the logic is that any man who does perform oral sex on a woman is a homosexual, colloquially termed a "fish." For a fuller reading of this song see Hutton (2014, 21–45).

1 Although *Oscar Wao* depicts a diasporic Hispanic Caribbean community, Díaz's depiction of the crossovers between queer and hypermasculine identities is a fascinating example of a queer Caribbean that speaks meaningfully to the other works in English discussed in this book. Including this text also makes a gesture to the concept of the "Cariglobal" that Rosamond King (2014) argues for as a method to explore: "How are people and cultures in different parts of the region in conversation with each other? If a phenomenon exists in both the region and the diaspora, does it exist in the same way? And, equally important, if a phenomenon exists in one area and not another, how has it evolved in its location, and why has it *not* moved?" (6).

2 Lorgia García Peña explains that "The works of Aída Cartagena Portalatín (1918–1994), Angela Hernández (1954–), Chiqui Vicioso (1948–) and Aurora Arias (1962–) during the second half of the 20th century and the newer transnational/diasporic literature of Julia Alvarez, Rita Indiana Hernández, Rey Emmanuel Andújar, Frank Báez, Homero Pumarol, Josefina Báez, Junot Díaz,

Loyda Maritza Pérez, Angie Cruz, and Nelly Rosario are among the most prominent examples of this new direction in Dominican literature" (2018, 10).

3 Although my discussion here is focused on Yunior as he is narrated and narrates in *The Brief Wondrous Life of Oscar Wao*, it is relevant to note that Yunior also appears in Díaz's two short-story collections *Drown* (1996) and *This Is How You Lose Her* (2012).

4 The longer history of disciplining male same-sex acts and desires in Jamaica is addressed in chapter 5.

5 Given the accelerated critical engagement with issues of masculinity within Caribbean gender studies in the last two decades, it is interesting that, as Michael A. Bucknor (2012) has observed, research studies "on the role of masculinities in Caribbean culture have been modest in literary and cultural studies" (x) of the Anglophone Caribbean. Indeed, this relative lack of attention is even more interesting given Lewis's (2014) comment that "Caribbean creative writers . . . have been reflecting on matters of masculinity and sexuality for a very long time" (64). The subject of Caribbean masculinities was central to two special journal issues edited from within the Anglo-Caribbean—the *Journal of West Indian Literature* in 2012/2013 and *Caribbean Quarterly* in 2014—and generated a flurry of literary critical approaches; however, even in these collections, the attention was often on an interdisciplinary reading of textual works alongside music and popular cultural forms. Michael A. Bucknor, ed. *Journal of West Indian Literature* "Caribbean Masculinities" 21, nos. 1/2 (2012); and Michael A. Bucknor and Conrad James, eds. *Caribbean Quarterly* "Caribbean Masculinities" 60, no. 4 (2014). A much more established and vibrant field of Hispanophone masculinity studies intersecting with literary studies exists, including important works by Efraín Barradas, Arnaldo Cruz-Malavé, and Lawrence La Fountain-Stokes.

6 While Shivani's detailed assessment of each book has been taken down, you can access some of the text relating to Junot Díaz here https://isteve.blogspot.com /2014/05/junot-diaz-on-unbearable-lightness-of.html.

7 "Nobody is ever one thing" is a quotation from Marlon James in his interview with Jeff Vasishta. See Jeff Vasishta, "Marlon James and the Spirit of '76— *Interview Magazine*," 2014, https://www.interviewmagazine.com/culture/marlon -james-a-brief-history-of-seven-killings.

8 See Mimi Sheller's discussion of Jamaican hypermasculinity and daggering in *Citizenship from Below: Erotic Agency and Caribbean Freedom* (2012, 276).

9 For more information on this letter see "A E Dyson—LGBT Archive," Lgbtarchive.Uk, accessed February 13, 2019, http://www.lgbtarchive.uk/wiki /A_E_Dyson.

10 Josey Wales does later express a more conventional view on heterosexual sex as a corrective function in relation to Weeper's sexual attraction to men: "Every time he fuck a woman I hope she is the woman that fix him. Because some disease lick him in prison, something that make him not normal" (James 2014, 137–138).

11 See Hanna (2010); Harford Vargas (2014); and Patteson (2012).

12 In her introduction to a special section of *Small Axe* 56 on "Critical Currents in Dominican Gender and Sexuality Studies, Maja Horn (2014) draws attention to Silvio Torres-Saillant's emphasis on "the homosociality and homoeroticism of the Trujillato," which "tends to be drowned out by the many anecdotal literary accounts of the dictator's voracious heterosexual exploits" (66) in his 1999 work *El retorno de las yolas: ensayos sobre diáspora, democracia y dominicanidad.*

Chapter 5 Imagining Impossible Possibilities

1 In this essay, originally a paper presented at the Fourth Berkshire Conference on the History of Women, Mount Holyoke College, 25 August 1978, Lorde is centrally concerned with locating a decolonized erotic power for women.

2 King's (2014) work on trans identities expressed both in Caribbean literary works and in Caribbean festivals is also attentively focused on how "class, color, and race play roles in determining the life possibilities open to a Caribbean trans individual" (60). In relation to *Moving Forward Sideways*, the economic privilege that Sydney enjoys is clearly crucial to his ability to enjoy social invisibility and visibility as he wishes. The significance of his ethnicity as an Indian Caribbean subject is the focus of Chatterji's (2016) "'Mini Death, and a Re-birth': Talking the Crossing in Shani Mootoo's *Moving Forward Sideways Like a Crab*."

3 It is Zain who points out to Sid that she walks sideways like a crab (Mootoo 2014, 90).

4 Perhaps not insignificantly the dedication to this novel states, "Time to think is the truest luxury" (Mootoo 2014).

5 The comparison in technique and effect in Powell's *The Pagoda* is made clear in Valens's (2016) reading: "Indeed, *The Pagoda* proceeds through revelatory flashbacks as if it might lead to an original personal identity, but the search turns into a dizzying endless regress. Each step back requires another, and each time we land on something that seems like it must be the 'true' Lowe, we find only someone else's coercive construction. Lowe realizes that 'Nobody had ever asked him. He had just lived out all their fantasies. There was his father, who used to dress Lowe the same way he dressed himself. . . . Then it was Cecil's fantasies and his grand plans for both Lowe and Miss Sylvie (Powell 1998, 99)" (Valens 2016, 70–71).

6 In his final notebook entry, Sydney does try to translate a nonbinary, unresolved experience of gender and sexual identity when describing his young self as "an undecided, half-formed thing" (Mootoo 2014, 7).

7 The night before Zain's funeral, Sid relates a dream about her that she has had "a thousand times before" (Mootoo 2014, 78). "We're in a constant state of moving towards each other, and we look at each other's lips, but our lips never touch. A hollow plastic pipe, the kind used in plumbing has replaced my backbone. It runs from my vagina to my chest. Its large hole makes a whooshing sound as air rushes through it unimpeded. I keep reaching behind my back to try to touch the hollow space, but it is as if I am backless. I want Zain to enter the pipe and fill me up so that I know I exist" (Mootoo 2014, 78). The dream queers the idea of the human body, imagining a transition to being invertebrate, a vessel. This seems to confirm the estranging, turbulent character of erotic being that undoes the illusion of identity: disorganized and disorganizing, making people available to each other in unpredicted and unpredictable ways.

8 The term *sexile* was coined by Manuel Guzman (1997) in "Contesting Terrains of the Nation and Sexual Orientation" to denote the specific exile of those who must leave their homelands because of the threat of persecution on account of their sexual orientation.

9 The accepted fluidity in relation to faith identities is also pointed out in the narrative, for example, in relation to Zain's conversion to marry Angus, which Sid suspects will mean that she is "Catholic in public, but Muslim at home and in her heart" (Mootoo 2014, 157).

10   In many ways, Jamaica represents the most extreme version of Anglophone
     Caribbean homophobia in the global imagination: the dancehall lyrics of Buju
     Banton's now infamous "Boom Bye Bye" from 1992—alongside T. O. K.'s 2001
     infamous song "Chi Chi Man" and Elephant Man's 2001 "Log On"—incited
     violence against homosexuals. The 1997 riots in St. Catherine's District Prison and
     Kingston's General Penitentiary led to the deaths of sixteen prisoners targeted as
     gay after the commissioner of corrections announced the distribution of condoms;
     and gay Jamaicans were granted asylum in Europe, Canada, and the U.S.—
     including a former J-FLAG founding member and founder of the 1978 Gay
     Freedom Movement (GFM), Larry Chang—on the grounds that it would
     endanger their lives to return. All these incidents brought the island's homopho-
     bia to European and North American scrutiny at the turn of the twentieth
     century, culminating in Tim Padgett's (2006) headline question in the April
     edition of *Time* magazine which asked: Is Jamaica "The Most Homophobic Place
     on Earth?" While no social landscape remains static, the possibilities for trans-
     forming attitudes and legal frameworks around same-sex relations in Jamaica
     remain significantly constrained despite notable signs of changing attitudes.
     Indeed, while the public defender, Arlene Harrison Henry, and the former
     minister of justice, Mark Golding, have both spoken about the need to protect the
     human rights of LGBTI citizens in recent years, the then prime minister Portia
     Simpson-Miller failed to pursue her 2011 campaign promise to review current
     legislation before demitting office in 2016. A more inclusive gesture came from
     within the religious community when Anglican priest Father Sean Major-
     Campbell made "an unprecedented act within local church ministry" by washing
     the feet of lesbian congregants in a gesture of welcome to all. However, his actions
     provoked an angry response from other religious groups (Serju 2014, n.p.).
     Certainly, the many organizations supporting LGBTI people in Jamaica and
     advocating for an end to discrimination based on sexual orientation (including
     J-FLAG, Quality of Citizenship Jamaica, Caribbean Dawn, and EVE for Life)
     testify to a shifting social scene and an expanded space for discussions around
     sexual and gender rights, as well as to personal lives lived in resilience and varying
     degrees of fulfilment. All the same, the ongoing prejudice and violent sanction
     facing same-sex-loving subjects continue. Indeed, in 2014 sexual rights activist
     Javed Jaghai launched a legal challenge to Jamaica's so-called buggery laws (little
     changed since 1864) in the country's Supreme Court, but eventually withdrew the
     action following threats of extreme violence (Lavers 2014).

11   Exploring the historical factors that informed a spike in the prosecutions for
     sexual crimes in 1840s and early 1850s Jamaica, Dalby (2014) considers this change
     in the patterns of criminalization and bodily discipline within the wider context
     of a postemancipation Jamaica and its changing racial dynamics. He draws
     attention to the fact that, in the century leading up to emancipation, the slave
     courts (established to try the enslaved for criminal offenses) identified and
     punished crimes in accordance with how seriously they threatened the planter's
     financial health or power, and that hence "prosecutions for running away,
     rebellion and larceny predominate[d]" (Dalby 2014, 139). In the postemancipation
     period both the court system and the attention paid to sexual crimes in Jamaica
     changed substantially and rapidly: "In the two decades after 1834, there were 183
     assize prosecutions for rape, 81 for bestiality, 77 for carnal abuse and 30 for
     sodomy, representing together over 14 per cent of the total prosecutions. In the

early 1850s, one-quarter of all assize cases tried were for sex offences. In the peak year of 1853, sex cases represented fully one-third of the total" (Dalby 2014, 137). This increase was not only dramatic given Jamaica's historical precedent, but also given global comparators.

12 Probably to be read as an accessory to this war of representation, in January 1950, the "Whipping Act" returned corporal punishment to Jamaica. At the same time, "judges' presentments and newspaper commentaries by a harsh and racist rhetoric . . . repeatedly harped upon the gulf between European 'civilization' and African 'barbarism'—a gulf which, it was implied, was becoming increasingly unbridgeable" (Dalby 2014, 153). This law "permitted sentences of up to 117 lashes (with a maximum of 39 at any one time) on conviction for rape, attempted rape, sodomy and attempted sodomy, carnal abuse and attempted carnal abuse, bestiality and attempted bestiality, and arson" (Dalby 2014, 153). It hardly needs to be pointed out that these lashings are a recognizable echo of the lashes dispensed during slavery and integral to the perverse masteries of empire. The fact that a discursive return to the racialized discourses of "barbarism" coincided with the return of sadistic corporal punishments indicates the heightened attention to and punishment of "unnatural bodies" as a coordinated expression of elite power. As Foucault (1975) reminds us in *Discipline and Punish: The Birth of the Prison*, the intention of such bodily torture was not just to punish, but to discipline and to define: "It must mark the victim: it is intended, either by the scar it leaves on the body, or by the spectacle that accompanies it, to brand the victim with infamy; even if its function is to 'purge' the crime, torture does not reconcile; it traces around or, rather, on the very body of the condemned man signs that must not be effaced" (34).

13 When penal codes became more commonplace in British colonies in the 1860s, the Indian Penal Code of 1860, in which buggery was named under "unnatural offences" in Chapter XVI, section 337, became particularly influential (Kirby 2013, 66). The naming of an "abominable crime" was the particular linguistic preference of Edward Coke and William Blackstone, the British law-writers of the mid- to late eighteenth century (Kirby 2013, 63). Michael Kirby's (2013) essay, "The Sodomy Offence: England's Least Lovely Criminal Law Export?" shows how Jamaica's 1864 Act substantially ventriloquized the colonial British "Offences Against the Person Act of 1861," which also defined punishments for "the abominable crime of buggery, committed either with mankind or with any animal" (British Act: Article 61; Jamaican Act: Article 76, 26) as punishable by life imprisonment.

14 As M. Jacqui Alexander (1994) has argued, the issue of policing indecency remains relevant at the independence moment a whole century later when "naturalized heterosexuality shape[d] the definitions of respectability, Black masculinity, and nationalism" (7). This claim is given closer historical scrutiny in the work of Caribbean legal historian Tracy Robinson (2009), who contends that it is the ongoing value placed on heterosexual reproductive couples that shaped the outlaw culture of same-sex activity and the hardening of attitudes over time. She explains that in "the early- to mid-twentieth century Caribbean criminal codes did not target homosexuality per se, the focus was unnatural, non-procreative sex. Same-sex sexuality was included, but it was not a singular object of laws prohibiting unnatural crimes" (T. Robinson 2009, 6). As T. Robinson also explains, "a central idea of Caribbean nationalism was that men and women could be *made*

into worthy citizens through marriage, social uplift, awakening their ambition, reproducing responsibly in marriage and living proper lives for the betterment of their children" (7). Not insignificantly, T. Robinson argues that, in the Caribbean more widely, the legal framework that has been refined in the late twentieth century in relation to crimes and the family is progressively more punitive toward those who step outside the boundaries of what is deemed acceptable sex and affirming of those who meet heteronormative standards of family (19).

15 The emphasis on aquatic ecstasy is also interesting given that "fish" is one of many pejorative terms used in Jamaica for men who have sex with men.

16 As Mimi Sheller (2012) argues, "One of the greatest silences in Caribbean historiography is the invisibility of queer subjectivities" (3), and the imaginative rendering of queer subjects in the early history of the Caribbean through literature is also notably rare. In this regard, Glave's story sits alongside Patricia Powell's *The Pagoda* "set in colonial Jamaica after the 1834 abolition of slavery and in the midst of the subsequent expansion of the 'coolie trade' that brought Chinese and Indian workers to the Caribbean (Walters 2010; Yun 2004)" (Valens 2016, 68). In Valens's (2016) reading of Powell's novel, the backgrounding of a queer milieu is also part of the novel's gesture toward a sexual fluidity that cannot be officially sanctioned: "Throughout the novel, relationships between men and relationships between women as well as crossings of the gender binary appear as common and as common knowledge, even if always marginal" (76).

17 The mission, vision, values, and history of J-FLAG can be accessed on the organization's website (J-FLAG, "About," 2019, https://jflag.org/about/).

18 First published in Glave's (2005) *Words to Our Now: Imagination and Dissent* and then selected to be republished in Glave's (2008a) *Our Caribbean*.

19 The term *all-sexual* was chosen by both C-FLAG (1995) and J-FLAG (1998) to indicate a continuum of sexual desires, preferences, and practices that cannot be organized around binarisms and categories without the inevitably of exclusion—hence the emphasis on *all*.

20 For more on the subject of a challenge to Western humanism and its assault on Black humanity see Katherine McKittrick's *Sylvia Wynter: On Being Human as Praxis* (2015).

21 Other works by Caribbean writers can also be usefully read as part of a wider literary project that questions the configuration of imposed gender, sexual, and species demarcations, including Lawrence Scott's *Witchbroom* (1992), Shani Mootoo's *Cereus Blooms at Night* (1996), and Nalo Hopkinson's *Midnight Robber* (2000).

References

Achebe, Chinua. 1997. *Conversations with Chinua Achebe*, edited by Berth Lindfors. Jackson: University of Mississippi.

Agard-Jones, Vanessa. 2009. "'Le Jeu de Qui?' Sexual Politics at Play in the French Caribbean." *Caribbean Review of Gender Studies* 3: 1–19.

———. 2012. "What the Sands Remember." *GLQ* 18, nos. 2–3: 325–346.

Ahmed, Sarah. 2006. *Queer Phenomenology: Orientations, Objects, Others*. Durham: Duke University Press.

Alexander, M. Jacqui. 1994. "Not Just (Any) Body Can Be a Citizen: The Politics of Law, Sexuality and Postcoloniality in Trinidad and Tobago and the Bahamas." *Feminist Review* 48 (Autumn): 5–23.

———. 1997. "Erotic Autonomy as a Politics of Decolonization." In *Feminist Genealogies, Colonial Legacies, Democratic Futures*, edited by M. Jacqui Alexander and Chandra Talpade Mohanty, 63–100. New York and London: Routledge.

Allen, Jafari S. 2012. "Black/Queer/Diaspora at the Current Conjuncture." *GLQ: A Journal of Lesbian and Gay Studies* 18, nos. 2–3 (April): 211–248.

———. 2016. "Black/Queer Rhizomatics: Train Up a Child in the Way Ze Should Grow." In *No Tea, No Shade: New Writings in Black Queer Studies*, edited by E. Patrick Johnson, 27–47. Durham: Duke University Press.

Allen, Jafari S., and Omise'eke Natasha Tinsley. 2012. "A Conversation 'Overflowing with Memory': On Omise'eke Natasha Tinsley's 'Water, Shoulders, into the Black Pacific.'" *GLQ* 18, nos. 2–3: 249–262.

Balutansky, Kathleen, and Marie-Agnes Sourieau, eds. 1998. *Caribbean Creolization: Reflections on the Cultural Dynamics of Language, Literature, and Identity*. Gainesville: University Press of Florida, and Barbados: University Press of the West Indies.

Baron, Robert, and Ana C. Cara. 2011. *Creolization as Cultural Creativity*. Jackson: University Press of Mississippi.

Barradas, Efraín. 1977. "El machismo existencialista de Rene Marqués." *Sin Nombre* 8, no. 3: 69–81.

Baugh, Edward. 2011a. "'The History That Had Made Me': The Making and Self-Making of V.S. Naipaul." In *Created in the West Indies: Caribbean Perspectives on*

V.S. Naipaul, edited by Jennifer Rahim and Barbara Lalla, 3–19. Kingston, Jamaica: Ian Randle.

———. (1977) 2011b. "The West Indian Writer and His Quarrel with History." *Small Axe* 16, no. 2: 60–74.

Beckett, Greg. 2017. "The Politics of Disjuncture, or Freedom from a Caribbean Point of View." *Small Axe* 21, no. 2 (53): 184–192. doi: 10.1215/07990537-4156906.

Benítez-Rojo, Antonio. (1992) 1996. *The Repeating Island: The Caribbean and the Postmodern Perspective*. 2nd ed. Translated by James E. Maraniss. Durham: Duke University Press.

Berlant, Lauren, and Michael Warner. 1998. "Sex in Public." *Critical Inquiry* 24, no. 2 (Winter): 547–566.

Bernabé, Jean, Patrick Chamoiseau, and Raphaël Confiant. 1993. *Eloge de la créolité / In Praise of Creoleness, Edition Bilingue*. Translated by M. B. Taleb-Khyr. Paris: Gallimard.

Bersani, Leo. 1996. *Homos*. Cambridge: Harvard University Press.

Brand, Dionne. 1990. *No Language Is Neutral*. Toronto: Coach House Press.

———. 1996. *In Another Place, Not Here*. London: The Women's Press.

———. 2001. *A Map to the Door of No Return*. Toronto: Vintage Canada.

Brathwaite, E. K. 1971. *The Development of Creole Society in Jamaica 1770–1820*. Oxford: The Clarendon Press.

———. 1974. *Contradictory Omens: Cultural Diversity and Integration in the Caribbean*, Monograph 1. Kingston, Jamaica: Savacou.

———. 1975. "Caribbean Man in Space and Time." *Savacou* 11, no. 12: 1–11.

Brennan, Timothy. 1989. *Salman Rushdie & the Third World: Myths of the Nation*. New York: St. Martin's Press.

Bucknor, Michael A. 2012. "Dangerous Crossings: Caribbean Masculinities and the Politics of Challenging Gendered Borderlines." *Journal of West Indian Literature* 21, nos. 1/2: vii–xxx.

Bucknor, Michael A., and Conrad James. 2014. "'Cock Mouth Kill Cock': Language, Power, and Sexual Intimacy." *Caribbean Quarterly* 60, no. 4: 1–7. doi:10.1080/000 86495.2014.11672532.

Butler, Judith. 1990. *Gender Trouble: Feminism and the Subversion of Identity*. New York: Routledge.

———. 1993. *Bodies That Matter: On the Discursive Limits of Sex*. New York and London: Routledge.

Celayo, Armando and David Shook. 2008. "In Darkness We Meet: A Conversation with Junot Diaz." *World Literature Today*, 2, no.82: 12–17.

Chariandy, David. 2018. *Brother*. London: Bloomsbury.

Chatterji, Tuli. 2016. "'Mini Death and a Re-birth': Talking the Crossing in Shani Mootoo's *Moving Forward Sideways Like a Crab*." In *Indo-Caribbean Feminist Thought: Genealogies, Theories, Enactments*, edited by Gabrielle Jamela Hosein and List Outar, 113–130. New York: Palgrave.

Chin, Staceyann. 2009. *The Other Side of Paradise: A Memoir*. New York: Scribner.

Chin, Timothy S. 2007. "The Novels of Patricia Powell: Negotiating Gender and Sexuality across the Disjunctures of the Caribbean Diaspora." *Callaloo* 30, no. 2: 533–545.

Cliff, Michelle. (1987) 1996. *No Telephone to Heaven*. New York: Plume.

———. 1980. *Claiming an Identity They Taught Me to Despise*. Watertown, MA: Persephone Press.

———. (1982) 2008. *If I Could Write This in Fire*. Minneapolis: University of Minnesota.

Cobham-Sander, Rhonda. 2011. "Consuming the Self: V.S. Naipaul, C.L.R. James, and *A Way in the World*." In *Created in the West Indies: Caribbean Perspectives on V.S. Naipaul*, edited by Jennifer Rahim and Barbara Lalla, 51–76. Kingston, Jamaica: Ian Randle.

Cohen, Cathy J. 1997. "Punks, Bulldaggers, and Welfare Queens: The Radical Potential of Queer Politics?" *GLQ* 3, no. 4: 437–465.

Collado, Lipe. 1981. *El Tiguere dominicano*. Dominican Republic: Talleres Gráficos de la UASD.

Collier, Gordon, and Ulrich Fleischmann, eds. 2003. *A Pepper-Pot of Cultures: Aspects of Creolization in the Caribbean*. Amsterdam and New York: Rodopi.

Crichlow, Wesley. 2014. "Hyperheterosexualization and Hypermasculinity: Challenges for HIV/AIDS Intervention in the Caribbean, Trinidad and Tobago." *International Journal of Sociology and Anthropology* 6, no. 10: 28–41.

Cruz-Malavé, Arnaldo. 1996. "What a Tangled Web! Masculinity, Abjection, and the Foundations of Puerto Rican Literature in the United States." *differences* 8, no. 1: 132–151.

Cruz-Malavé, Arnaldo, and Martin F. Manalansan IV. 2002. *Queer Globalizations: Citizenship and the Afterlife of Colonialism*. New York: New York University Press.

Cudjoe, Selwyn. 1988. *V.S. Naipaul: A Materialist Reading*. Amherst: University of Massachusetts Press.

Cummings, Ronald. 2012/13. "Jamaican Female Masculinities: Nanny of the Maroons and the Genealogy of the Man-Royal." *Journal of West Indian Literature* 21, nos. 1/2: 129–154.

———. 2018. "Johnnie's Letters: Epistolary Practice in Andrew Salkey's *Escape to an Autumn Pavement*." *SX Salon* 29. http://smallaxe.net/sxsalon/discussions/johnnies -letters.

Cummings, Ronald, and Faizal Deen. 2021. *"Sexual Subjects" in Caribbean Literature in Transition, Volume 3 1970–2020*. New York: Cambridge University Press.

Cummings, Ronald, and Nalini Mohabir. 2018. "The Anger of Very, Very Restless Spirits': Plantation Arrivals, Diasporic Departures and Other Queer Narratives of Caribbean Becoming—a Conversation with Faizal Deen" *Journal of West Indian Literature* 26, no. 1: 10–24.

Dalby, Jonathan R. 2014. "'Such a Mass of Disgusting and Revolting Cases': Moral Panic and 'Discovery' of Sexual Deviance in Post-emancipation Jamaica (1835–1855)." *Slavery & Abolition* 36, no. 1: 136–159.

Dawson, Ashley. 2007. *Mongrel Nation: Diasporic Culture and the Making of Postcolonial Britain*. Ann Arbor: University of Michigan Press.

deCaires Narain, Denise. 2012. "Naming Same-Sex Desire in Caribbean Women's Texts: Towards a Creolizing Hermeneutics." *Contemporary Women's Writing* 6, no. 3: 194–212.

Deckard, Sharae. 2018. "'Always Returning From It': Neoliberal Capitalism, Retrospect, and Marlon James's *A Brief History of Seven Killings*." *Countertext* 4, no. 2: 169–191. doi:10.3366/count.2018.0126.

Deen, Faizal. 1999. *Land without Chocolate: A Memoir*. Hamilton, Ontario: Wolsak and Wynn.

Dhondy, Farrukh. 2001. "Interview: Farrukh Dhondy Talks to V.S. Naipaul." *Literary Review* 278: 29–37.

Díaz, Junot. 2007. *The Brief Wondrous Life of Oscar Wao*. New York: Riverhead Books.

———. 2016. "The Search for Decolonial Love: A Conversation between Junot Díaz and Paula M. L. Moya." In *Junot Díaz and the Decolonial Imagination*, edited by Monica Hanna, Jennifer Harford Vargas, and José David Saldívar, 391–402. Durham: Duke University Press.

Duggan, Lisa. 2003. *The Twilight of Equality? Neoliberalism, Cultural Politics and the Attack on Democracy*. Boston: Beacon Press.

———. 2007. "Afterword." In *The Invention of Homosexuality*, Jonathan Ned Katz, 193–196. Chicago: University of Chicago Press.

Edelman, Lee. 2004. *No Future: Queer Theory and the Death Drive*. Durham and London: Duke University Press.

Ellis, Nadia. 2011. "Out and Bad: Toward a Queer Performance Hermeneutic in Jamaican Dancehall." *Small Axe* 15, no. 2 (35): 7–23. doi: 10.1215/07990537-1334212.

———. 2015a. "Marlon James's Savage Business." *Public Books*. https://www.publicbooks.org/marlon-jamess-savage-business/.

———. 2015b. *Territories of the Soul: Queered Belonging in the Black Diaspora*. Durham: Duke University Press.

Espinet, Ramabai. 2003. *The Swinging Bridge*. Toronto: Harper Collins.

Fallon, Amy. 2011. "V.S. Naipaul Finds No Woman Writer His Literary Match—Not Even Jane Austen." *The Guardian*. https://www.theguardian.com/books/2011/jun/02/vs-naipaul-jane-austen-women-writers.

Fanon, Frantz. 1988. *Toward the African Revolution: Political Essays*. Translated by Haakon Chevalier. New York: Grove Press.

Fantina, Richard, ed. 2006. *Straight Writ Queer: Non-normative Expressions of Heterosexuality in Literature*. Jefferson, NC: McFarland.

Figueroa, John. 1960. "A Choice of Lives." *Tribune*. 5 August.

Forbes, Curdella. 2005. *From Nation to Diaspora: Samuel Selvon, George Lamming, and the Cultural Performance of Gender*. Kingston, Jamaica: University of the West Indies Press.

———. 2008. "A Permanent Freedom" in *A Permanent Freedom*. Leeds, UK: Peepal Tree.

Forbes, Curdella, and Sheryl Clifford. 2014. "A Community of the Self: A Conversation with Curdella Forbes." Interview by Sheryl Clifford. *SX Salon* 17. http://smallaxe.net/sxsalon/interviews/community-self.

Forrester, Faizal. 1994. "'Revolting Bodies': Homosexual Dream & Masculine Anxiety in Edgar Mittelholzer's *A Morning at the Office* and Caryl Phillips's *Higher Ground*." *Caribbean Studies* 27, nos. 3/4: 311–330.

Foucault, Michel. 1975. *Discipline and Punish: The Birth of the Prison*. Translated by Alan Sheridan. London: Penguin Books.

Fraser, Nancy, and Axel Honneth. 2003. *Redistribution or Recognition? A Political-Philosophical Exchange*. London: Verso.

French, Patrick. 2008. *The World Is What It Is*. London: Picador.

Fumagalli, Maria Christina, Bénédicte Ledent, and Roberto del Valle Alcalá, eds. 2013. *The Cross-Dressed Caribbean: Writing, Politics, Sexualities*. Charlottesville: University of Virginia Press.

García Peña, Lorgia. 2018. "Dominican Ethnic Identities, National Borders, and Literature." In *Oxford Research Encyclopedia of Literature*. Oxford: Oxford University Press, 1–18. DOI:10.1093/acrefore/9780190201098.013.375.

Gaskins, Joseph. 2013. "'Buggery' and the Commonwealth Caribbean: A Comparative Examination of the Bahamas, Jamaica, and Trinidad and Tobago." In *Human Rights, Sexual Orientation, and Gender Identity in the Commonwealth*, edited by Lennox Corinne and Waites Matthew, 429–454. London: School of Advanced Study, University of London.

General, Ricky. 1999. "A Wha Dis." Vinyl. London: Greensleeves Records.

Gill, Lyndon. 2018a. *Erotic Islands: Art and Activism in the Queer Caribbean.* Durham: Duke University Press.

———. 2018b. "I Am a Messenger: Spiritual Baptism and the Queer Afterlife of Faith" *Small Axe* 22, no. 1 (55): 71–84.

Glave, Thomas. 2005. *Words to Our Now: Imagination and Dissent.* Minneapolis: University of Minnesota Press.

———. 2007. "He Who Would Have Become 'Joshua,' 1791." *Callaloo* 30, no. 2: 420–438.

———. ed. 2008a. *Our Caribbean: A Gathering of Lesbian and Gay Writing from the Antilles.* Durham: Duke University Press.

———. 2008b. "Whose Caribbean? An Allegory, in Part." In *Our Caribbean: A Gathering of Lesbian and Gay Writing from the Antilles*, edited by Thomas Glave. Durham: Duke University Press. First Published *Callaloo* 27, no. 3 (2004): 671–681.

———. 2009. "Introduction." In *Escape to an Autumn Pavement*, Andrew Salkey. Leeds, UK: Peepal Tree.

———. 2012. "Jamaican, Octopus." *Callaloo* 35, no. 2: 368–375.

———. 2013a. "Again, a Book of Dreams," in *Among the Bloodpeople: Politics and Flesh.* New York: Akashic Books: 76–90.

———. 2013b. *Among the Bloodpeople: Politics and Flesh.* New York: Akashic Books.

Glissant, Édouard. 1989. *Caribbean Discourse: Selected Essays.* Translated by J. Michael Dash. Charlottesville: University Press of Virginia.

———. 1995 "Creolization in the Making of the Americas." In *Race, Discourse, and the Origin of the Americas: A New World View*, edited by V. Hyatt and R. Nettleford, 268–275. Washington: Smithsonian Institution Press.

———. 1997. *Poetics of Relation*, translated by Betsy Wing. Ann Arbor: University of Michigan Press.

Gussow, Mel. 1994. "V.S. Naipaul in Search of Himself: A Conversation." *New York Times.* http://www.nytimes.com/books/98/06/07/specials/naipaul-conversation.html.

Guzman, Manuel. 1997. "Contested Terrains of the Nation and Sexual Orientation." In *Puerto Rican Jam: Rethinking Colonialism and Nationalism*, edited by Frances Negron-Muntaner and Ramon Grosfoguel, 109–228. Minneapolis: University of Minnesota Press.

Halberstam, J. 2005. *In a Queer Time and Place: Transgender Bodies, Subcultural Lives.* New York: New York University Press.

Hall, Stuart. 2017. *Familiar Stranger: A Life between Two Islands.* London: Allen Lane.

Hanna, Monica. 2010. "'Reassembling the Fragments': Battling Historiographies, Caribbean Discourse, and Nerd Genres in Junot Díaz's *The Brief Wondrous Life of Oscar Wao.*" *Callaloo* 33, no. 2: 498–520.

Harford Vargas, Jennifer. 2014. "Dictating a Zafa: The Power of Narrative Form in Junot Díaz's *The Brief Wondrous Life of Oscar Wao.*" *MELUS* 39, no. 3: 8–30.

Harris, Wilson. 1960. *Palace of the Peacock*. London: Faber and Faber.

Harrison, Sheri-Marie. 2015. "Excess in *A Brief History of Seven Killings*." Post45, October. http://post45.research.yale.edu/2015/10/excess-in-a-brief-history-of-seven-killings/.

Henderson, Mae G., and. E. Patrick Johnson, eds. 2005. *Black Queer Studies: A Critical Anthology*. Durham, NC: Duke University Press.

Hope, Donna P. 2010. *Man Vibes: Masculinities in the Jamaican Dancehall*. Kingston, Jamaica: Ian Randle.

———. 2012. "'Pon Di Borderline': Exploring Constructions of Jamaican Masculinity in Dancehall and Roots Theater." *Journal of West Indian Literature* 21, nos. 1/2: 105–128.

Hopkinson, Nalo. 2000. *Midnight Robber*. New York: Warner Books.

Horn, Maja. 2014. *Masculinity after Trujillo: The Politics of Gender in Dominican Literature*. Gainesville: University Press of Florida.

———. 2018. "Introduction: Critical Currents in Dominican Gender and Sexuality Studies." *Small Axe* 22, no. 2 (56): 64–71.

Houlbrook, Matt. 2005. *Queer London: Perils and Pleasures in the Sexual Metropolis, 1918–1957*. Chicago: University of Chicago Press.

Houlden, Kate. 2013. "Andrew Salkey, the British Home, and the Intimacies In-Between." *Interventions* 15, no. 1: 95–109.

Howard, John. 1999. *Men Like That: A Southern Queer History*. Chicago: University of Chicago Press.

Hutton, Clinton. 2014. "The Gyalification of Man: The Expression of Male-Male Conflict in Jamaica and the Roots of Homoeroticism in the Political Ideology, Ontology, and Praxis of White Supremacy." *Caribbean Quarterly* 60, no. 4. doi: 10.1080/00086495.2014.11672534.

James, Marlon. 2014. *A Brief History of Seven Killings*. New York: Riverhead Books.

Johnson, Barbara. 1987. *A World of Difference*. Baltimore: Johns Hopkins University Press.

Johnson, E. Patrick. 2005. "'Quare' Studies or Almost Everything I know about Queer Studies I Learned from My Grandmother." In *Black Queer Studies: A Critical Anthology*, E. Patrick Johnson and Mae Henderson, 124–157. Durham, NC: Duke University Press.

Kamugisha, Aaron. 2012. "Austin Clarke's Bajan Boyhood: Coming of Age In: Amongst Thistles and Thornes, Growing Up Stupid Under the Union Jack, and Proud Empires." *Journal of West Indian Literature* 21, nos. 1/2: 42–59.

Katz, Jonathan Ned. (1996) 2007. *The Invention of Heterosexuality*. Chicago: University of Chicago Press.

Keeling, Kara. 2019. *Queer Times, Black Futures*. New York: New York University Press.

Kempadoo, Kamala. 2009. "Caribbean Sexuality: Mapping the Field." *Caribbean Review of Gender Studies* 3: 1–18.

Kempadoo, Oona. 2013. *All Decent Animals*. New York: Farrar, Straus & Giroux.

King, Rosamond S. 2014. *Island Bodies: Transgressive Sexualities in the Caribbean Imagination*. Gainesville: University Press of Florida.

King, Rosamond S., and Angelique V. Nixon. 2012. "Introduction by Rosamond S. King and Angelique V. Nixon," part of the multimedia presentation "Theorizing Homophobias in the Caribbean." http://www.caribbeanhomophobias.org/node/6.

Kirby, Michael. 2013. "The Sodomy Offence: England's Least Lovely Criminal Law Export?" In *Human Rights, Sexual Orientation, and Gender Identity in The Commonwealth*, edited by Lennox Gorinne and Waites Matthew, 61–82. London: School of Advanced Study, University of London. http://www.jstor.org/stable/j.ctv512st2.6.

La Fountain-Stokes, Lawrence. 2009. *Queer Ricans: Cultures and Sexualities in the Diaspora*. Minneapolis: University of Minnesota Press.

Lamming, George. 1960. *The Pleasures of Exile*. London: Allison and Busby.

———. (1963) 1991. *In the Castle of My Skin*. Ann Arbor: University of Michigan Press.

———.1971. *Water with Berries*. Harlow, UK: Longman.

Lavers, Michael. 2014. "Gay Jamaica Man Withdraws Challenge of Anti-sodomy Law." *Washington Blade*. https://www.washingtonblade.com/2014/09/02/gay-jamaica-man-drops-lawsuit-against-anti-sodomy-law/.

Lewis, Linden. 2003a. "Caribbean Masculinity: Unpacking the Narrative." In *The Culture of Gender and Sexuality in the Caribbean*, edited by Linden Lewis, 94–125. Gainesville: University of Florida.

———. 2003b. "Exploring Intersections of Gender, Sexuality, and Culture in the Caribbean: An Introduction." In *The Culture of Gender and Sexuality in the Caribbean*, edited by Linden Lewis, 1–24. Gainesville: University Press of Florida.

———. 2014. "Caribbean Literary Discourses on the Polyvalence of Masculinity." *Caribbean Quarterly* 60, no. 4: 64–83. doi:10.1080/00086495.2014.11672536.

Lokaisingh-Meighoo, Sean. 2000. "Jahaji Bhai: Notes on the Masculine Subject and Homoerotic Subtext of Indo-Caribbean Identity." *Small Axe* 4, no. 1 77–92.

Lorde, Audre. 1984a. "The Master's Tools Will Never Dismantle the Master's House." In *Sister Outsider: Essays and Speeches*, Audre Lorde, 110–114. Berkeley: Crossing Press.

———. 1984b. "Uses of Erotic: The Erotic as Power." In *Sister Outsider: Essays and Speeches*, Audre Lorde, 53–59. Berkeley: Crossing Press.

———. 1984c. "Poetry Is Not a Luxury." In *Sister Outsider: Essays and Speeches*, Audre Lorde, 36–39. Berkeley: Crossing Press.

Love, Heather. 2007. *Feeling Backwards: Loss and the Politics of Queer History*. Cambridge, MA: Harvard University Press.

Lugones, Maria. 2007. "Heterosexualism and the Colonial/Modern Gender System." *Hypatia* 22, no. 1: 186–209.

Lutes, Michael A. 2000. "Wolfenden Report." In *Reader's Guide to Lesbian and Gay Studies*, edited by Timothy F. Murphy, 642–644. Chicago: Fitzroy Dearborn Publishers.

Machado Sáez, Elena. 2011. "Dictating Desire, Dictating Diaspora: Junot Díaz's *The Brief Wondrous Life of Oscar Wao* as Foundational Romance." *Contemporary Literature* 52, no. 3: 522–555.

Maharaj, Clem. 1992. *The Dispossessed*. Oxford: Heinemann Educational Books.

Markham, E. A. 2002. "Lines Composed to Test the Idea of Montserrat." In *A Rough Climate*, E. A. Markham. London: Anvil Press Poetry, 34–37.

Martínez-San Miguel, Yolanda. 2011. "Female Sexiles? Toward an Archeology of Displacement of Sexual Minorities in the Caribbean," *Signs* 36, no. 4: 813–836.

———. 2014. *Coloniality of Diasporas: Rethinking Intra-colonial Migrations in a Pan-Caribbean Context*. New York: Palgrave Macmillan.

Martínez-San Miguel, Yolanda, and Sarah Tobias. 2016. "Conclusion: Trans Fantasizing: From Social Media to Collective Imagination." In *Trans Studies: The*

Challenge to Hetero/Homo Normativities, edited by Yolanda Martínez-San Miguel and Sarah Tobias. New Brunswick, NJ: Rutgers University Press, 230–242.

McKittrick, Katherine. 2015. *Sylvia Wynter: On Being Human as Praxis*. Durham, NC: Duke University Press.

McLeod, John. 2004. *Postcolonial London: Rewriting the Metropolis*. New York: Routledge.

Mehta, Rini Bhattacharya, and Debali Mookerjea-Leonard. 2015. "Introduction." In *The Indian Partition in Literature and Films: History, Politics, and Aesthetics*, edited by Rini Bhattacharya Mehta and Debali Mookerjea-Leonard, 1–10. New York: Routledge.

Miller, Kei. 2013. "Maybe Bellywoman Was on 'Di Tape (2011).'" In *Writing Down the Vision: Essays and Prophecies*, Kei Miller, 96–108. Leeds, UK: Peepal Tree.

———. 2014. "On That Island of Broken Penises." *Caribbean Quarterly* 60, no. 4: 101–105. doi:10.1080/00086495.2014.11672538.

———. 2016. *Augustown*. London: Weidenfeld and Nicholson.

Mintz, Sidney W. 1996. "Enduring Substances, Trying Theories: The Caribbean Region as Oikoumenê." *Journal of the Royal Anthropological Institute* 2, no. 2: 289–311.

Mittelholzer, Edgar. 1950. *A Morning at the Office*. London: Hogarth Press.

Mootoo, Shani. 1996. *Cereus Blooms at Night*. New York: Arcade Books.

———. 2008a. "On Becoming an Indian Starboy." *Canadian Literature* 196: 83–94.

———. 2008b. *Valmiki's Daughter*. Toronto: Anansi.

———. 2014. *Moving Forward Sideways Like a Crab*. Toronto: Doubleday Canada.

Morris, Pam. 2003. *Realism*. New York: Routledge.

Mort, Frank. 1998. "Cityscapes: Consumption, Masculinities, and the Mapping of London since 1950." *Urban Studies* 35, nos. 5/6: 889–907.

Muñoz, José Esteban. 2006. "Forum: Conference Debates. The Antisocial Thesis in Queer Theory." *PMLA* 121, no. 3: 819–828.

———. 2009. *Cruising Utopia: The Then and There of Queer Futurity*. New York: New York University Press.

Murdoch, H. Adlai. 2013. "Édouard Glissant's Creolized World Vision: From Resistance and Relation to Opacité." *Callalloo* 36, no. 4: 875–889.

Murray, David. 2002. *Opacity: Gender, Sexuality, Race, and the "Problem" of Identity in Martinique*. New York: P. Lang.

Naipaul, V. S. (1961) 1983. *A House for Mr. Biswas*. New York: Alfred A. Knopf.

———. 1962. *The Middle Passage: Impressions of Five Societies—British, French, and Dutch in the West Indies and South America*. London: Deutsch.

———. 1969. *The Loss of El Dorado—a Colonial History*. London: Deutsch.

———. 1981 *Among the Believers: An Islamic Journey*. London: Andre Deutsch.

———. 1984. *Finding the Center: Two Narratives*. London: Andre Deutsch.

———. 1987. *The Enigma of Arrival*. London: Viking.

———. (1994) 1995. *A Way in the World*. London: Minerva.

———. 2001. "Nobel Lecture: Two Worlds." Nobelprize.org. http://www.nobelprize.org/nobel_prizes/literature/laureates/2001/naipaul-lecture-e.html.

Nair, Supriya. 2011. "Caribbean Ecopoetics: Dwellings in George Lamming's *In the Castle of My Skin*, Wilson Harris's *Palace of the Peacock*, and V.S. Naipaul's *A House for Mr. Biswas*." In *Routledge Companion to Anglophone Caribbean Literature*, edited by Alison Donnell and Michael Bucknor, 173–180. London: Routledge.

Nasta, Susheila, ed. 1988. *Critical Perspectives on Sam Selvon*. Washington: Three Continents Press.

———. 2002. *Home Truths: Fictions of the South Asian Diaspora in Britain*. London: Palgrave.

———. 2006. "Introduction." In *The Lonely Londoners*, Sam Selvon, v–xvii. London: Penguin.

Nelson, Alondra. 2002. "Making the Impossible Possible": An Interview with Nalo Hopkinson. *Social Text* 20, no. 2 (71): 97–113.

Offences Against the Person Act. 2010. Jamaica: Government of Jamaica, Ministry of Justice.

Offences Against the Person Act of 1861. United Kingdom: Government of the United Kingdom and Ireland.

O'Rourke, Meghan. 2007. "*The Brief Wondrous Life of Oscar Wao*: Questions for Junot Díaz." *Slate Magazine*. https://slate.com/news-and-politics/2007/11/questions-for-junot-diaz.html.

O'Rourke, Michael. 2005. "On the Eve of a Queer-Straight Future: Notes toward an Antinormative Heteroerotic." *Feminism & Psychology* 15, no. 1: 111–116. doi:10.1177/0959353505049713.

Oyěwùmí, Oyeronke. 1997. *The Invention of Women: Making an African Sense of Western Gender Discourses*. Minneapolis: University of Minnesota Press.

Padgett, Tim. 2006. "The Most Homophobic Place on Earth?" *Time*. http://content.time.com/time/world/article/0,8599,1182991,00.html.

Paquet, Sandra Pouchet. 2002. *Caribbean Autobiography: Cultural Identity and Self-Representation*. Madison: University of Wisconsin Press.

Patterson, Orlando. 1982. *Slavery and Social Death: A Comparative Study*. Cambridge: Harvard University Press.

Patteson, Richard. 2012. "Textual Territory and Narrative Power in Junot Díaz's *The Brief Wondrous Life of Oscar Wao*." *Ariel* 42, no. 4: 5–20.

Poupeye, Veerle. 2014. "Gangstas and Bush Cockerels: The Body, Gender, and Masculinity in the Work of Ebony G. Patterson. *Caribbean Quarterly* 60, no. 4: 8–20. doi:10.1080/00086495.2014.11672533.

Powell, Patricia. 1994. *A Small Gathering of Bones*. Oxford: Heinemann Educational Books.

———. 1998. *The Pagoda*. New York: Alfred A. Knopf.

Procter, James. 2003. Dwelling Spaces: Postwar Black British Writing. Manchester: Manchester University Press.

Puri, Shalini. 2004. *The Caribbean Postcolonial: Social Equality, Post-nationalism, and Cultural Hybridity*. New York: Palgrave Macmillan.

Rahim, Jennifer, ed. 2007. *Anthurium: A Caribbean Studies Journal* 5, no. 2. Special issue on V.S. Naipaul.

Ramírez, Dixa. 2018. *Colonial Phantoms: Belonging and Refusal in the Dominican Americas, from the 19th Century to the Present*. New York: NYU Press.

Ramirez, Rafael L. 2003. "Masculinity and Power in Puerto Rico." In *The Culture of Gender and Sexuality in the Caribbean*, edited by Linden Lewis, 234–250. Gainesville: University Press of Florida.

Robinson, Colin. 2016. *You Have You Father Hard Head*. Leeds, UK: Peepal Tree.

———. 2020. "Colin Robinson: In His Own Words." *Trinidad and Tobago Newsday*. https://newsday.co.tt/2020/05/26/colin-robinson-in-his-own-words/.

Robinson, Tracy. 2009. "Authorized Sex: Same-sex Sexuality and Laws in the Caribbean." In *Sexuality/Social Exclusion and Human Rights: Vulnerability in the Context of HIV*, edited by Christine Barrow, Marian de Bruin, and Robert Carr, 3–22. Kingston, Jamaica: Ian Randle.

Rowe-Evans, Adrian, and V. S. Naipaul. 1971. "An Interview with V.S. Naipaul." *Transitions* 40: 56–62.

Russell, Bertrand. 1946. *A History of Western Philosophy and Its Connection with Political and Social Circumstances from the Earliest Times to the Present Day*. New York: Simon and Schuster.

Said, Edward. 1986. "Intellectuals in the Post-colonial World." *Salmagundi* 70/71 (Spring/Summer): 44–64.

———. 2001. "Bitter Dispatches from the Third World." In *Reflections on Exile*, Edward Said, 98–104. London: Granta Books.

Sairsingh, Marie. 2013. "Reclaiming Sexual Identities in Patricia Powell's *A Small Gathering of Bones* and Curdella Forbes's *A Permanent Freedom*." *Journal of West Indian Literature* 22, no. 1: 63–84.

Salkey, Andrew, ed. 1967. *Caribbean Prose: An Anthology for Secondary Schools*. London: Evans Brothers.

———, ed. (1960) 1969a. *West Indian Stories*. London: Faber and Faber.

———. 1969b. *The Adventures of Catullus Kelly*. London: Hutchinson.

———. 1970. *Island Voices: Stories for the West Indies*. New York: Liveright.

———, ed. (1965) 1972. *Stories from the Caribbean: An Anthology*. London: P. Elek Books.

———. 1973. *Anancy's Score*. London: Bogle-L'Ouverture Press.

———. 1976. *Come Home, Malcolm Heartland*. London: Hutchinson.

———. (1959) 1978. *A Quality of Violence*. London: New Beacon Books.

———. (1964) 1979a. *Hurricane*. Oxford: Oxford University Press.

———. 1979b. *The River That Disappeared*. London: Bogle-L'Ouverture Press.

———. (1968) 1982. *The Late Emancipation of Jerry Stover*. Harlow, UK: Longman.

———. 1992. *Anancy Traveller*. London: Bogle-L'Ouverture Press.

———. (1960) 2009. *Escape to an Autumn Pavement*. Leeds, UK: Peepal Tree.

Santos-Febres, Mayra. 2000. *Sirena Selena vestida de pena*. Translated by Stephen A. Lytle. New York: Picador.

Scott, Lawrence. 1992. *Witchbroom*. London: Allison & Busby.

———. (1998) 2014. *Aelred's Sin*. London: Allison & Busby.

———. 2011. "The Novelist and History—Pleasures and Problems: V.S. Naipaul's *The Loss of El Dorado—A History*, *The Enigma of Arrival—A Novel*, and *A Way in the World—A Sequence*." In *Created in the West Indies: Caribbean Perspectives on V.S. Naipaul*, edited by Jennifer Rahim and Barbara Lalla, 165–182. Kingston, Jamaica: Ian Randle.

Sedgwick, Eve Kosofsky. 1993 *Tendencies*. Durham: Duke University Press.

Selvon, Samuel. (1956) 1979. *The Lonely Londoners*. London: Longman Drumbeat.

Serju, Christopher. 2014. "Righteous Anger—Church Members Upset of Priest's Embrace over Gays in Worship Service." *The Gleaner*. http://jamaica-gleaner.com /article/lead-stories/20141208/righteous-anger-church-members-upset-over-priests -embrace-gays-worship.

Sheller, Mimi. 2012. *Citizenship from Below: Erotic Agency and Caribbean Freedom*. Durham: Duke University Press.

Shivani, Anis. 2011. "The 15 Most Overrated Contemporary American Writers." Huffington Post. https://www.huffingtonpost.com/anis-shivani/the-15-most-overrated-con_b_672974.html#s123717&title=William_T_Vollmann.

Silvera, Makeda. 1992. "Man Royals and Sodomites: Some Thoughts on the Invisibility of Afro-Caribbean Lesbians." *Feminist Studies* 18, no.3: 521–532.

Smith, Faith. 2011. "Introduction." In *Sex and the Citizen*, Faith Smith, 1–17. Charlottesville and London: University of Virginia Press.

Smith, Ian. 1999. "Critics in the Dark." *Journal of West Indian Literature* 8, no. 2: 2–9.

Smith, Miriam. 1999. *Lesbian and Gay Rights in Canada: Social Movements and Equality-Seeking, 1971–1995*. Toronto: University of Toronto Press.

Srinivasan, Amia. 2017. "The Sucker, the Sucker!" *London Review of Books*, 39, no. 17 (September 7). https://www-lrb-co-uk.uea.idm.oclc.org/the-paper/v39/n17/amia-srinivasan/the-sucker-the-sucker

Thomas, Calvin. 2000. *Straight with a Twist*. Champaign: University of Illinois Press.

Thomas, H. Nigel. 1993. *Spirits in the Dark*. Oxford: Heinemann Educational Books.

Tinsley, Omise'eke Natasha. 2008. "Black Atlantic, Queer Atlantic: Queer Imaginings of the Middle Passage," *GLQ* 14, no. 2–3: 191–215.

———. 2010. *Thiefing Sugar: Eroticism between Women in Caribbean Literature*. Durham, NC: Duke University Press.

———. 2018 *Ezili's Mirrors: Imagining Black Queer Genders*. Durham, NC: Duke University Press.

Torres-Saillant, Silvio. 1999. *El retorno de las yolas: ensayos sobre diáspora, democracia y dominicanidad*. Dominican Republic: Libreria La Trinitaria.

Trouillot, Michel-Rolph. 1995. *Silencing the Past, Power and the Production of History*. Boston: Beacon Press.

Valens, Keja. 2013. *Desire between Women in Caribbean Literature*. New York: Palgrave Macmillan.

———. 2016. "Excruciating Improbability and the Transgender Jamaican." In *Trans Studies: The Challenge to Hetero/Homo Normativities*, edited by Yolanda Martínez-San Miguel and Sarah Tobias, 65–81. New Brunswick, NJ: Rutgers University Press.

Walcott, Derek. 1979. "The Schooner Flight." In *The Star-Apple Kingdom*. New York: Farrar, Straus & Giroux.

———. 1974. "The Caribbean: Culture or Mimicry?" *Journal of Interamerican Studies and World Affairs* 16, no. 1: 3–13.

———. 1993. *The Antilles: Fragments of Epic Memory: The Nobel Lecture*. New York: Farrar Straus & Giroux.

———. 1998. *What the Twilight Says: Essays*. London: Faber and Faber.

Walcott, Rinaldo. 2009. "Queer Returns: Human Rights in the Anglo-Caribbean and Diaspora Politics." *Caribbean Review of Gender Studies* 3, no. 4: 1–19.

Walonen, Michael K. 2018. "Violence, Diasporic Transnationalism, and Neo-imperialism in *A Brief History of Seven Killings*." *Small Axe* 22, no. 3: 1–12.

Wekker, Gloria. 1999. "What's Identity Got to Do with It? Rethinking Identity in Light of the Mati Work." In *Female Desires: Same-Sex Relations and Transgender Practices across Cultures*, edited by Evelyn Blackwood and Saskia E. Wieringa, 119–138. New York: Columbia University Press.

———. 2006. *The Politics of Passion*. New York: Columbia University Press.

———. (1996) 2008. "Mati-ism and Black Lesbianism: Two Idealtypical Expressions of Female Heterosexuality in Black Communities of the Diaspora." In *Our Caribbean: A Gathering of Lesbian and Gay Writing from the Antilles*, edited by Thomas Glave, 368–381. Durham, NC: Duke University Press.

Williams, Joseph J. 1932. *Whence the "Black Irish" of Jamaica?* New York: Dial Press Inc.

Wolfenden, John. 1957. *Report of the Departmental Committee on Homosexual Offenses and Prostitution*. London: HMSO.

Wynter, Sylvia. 1968. "We Must Learn to Sit Down Together and Talk About a Little Culture: Reflections on West Indian Writing and Criticism I." *Jamaican Journal* 2, no. 4: 23–32.

———. 1970. "Jonkonnu in Jamaica: Towards the Interpretation of Folk Dance as a Cultural Process." *Jamaica Journal* 3, no. 4: 34–48.

———. 2006. "On How We Mistook the Map for the Territory, and Reimprisoned Ourselves in Our Unbearable Wrongness of Being, of Desêtre: Black Studies toward the Human Project." In *A Companion to African-American Studies*, edited by Lewis R. Gordon and Jane Anna Gordon, 107–118. Malden, MA: Blackwell.

Zehnder, Martin. 2003. *Something Rich and Strange: Selected Essays on Sam Selvon*. Leeds, UK: Peepal Tree.

Index

About the Author

ALISON DONNELL is professor of modern literatures in English and head of the School of Literature, Creative Writing, and Drama at the University of East Anglia. She has published widely on Caribbean and Black British writings, with a particular emphasis on challenging orthodox literary histories and recovering women's voices. She is the author of *Twentieth Century Caribbean Literature: Critical Moments in Anglophone Literary and Critical History* and general editor of *Caribbean Literature in Transition, 1800–2020* (3 volumes), as well as coeditor (with Michael A. Bucknor) of *The Routledge Companion to Anglophone Caribbean Literature*. She is the lead researcher on a major research project funded by the Leverhulme Trust: Caribbean Literary Heritage: Recovering the Lost Past and Safeguarding the Future, www.caribbeanliteraryheritage.com.

Available titles in the Critical Caribbean Studies series:

Printed and bound by CPI Group (UK) Ltd, Croydon, CR0 4YY

09/06/2025

14685722-0001